BEATING AROUND THE BUSH

BEATING AROUND THE BUSH

A LIFE IN THE NORTHERN FOREST

Wilf Taylor & Alan Fry

with best wishes,

Alan Fry

HARBOUR PUBLISHING

Harbour Publishing Co. Ltd.
P.O. Box 219
Madeira Park, BC
Canada V0N 2H0

Cover design by Roger Handling
Line illustrations by Donald C. Watt

Printed and bound in Canada by Friesen Printers

Canadian Cataloguing in Publication Data

Taylor, Wilf.
   Beating around the bush

   ISBN 1-55017-015-5

   1. Taylor, Wilf.   2. Trappers — Canada,
Western — Biography.   3. Park rangers — Canada,
Western — Biography.   4. Outdoor life — Canada,
Western.   I. Fry, Alan, 1931–   II. Title.
SK17.T39A3 1989   796.5'749'09711   C89-091503-2

CONTENTS

INTRODUCTION

Wilf Taylor's active life in the outdoors began in the foothills of Alberta over sixty years ago and continues in the Peace River country of British Columbia today.

When Wilf was a boy in the foothills, Canada was largely a rural nation. A few Canadians lived in places such as Toronto and Montreal; most Canadians lived on farms and ranches or in logging and mining camps or in remote fishing villages. Many could be found in the bush or the treeless north, hunting and trapping for their living.

Nowadays Canada is largely an urban nation. Most people live in cities in a lifestyle far removed from the rural origins of their parents or their grandparents.

So far removed are many of the city dwellers that they have turned against the few still found on the land.

The Inuit hunters in the north can no longer sell the pelts of the seals which they kill for food because opinion in the cities has been turned against the harvest of wild animals, depriving these hunters of one of the few sources of cash income they might use to supplement the meagre living they make from the land.

Centuries ago, the demand for North American furs led to the European occupation of this continent. Native people and pioneering Europeans built an economy on the fur trade, an economy still vital to the people who live in scattered villages throughout the Canadian bush. But the tide of public sentiment turns against these people too, and soon they may have no market for their furs, no economic base for their way of life.

When Wilf, emerging from his boyhood, took up market hunting to make a living, what he did was no longer legal (though not many years before, it had been) but it was respected. Wilf hunted the bucks and dry does which could be taken without harm from the mule deer herds in the foothills.

When Wilf set traps for weasels in the hope of selling the pelts for cash with which to support his family, he pursued a respected tradition of self-reliance. That the venture failed was not due to opinion-makers in the cities turning urban populations against buying furs but to some unconscionable scoundrel stealing his furs and his traps.

I explain these matters so that whatever feeling you might hold about hunting and trapping today, you might better understand the context in which Wilf began his working life, a life in which his Winchester rifle was the basic tool of his trade.

Many men of Wilf's generation began life in a rural setting, came of age in time to serve in the forces in the Second World War, then found, on returning to civilian life, that rural Canada no longer had room for them. After scraping along in the country for a while, they joined the great shift of population to the cities.

Wilf, rooted in the bush and the ranch country of the foothills, had hoped to secure land of his own on returning from the war. When this hope was thwarted he scraped along for a while, breaking horses and taking odd jobs on the ranches and in the bush.

But in time it became clear that he needed a more reliable livelihood than these casual employments offered. He had married Vera in Halifax on his way overseas and now they had Joanne, born in December of 1946; Charles, born in August of 1948; and Hugh, born in February of 1950.

Something had to be done, but at the same time working with horses, hunting and generally beating around in the bush were not simply the means of making a living for Wilf, they were the fibre of his lifestyle.

In a stroke of good fortune, in 1950 Wilf hired on with the National Parks Service working out of Banff, Alberta. From that day to this he has managed to earn a reliable living, yet for the most part keep beating around in the bush. His employments have taken him as far afield as Inuvik and the Arctic islands but — except for a few years behind a desk just before he retired — have let him keep his essential connection with bush life and the people and animals who are central to its character.

Now, about Wilf's stories.

Men who enjoy their growing up and their working lives collect memories as they go along which they later like to tell about, most often in anecdotes suitable over a cup of coffee or a glass of beer.

Of course a man is always on the lookout for a fresh audience for his stories, but often his wife or his children will be on hand when *such an audience is found. Then, as he launches into a wonderful tale, there will be considerable rolling of eyes and even a few anguished cries of, "Oh, Daddy, not again!"*

Be that as it may, I found Wilf's stories highly entertaining and I present them here as accurately as I can from his telling.

Now these stories are not a factual account of Wilf's career, nor do they tell much of family life as it was shared among Wilf, Vera and their six children. These are the collected memories, mainly but not always humourous, out of Wilf's working life.

The main divisions in Wilf's working life are presented in chronological order. However, beginning with his employment in the National Parks Service and the Alberta Wildlife and Alberta Forestry Services, the anecdotes within the divisions are presented more by type than in chronological order.

Those of us who beat around in the bush are in a minority these days and inevitably so. The crushing populations now inhabiting the planet can only survive by industrial technologies which compel us to live mainly in cities.

For a refreshing look at a different life, I invite you to beat around the bush with Wilf Taylor.

Alan Fry
Whitehorse, Yukon Territory

I

BEFORE THE WAR

This period in Wilf's life begins with the high spirits of boyhood and concludes with his enlistment in the Canadian Army in 1941.

It was a carefree time, even though Wilf began working and earning his own living at an early age.

Apart from his success as a market hunter, Wilf's growing up was not unusual in ranch life in those years. Many boys began working full days in the harvest or working cattle as young as twelve, although the heaviest work would not usually be given them for another two or three seasons.

Most boys longed, above all, to be a man as soon as possible, and the way to be a man was to do a man's work.

High-Jinks

In the lean years of the thirties throughout rural Canada young boys had few toys with which to amuse themselves. Most had a pocket knife, a few had single-speed bicycles and in some schoolyards glass marbles would appear for a couple of weeks in the muddy season in the spring.

But in much of the west we had splendid alternatives. We had the use of horses, we had access to basic tools with which to make things, we were early introduced to the responsible use of firearms, we had an abundance of open country and we could always scrape together enough canvas, bedding and frying pans to go camping.

Also, as with boys everywhere, our imaginations were generally running a long way in front of our better judgement, frequently getting us in trouble with the authorities—our parents, the school-teacher, occasionally the game warden.

Mind you, we had work to do much of the time, a matter of practical necessity in rural family life in those years, but a shortage of time to devote exclusively to our own amusement hardly kept us out of trouble.

My brother Jim was a year and a half older than I, and when we were still half-grown boys we would ride double on a horse, Jim in the saddle and me behind.

Assigned on one occasion to drive a few cows along a lane which bordered the railway track, we rode in this fashion on a stout horse which was of decent disposition but which nevertheless could be provoked to buck. The lane was fenced and the cows needed little attention to keep them moving.

My brother and I got into an argument about which of us was the better rider. The argument soon deteriorated to the level of are not, am so, asserted with increasing volume and belligerence. While the debate proceeded I tied the stout saddle strings at the base of the cantle into tight loops, then slid my hands through the loops.

That done, I slapped my heels into the horse's flanks and the contest was on. Jim, with the reins in one hand, grabbed the saddle horn with the other. We settled in to see who was going to outlast

The horse exploded in every direction at once.

the other and as the agitated horse bucked vigorously down the middle of the road, scattering cows to both sides, it might have been a fair guess that the horse would outlast us both.

Now many horses have two levels of bucking, one that is moderately rough when the horse is moderately agitated and the next which is violently rough, frequently brought on by the horse catching one hell of a fright from some external source.

Jim and I were settling in quite nicely to a moderately rough ride, but just then the train hove into view, barrelling up the track toward us. When the engineer, leaning out the side window of the steam locomotive, saw two boys on a bucking horse and cows running in every direction, he decided, it appeared, to applaud. First, he took off his cap and waved it toward us in general encouragement. Then, just as he came broadside and with only a few yards separating our bucking horse from his steam engine, he hauled on the whistle lanyard.

The piercing howl of a steam whistle at close quarters is enough to scare the wits out of any horse, and immediately we had twice the fight on our hands to stay the ride. The horse exploded in every direction at once.

But the first stage of this contest had given us some advantage. We had got the feel of the horse and had improved our purchase on the rigging. Besides, we were each stubbornly determined not to be first to be bucked off.

Fortunately the rigging held. My saddle string loops did not come unstuck, the bridle did not separate and the saddle cinch endured the stress without breaking. In time the horse wound down and the freight train disappeared into the distance.

An alert neighbour working in his fields had witnessed the event, and soon the story spread. The schoolyard next day buzzed with varying accounts, none of which we denied since the key phrase in each was, "Wow, can them Taylor boys ever ride a buckin' horse!"

The story reached home as well, and we did not have anything to say then either. When the senior Taylor in the family was asking things like what the hell were you boys doing anyway, spooking that horse to buck, we knew that silence was the only permitted response.

It was common on the ranches and smaller homesteads to build a shed, open at one end, against a side of the barn, as a shelter for loose stock. The shelter would be used in different seasons for different purposes. In high summer the shed offered refuge from the heat of the sun and certain pestering flies which are partially discouraged by shade.

On a vacant place near our home there was just such a shed, but this one had been built only of poles with a brush roof, in the absence, no doubt, of cash with which to buy lumber. It served in those years as summer shade for a few unbroken, half-wild horses.

We found you could climb onto the roof without frightening the horses and then, if you worked at it patiently, you could separate the brush enough to drop through and onto a horse. The moment you landed you grabbed for a handful of mane, but seldom did you advance to even this modest purchase on your mount, for the moment you landed on it, the horse shot through the open end of the shed into a running and bucking pattern across the field. Whether the boy would stay on the horse was never a question. The point of interest was how many jumps and how high before you sailed off into the air to practise yet another landing.

Much of the time we would ride bareback, rigging our horses with only a bridle or a hackamore, a headgear similar to a bridle but lacking a bit in the horse's mouth.

Now a meandering stream worked its way through the bottom-land near our home, and where the oxbow curves of the stream reached into the rising ground at the meadow's edge, the land had eroded, leaving steep cut-banks. These cut-banks occurred in a series, and in the stream at the foot of each, a deep pool would be found, suitable for swimming.

Livestock travelling along the stream in the course of going to and fro would not follow every meandering curve but would take the short route from one cut-bank to the next. The trail, therefore, came close by the stream only at the cut-banks, and it was common practice when swimming in one of the pools to dive in from the top of the bank.

I do not know how it started, probably on a dare—and no twelve year old boy, as everyone knows, can possibly refuse a dare. Inevitably the bareback horse and the well-made trail passing the cut-bank with the swimming pool at the foot came together in a stunt requiring agility, timing and foolishness in roughly equal proportions.

You mounted the horse, rode up the trail at full speed and then, just as you approached a cut-bank, quickly gathered your feet to the horse's back in a sort of vaulting crouch and leapt off into space. The momentum of the horse and your thrust to the side carried you out and down, in a gentle arc, into the pool.

Good luck prevailed with that game. No one ever missed the pool and no one's parents ever found out.

My brother and I liked to go camping in the semi-open bush and hill country which surrounded the thin sprinkling of homesteads and ranch quarters in the Rocky Mountain foothills. Abundant good camping places could be found at hand, so we seldom strayed far from a homestead or country road.

We liked to live in some measure from the land by catching fish, picking berries and killing grouse with our slingshots, and our ingenuity often had us in trouble.

On one occasion in the heat of midsummer we set off with a friend, using our pony and cart to haul ourselves and our outfit.

Now three boys and their canvas, blankets, pots, frying pans and sundry possessions more than filled the cart, leaving insufficient room for grub. By the second day out we were scouring the landscape for food but finding only Saskatoon berries.

Of course we always camped by water and on this occasion we were also not far from the house and outbuildings of a neighbour, Nels Jensen. He kept a small herd of milk cows, enough to provide milk, cream and butter for the family, skim milk to feed some hogs and surplus cream to ship to the creamery in town for a little cash income.

Homesteads in those years had no electricity and in order to keep cream fresh between deliveries farm families would stand creamers, five-gallon stainless steel containers holding the cream, in pools in a nearby stream. The chosen pool would always be well shaded with streamside willow growth.

So it happened that while scouting the creek near which we had camped, we came on Nels Jensen's cream cache. Now cream and Saskatoon berries has a heap more to be said for it than plain berries, and we knew there would be no harm in taking just a *little* cream, which we did.

But of course a little cream led to a little *more* cream and, just to be sure not to cause Nels Jensen any alarm, we put a little of the sparkling clean stream water into the creamer to maintain the level. It was such good, rich cream that you could hardly imagine a cup of water — or two, or even three or perhaps just a *little* bit more than that — making any difference in the best part of a creamer full.

We put a little of the sparkling clean stream water into the creamer...

Little did we dwell, of course, on the precision with which the cream would be measured on delivery at the creamery for remote qualities such as specific gravity and butterfat content.

But Nels Jensen did dwell on these things, with great attention, for they mattered substantially to his cream cheque. Having watered down his cream we had, unintentionally, also watered down his modest income.

Now Nels had seen us only at a distance with our pony and cart so he could hardly have said whose boys we were, except that he knew whose pony that was, even at a distance.

Nels had a discussion with the senior Taylor who in turn had a discussion with us, and we boys weeded garden for some days at Nels Jensen's place to compensate him for his losses at the creamery.

On another camping venture along a different water course, we found no berries on the hillsides but did discover an abundance of trout in the stream.

Now we knew about a hook and line and a willow stick for a fishing pole, but when the food we had brought with us ran out we had either to make the tedious journey home for more or increase the rate at which we caught fish.

We concentrated on our fishing. We knew that fish, when resting in still, clear sidepools, will tolerate movement in their vicinity provided it is very slow and even. We knew that in shallow water you could actually slide your hand into the water and under a fish, if you were sufficiently patient, then quickly flip it out on the bank.

We also knew that neither hook and line nor hand flipping had a patch on snaring fish in somewhat deeper water, if it was straight production you sought. Faced with a food shortage or a tedious trek home we cut long poles, then attached to the ends squirrel snares, light malleable wire loops which hold their shape until the snare is tightened around captured prey.

We set to work, slowly and with impeccably steady movement, each putting a snare into a deeper pool, then slowly sliding it around a trout until, with one decisive flip of the snare pole, the fish would be caught around the mid-section and brought out on the stream bank.

In short order we had enough fish for the day. The next day we repeated the exercise.

Now there were two shortcomings to this procedure: first, it was illegal, although that hardly mattered in itself, but second, the snare invariably left a telltale ring around the body of the captured fish.

So it happened on about the third day, just as I was frying a panful of trout over the campfire for our lunch, that Dunc Cromie, the game warden, came sauntering along the creek.

"Well, how are you boys?"

"Oh, fine. Just fishin' for a little grub here. We run outa stuff from the house."

"You been out long?"

"Few days."

"Well, don't forget to go home," he joked, as he turned to leave, and I heaved a sigh of relief. I could see the snare marks still as plain as day on the fish in the frying pan, but perhaps he had not looked very hard at our fish.

Then he paused and turned back to speak one more time before leaving: "You'd better quit using your snares to catch fish. Use a hook and line. It takes longer but it's legal."

It was some years later that I discovered our parents had sent the game warden to check on us, just to see if we were all in order, as it were.

Even on a day hike we would look for food from the land since the food we brought with us, however adequate it seemed on setting off, rarely lasted beyond mid-morning.

We made slingshots with a forked stick, two strips of rubber inner tube and a leather pouch. We invariably set off with our pockets bulging and heavy with the small rounded stones which were the essential ammunition for our weapons.

Should we come on a covey of grouse we would kill as many as we could before the rest flew off in alarm. At once we would make a campfire and cook the meat on a hand-held spit, then eat the lot before moving on.

Now these small rounded stones we used were not at hand everywhere. Much of the hill country was composed of rich soil, supporting grass and aspen and willows and, in higher country, the pine forests. There were few stones lying about, and we were obliged to carry with us the day's supply of shot from the creek bottoms in the valley floor.

But of course we would use up our supply as the day wore on, and not only on game when game appeared. By far the bulk of the shot went into contests to see who could hit a particular cone standing out on a pine branch or some similar target.

One day, high on a burned-over ridge top, we came on a single grouse in a tangle of fallen, fire-killed timber. We were out of shot and, in a quick discussion of our problem, decided that I should take our hatchet in hand, the only hatchet we owned between us, creep as close to the grouse as I could, then throw the hatchet and cleave his ducking, bobbing head.

The rest takes little telling. I missed, of course, but though we searched for the next two hours, a good part of the time on our hands and knees, we could not find the hatchet.

We were a long time scrounging up another one. It was an expensive grouse that got away from us that day.

We seemed never to need much time to get into a fix.

We had an hour for lunch at school and would bolt down our sandwiches in less than five minutes to save most of the hour for play.

Now the schoolyard was large, but the railway yard adjoining offered more adventure, and we would slip out of sight between the boxcars in any moment the teacher was suitably distracted.

Tag on top of the boxcars was the best game, especially if there were many cars coupled together on one of the several siding tracks.

Leaping from one car to the next...

We would climb the ladder on an end car and then chase each other along the tops of the cars, leaping from one car to the next in a coupled string.

One day the boy I was chasing hesitated and lost both his nerve and his timing at the jump to the next car. He fell to the ground, knocking himself unconscious in the impact.

Fortunately he came around in a short while, but now we were faced with what to tell our different sets of parents. We were thoroughly scared kids, and in a round of mutual contrition we all said we would tell the truth.

Now contrition had worn off by the time my brother and I got home, so we did not tell the truth. On the other hand, we did not tell any lies, either. We simply said nothing.

For the other family it was not quite so easy. The injured boy carried a lump on his head you could see across a good-sized barnyard, so his older brother, called upon to explain, said he had fallen out of a tree. There were several trees in the schoolyard, so the story was plausible.

That might have been the end of it except that a week later my brother, while visiting this same family, climbed up and about in the limbs of a tree in their yard.

Suddenly the door burst open and the father of the family proceeded to order my brother back to ground level with the gruff admonition that enough people have been hurt around here lately climbing damned trees.

Now my brother felt spurred by the scolding to say something in defence of his presence in the tree and blurted out the first words which came to mind.

"Bob never fell outa no tree. He fell off'n a boxcar."

"He fell off *what?*"

"A boxcar." By now Jim knew he'd let a bad cat out of a bag in which it should have stayed indefinitely, but there was no pulling it back now.

"*What* was he doing on a boxcar?"

"Wilf was chasin' him."

Everybody got a dressing down then and we were ordered forever to keep off the boxcars.

My Dad Had Hunting Dogs

My dad raised cross-bred Russian wolfhounds. They were used to hunt coyotes. You could always get a few dollars for a coyote pelt, and a well trained hound would fetch a price.

These hounds hunted by sight, not by scent. In each pack there would be one spotter hound which would ride in the front of the buggy or light truck with the hunter. The remaining hounds would ride in the back in an enclosed box.

On seeing a coyote in the distance, the hunter would stop the rig and point the coyote out to the spotter. This hound would search the landscape until it spotted the coyote, then leap from the rig in pursuit. At this instant the remaining hounds would be turned loose. They would not try to locate the coyote but would simply pursue the spotter, usually catching up in time to land on the quarry together. They killed quickly, and it was argued to be an efficient way to take coyotes.

The hunting part of keeping hounds was no problem. The problem with hounds was that for the greater part of the time they weren't hunting but still had to be fed and exercised. Also these hounds were very large and tended to be blamed for any dog damage which might occur in the district, whether they were seen at the site or not. Although our hounds were always tethered, they were usually the prime suspects.

Exercising the hounds was a tedious daily chore which always had to be done just before a boy was about to set off on some activity of his own choosing. Two hounds could be handled at a time, just barely, on a single line with a spreader chain about fifteen inches long between their collars.

On one occasion I wanted to go to a friend's yard to play softball, but first I had to take the hounds for a run. In my impatience I put two hounds on the spreader chain, then turned loose the old bitch and three of her half-grown pups and headed down the lane.

All of a sudden we turned a corner and the lane ahead was full of turkeys belonging to a neighbour. There must have been fifty of them, and they scattered and squawked in every direction.

Now I weighed barely a hundred pounds, and the grown hounds weighed as much each. I couldn't control the hounds on the line, much less the old bitch, and as surely as she waded into the turkeys her pups followed.

My dad bought and paid for a lot of turkeys that day that he really did not want.

On another occasion my brother and 'I, with hounds on lead, came by an open haystack where some other boys were playing.

Playing on a haystack was worth a thrashing in itself, but these kids had their old collie dog up there, and the stack had only been started, so it was no trick to climb up on it.

In fact my brother was, for the most part, dragged up by the killer hound and the old bitch he had on a spreader. I followed close behind with our spotter and a pup on another spreader.

It was late summer, and the hounds had not done any hunting since March so they were generally easy to manage. But one of the boys on the stack cried "sick 'im!" to the old collie as the hounds bounded into view over the edge of the stack. The collie courageously attacked and in seconds the four hounds, only marginally impeded by the spreader chains, had torn the poor dog to pieces, and the hapless neighbour boys were in tears.

Now that was not an easy mess to resolve, never mind that the other kid had set his dog on our hounds at the start. We got the expected fresh set of instructions for our future behaviour from the senior Taylor but that was the beginning of the end of keeping hounds. My dad gradually sold off the older dogs and then the pups as well as they came of hunting age.

The Black Cow
and the Septic Tank

An old friend of my dad's was Doc Keene. Nobody had any money in the Depression, so Doc Keene took whatever he could get for medical services rendered.

So it was the case that from time to time Doc Keene would come into possession of some cattle and likewise of the odd place to pasture those cattle. It wasn't in the usual line of a medical practice, but again, he took what he could get.

One day a man named Austin, who managed some of Doc Keene's non-medical activities, came early to our house to explain that Doc had made a deal to pasture some cows north of town and wondered if I could help him herd these range cows past the town and safely on the other side. He told my mother that if I could be spared, he would make sure I was back to school in time for morning lessons. This was not a major cattle drive requiring cowboys on horseback. This was a simple task manageable by a man and a boy on foot.

So off I went with Austin who cautioned me emphatically to watch the black cow for she was a bunch quitter and, if she got away from us, would be a lot of trouble to fetch up again.

Now I knew the black cow personally — on several occasions I had milked her for a previous owner — and I found it hard to understand Austin's concern about this gentle old cow getting away from us.

But as it turned out, this old black cow did not like the company she was obliged to keep that day and at the first chance on the way by the town she bolted.

She ran down a back alley and I ran after her in hot pursuit. Finally I got alongside her and turned her against the fence.

All would have been well, but as luck would have it, Mrs. Ransom's gate was open. The old cow ran across Mrs. Ransom's yard and underneath her clothesline. The line had been slung barely high enough, and a low-hanging garment got caught in the old cow's

The whole line full of clothing came to the ground...

horns. The whole line full of clothing came to ground and beyond it the black cow disappeared.

But the black cow was hidden by more than the line full of clothing. She had gone through the lightly buried and thoroughly rotten top of an old wooden septic tank.

Austin hove up beside me, somewhat short of breath, as I watched the cow wallow about in the septic slush.

"Wilf," said Austin, in a restrained voice, "I think you had better hike off to school."

I did so, glad to escape the scene. Later in the day, when stories reached the schoolyard about a hoist truck beside an open septic tank and two men below rigging a sling around a cow that had somehow got in there, I kept my silence. I knew the two men must be Austin and my father.

Bullet-Holes in the Washtub

F‌irearms were in everyday use in the foothill country in my boyhood, but family practice differed on the question of how soon a boy could use a rifle or shotgun.

My dad favoured early access with firm instructions, and so my brother and I were using firearms at an age when other youngsters had to make do with their slingshots.

In retrospect it may not have been as safe as it looked at the time. Some irrepressible boyishness did compromise safety occasionally, but it all worked out in the end.

We once sneaked an 8-gauge shotgun out of the house with the idea of shooting a few ducks with it. We discharged that cannon once, then returned it as quietly to the house as we had taken it and never entertained the notion again.

One time my brother Jim and I were sitting together in the front room talking guns, and he had in his hands a Winchester slide-action rifle (commonly called a pump-action) in Winchester .22 Special calibre. He had it pointed at the ceiling, a usual safety rule for holding a firearm indoors.

I said, "If you hold the trigger down and pump, a Winchester will fire as fast as you can pump."

He responded, "Nah!"

I urged, "Try it."

He asked, "You mean like this?"

And I was right. The bullet went straight through the ceiling, hit a wall somewhere above and bounced back down the stairs. Jim said he heard it falling back down the stairs before he heard the rifle go off.

That put a damper on things for a while.

Groundwater from wells and streamwater in the foothills was hard and so there was a demand for soft water. Women wanted soft water for washing their hair and the mountain of clothing that their

27

men made grubby at work every day; men wanted soft water to put in the electrical batteries which were essential to the internal combustion engines becoming increasingly common around the farms and ranches.

The only way for most people to get soft water was to save it off the roof during rainy weather. Most houses, ours included, had a rain barrel or large washtub beneath every downpipe from the gutters.

On the wall in our house there was a revolver, and in our house existed a severe prohibition about anyone other than my dad daring to touch the weapon.

I longed to use it, even just once, but I was mightily afraid of the trouble I would be in if I were caught with it in my hands, let alone outside the house.

But my chance came. One day our old bitch came in heat and for some reason there were more than the usual number of stray dogs coming through the yard in search of her. To preserve the integrity of the hounds we raised we felt justified in shooting these stray dogs.

My mother was gathering eggs one day and I spotted a big stray dog with obvious designs on the bitch so I dashed to the wall, grabbed the big Colt revolver, ran outside and, just like Tom Mix in the comic books, I let him have it.

The dog got away, but my mother's precious soft water was spilling out through a bullet hole in the side of the washtub at the bottom of the downspout from the roof.

I never did find a plausible reason to use the revolver.

When I Was Twelve,
Mrs. Mackie Gave Me a Pup

When I was twelve, Mrs. Mackie of the 25 Ranch gave me a bitch pup out of her old sheep dog. This was one very smart pup. When still only a small ball of fur she began herding the chickens around our yard. It certainly looked as though I had a winner of a pup.

Now there were school buses operating in our district to pick up and deliver children who lived beyond a specified distance from the school. As it happened, we were just short of the distance and had to walk or ride our saddle-horses. A family a little further along the road lived just outside the distance and each day the bus would go by our place to pick up the children from this family and each day go by our place to deliver them home.

Undoubtedly there had to be a rule, but it seemed unfair that the bus should go by our place each day but not stop to pick us up. In consequence, some irrational bad feelings generated and the school bus driver, who had a reputation as a loud-mouthed bully, made it plain that he looked down on my brothers and me as lower-class kids.

One day my pup was standing by the side of the road watching my younger brother approaching across the field from school. I was a short distance off with a .22-calibre rifle in my hand. The school bus approached on the way to deliver the children who lived further down the road.

To my horror and disgust, the bus driver swung the bus clear off the wheel track to the side of the road to strike my pup, then swung back on the road to proceed on his way.

My pup was badly smashed up and I had no choice but to shoot her at once. We couldn't have saved her and she would have died a miserable death.

I stayed on the road, and when the bus returned on its way to town, I flagged down the driver, the rifle in my hands.

The driver stopped the bus, then shouted out the side window, "That'll teach you to keep your goddamned dogs tied up!"

I vented my feelings loudly. "You are a no-good son-of-a-bitch!"

He shouted back, "I'll get you!"

Then he started to ease the bus forward, and I quickly laid the barrel end of my rifle on the bus window. "You don't go anywhere 'til I say so," I declared.

Of course it was a pointless challenge. I wasn't about to shoot the man however much I hated him, and keeping him there served no purpose. I dropped the rifle and told him he could go, getting painfully little satisfaction from my short-lived assertion of power.

The story the bus driver later told was considerably embellished. I had not only held him up on the road at gunpoint, I had shot at him from short range and only because I had missed was he alive. I was as much offended by the implication that I was so bad a shot as to miss at such a range as by his lie that I had shot at all.

My old dad was in a storm. He went up one side of me and down the other, restating all the fundamental rules about responsible use of firearms and how I was only allowed to use them because I was thought to be responsible. I had been so hurt by the injustice of the bus driver deliberately running over my pup that I felt my brief threat with my rifle had been justified, but there was nothing I could say.

I kept a low profile for a long while after that, although in the small community in which we lived I could not avoid the bus driver, who took every opportunity to belittle me. In the bargain I felt hurt that my father had not given the slightest indication of understanding my own sense of justification for what I had done.

But perhaps my father understood the injustice more clearly than he let on.

One day in severely cold weather I was with my father late one evening while he spread water on the community skating rink. My job was to pull the hose behind him as he backed up from one end of the rink to the other, flooding the area before him as he did so. As he retreated from the progressively flooded area my attention to the hose kept it from contact with the newly laid water.

Into the enclosed rink came my adversary, the bus driver. He walked out on the ice, leaving his foot tracks in the half-frozen water which my father had so carefully spread about, and proceeded to bad-mouth the whole Taylor clan.

This went on for some time while my father patiently carried on spreading water on the rink surface, completely ignoring the bus driver's presence and everything he said.

As my father moved from one side of the rink to the other,

spreading water in his gradually retreating pattern, the bully followed, waving his arms and shouting his contempt.

I was offended by the bus driver's attacks on our family but more grievously hurt by my father's apparent indifference. I longed to take some decisive action in support of the Taylor name, but I had been in enough trouble over my earlier attempt to assert myself, and I decided to leave well enough alone.

Finally, his arms waving, his voice rising and his insults growing bolder, the bully stepped close to my father, all but nose to nose. My father, in a quick movement, but still hardly acknowledging the man's presence, grasped the front of his jacket and shoved the hose nozzle inside his clothing, soaking him from head to foot.

Then my father pushed the man out of the building into a prairie blizzard at minus thirty degrees Celsius. I slipped the bolt on the door to prevent his return, then watched his progress through a window.

In shock, stumbling and barely able to get to his feet after each fall, the bully worked his way slowly up the street toward the school garage, a distance of less than a town block. Two men working in the garage saw him as he approached and came out to carry him the last of the way into the warm.

I unlocked the door and returned to help my father make ice and to clean up the rough spots created by the bus driver tramping about on the half-frozen surface.

My father behaved as though nothing had happened, except that he asked, "Did he make it to the garage?"

"Yes," I said. I wanted to add "damnit!" but I thought I'd better not.

Half an hour later Mr. Gibson, an old friend of my father, who had been in the garage, came into the rink. As the two men shared some tea from a thermos bottle he said, "Bill, you almost killed that guy."

"What guy?" my father replied. Then he said, "Look, I'm making ice and some guy comes in here half-drunk and he slips and slides and falls down and gets himself all soaked up. I don't even get enough of a look at him to see who he is. Then he leaves and I'm glad when he leaves."

I listened to this play of words between old friends, in which both knew exactly what had happened but were now prepared to agree that it hadn't, and I knew that while I may have scared the bully a little bit momentarily, my father had scared the wits right out of him.

He kept his distance from all the Taylor family forever after that.

Reed Gordon, Who Hated Everyone from Ontario

Most rural people in the depression of the thirties were honest and decent, in spite of their hardships.

Even the best of people, however, could be crusty and quick to anger or carry smouldering resentments from wrongs done to them in earlier years.

A boy going out to work on the ranches had much to learn in all too little time, not least of which was to see through the gruffness of many of the men in order to estimate their fundamental goodness. Otherwise a boy could put his trust in someone not to be trusted or fail to have faith in a fine and reliable man.

One summer I had been exercising race horses for the Moran Ranch, some distance from home. I knew few people and few knew me. The Moran family treated me well, and as the time came to cut the grain crops they decided to send me for a few days to help Reed Gordon, a neighbour gather his rakings, the first cut swathes around the edges of the fields where the grain was mixed with weeds and grass. The rakings were an inexpensive source of feed for the big draft horses, and with these out of the way, the binders could start cutting in clean grain.

I would be needed again shortly at the Moran Ranch, but I could be spared for this short task at Reed Gordon's because Bill Moran had just hired three young men newly arrived from Ontario for the harvest.

As I saddled my horse first thing in the morning to leave, Buzz Moran, Bill's brother, came to give me some brief, last advice. "You may not get along very easily with Reed. He's pretty crusty."

That was that, and if I puzzled on why the Morans would send me to help a crusty man I might not get along with I was left to work it out for myself. I settled for my own assurance that they wouldn't send me to help unless Reed Gordon was a good man, however crusty.

When I arrived, Reed was ready to go to work, and the moment I had put my horse in the barn we started right in pitching rakings onto a hay wagon drawn by a team of magnificent, well-cared-for workhorses. They were just the sort of horses any boy would be delighted to have a turn to drive.

A couple of times I tried to start a casual conversation, but all I got for my trouble was a reluctant grunt, so soon I gave up and we worked on in silence through the morning. I would love to have been let to drive the big horses but I could see there was no chance of that.

At noon we drove to the farmyard to water and feed the horses and to have our own midday meal. While Reed unhooked his team I fetched my saddle horse from the barn to water him. Reed stopped long enough to look thoughtfully at my horse, then fetched a pan of oats and put it down for him to eat. Still not a word for me, mind you, but clearly he meant to be good to my horse.

We went into the house to wash and to eat. Mrs. Gordon was every bit as talkative as her husband was silent. She bubbled along in a steady flow of bright chatter, all in her strong Scottish accent. After about twenty minutes, as we neared the end of our meal, she asked me my name.

"I'm Wilf Taylor," I replied.

"And where would you be calling home, laddie?"

"My folks live west of Nanton. I went to school in Nanton."

Reed looked up in poorly concealed surprise, then with a trace of embarrassment began joining in the conversation. Mrs. Reed had a highly transparent I-told-you-so look on her face.

On our return to the barn to bring out the big team for the afternoon's work, Reed asked me if the horse I had was mine or did it belong to the Moran Ranch.

"He's mine," I said proudly.

"Well, you look after him and he'll take you a long way."

With that to open conversation, Reed talked freely through the afternoon, and close to quitting time I screwed up the courage to ask him why he had been so upset with me in the morning.

"Well, wasn't you really. I heard Moran hired some young fellows from Ontario and I thought you were one o' them."

"Oh no," I said, to further secure my identity. "I'm the guy who's been running racehorses by here all summer. You must have seen me plenty of times, but not up close."

I cranked my courage up another notch to ask the next question, carefully. "How come you don't like the guys from Ontario? They only just got here. You haven't had a chance to meet 'em yet.'"

That put the old man on the spot, so he told me his story.

"When I was a young fellow, green as the new heather, I came from Scotland to southern Manitoba. I had nothing but my labour, but I was willing to work as hard as any man. I worked for the farmers around there. They'd all come in from Ontario to take up land.

"They were mean bastards, and they treated me like dirt. They even took the board off the seed drill so I had to walk beside the rig. I worked eighteen hours a day. The bastards never said so much as thank you, and when the work was all done they cheated me on the wages.

"I didn't like 'em then and I don't like 'em now."

I didn't think it would do any good to suggest that maybe not everybody from Ontario was a mean bastard, and that possibly the young guys at Moran's should be given a chance to demonstrate their worth on their own. Reed's profound sense of grievance suggested little room was left for reason.

Nor was that the end of Reed's crustiness with me and his distaste of anyone from Ontario.

When the Moran Ranch began threshing, several teams were hired from other farms and ranches. Large racks, loaded high with the bundles, were drawn by the teams from the fields for threshing. Men heaved the bundles with pitchforks onto the racks in the field and then off the racks to the threshing machine in the threshing yard.

Now Reed Gordon had the best teams in the country and he too was asked to hire out what he could spare.

"You can take a team, but only if Wilf drives 'em."

The deal was made and to my delight, although I was the kid on the crew, I now drove the best team on the whole assembled Moran Ranch threshing outfit. I fairly burst with pride.

All went well as we worked our way through the more distant crops. In about three weeks of steady threshing we returned, late on a Saturday, to the home fields for the last stretch of this heavy work.

But as we returned a wind got up and the smell of snow was in the air. Sure enough, the wind began driving a wet sleet, and in a while it thickened into snow.

As the regular hand on the outfit I had some extra work to do in the move back to the home place, and I came in last at the end of the day. The barn was full and three teams already were tied by their halter ropes to the fence in the yard. I had no choice but to tie my team outside as well.

Now healthy, well-fed horses are done no harm by standing out-side in miserable weather provided they are not overheated when they are brought from work in the field. Even a couple of inches of snow sitting on their backs won't hurt them, but they look miserable as they endure the outdoors and wish they were in the barn.

I was putting out extra feed for the outside horses late on the Sunday when Reed Gordon came by. He was dismayed to see his prize horses outside the barn with snow on their backs. He snorted and complained and then he said, "Wilf, you are a hell of a man to leave horses with!"

With that he took his horses, leading them off up the road toward his own place.

Fortunately the early snow didn't last, and as the fields dried up we prepared to go back to threshing.

Reed showed up then, bringing his team back to work. He also brought two horse blankets and gruffly admonished me to ensure that I used them anytime there wasn't room in the barn for his hors-es.

As much as I liked driving the big team, I felt offended by Reed's harsh words, implying that I had mistreated his horses, so I asked Bill Moran if I could pitch into the thresher for a few days. This meant trading places with one of the young men from Ontario, and Bill said he didn't mind but doubted the man could drive a team.

"I'll teach him," I said. "He'll pick it up quickly and they're pretty easy horses to handle."

So I showed the Ontario chap the rudiments of driving a team and started pitching. As it happened, we were both pitching off the rack drawn by the team when Reed Gordon arrived to see how things were going.

He was standing nearby talking with Bill Moran when we finished the load. At this point I jumped off the rack to wait for the next load, and the Ontario man picked up the lines to drive away.

Reed exploded. "What the hell is that guy doing driving Wilf's team?"

"Oh, it's okay, Reed," Bill said. "I told Wilf to pitch for a while."

Well, that was not okay one damned bit with Reed. He shouted at Bill that unless Wilf drives his team, the team is going home right now. So Bill and Reed together came over to me and Bill said, "I guess you'd better go back driving the team, Wilf."

For reply, I turned to Reed and said, "You told me I was a hell of a man to leave horses with."

He gave me a steady look for a moment, then said, "I was hasty, lad. I didn't know the barn was full."

I'm sure that apology was hard to make, but clearly it was even harder for him to have some guy from Ontario drive his team.

I went back to driving the magnificent, big horses for the remainder of the threshing.

A Matter of Identity When Delivering a Letter to a Person Unknown

While I was working for the Moran Ranch, the Morans were leasing a tract of their land to Dude Henderson, another rancher in the district.

The lease contained a right of annual renewal unless a letter of termination was delivered to Dude one month prior to the annual renewal date.

Now the terms of the lease were quite favourable to Dude, and for some years he had managed to secure renewal by arranging to be a difficult man to whom to deliver a letter.

For the two months leading up to the renewal date he would stop picking up his mail and would avoid the Moran family like the plague. Attempts to deliver the letter to him at his own place failed, since he could identify anyone approaching in time to slip away before the unwanted knock came on the door.

Finally the Morans were determined to deliver the necessary letter, and it was drawn up and placed in an envelope. Then there was much debate as to how to deliver it, but finally everyone settled on the idea that I should set out on this all-important errand. With luck I would find Dude at his place. Since he did not know me he would not suspect that I carried the unwanted document until I had placed it in his hand.

There was, however, the awkward problem that neither did I know Dude. "Tell me what he looks like," I said, "or I'll end up delivering it to the wrong person. Suppose he's suspicious and he sends someone else to answer the door. Or suppose he isn't home and I go looking for him at the store. Maybe I'll meet him on the road on the way to his place. How will I know him?"

None of the Moran family could come up with much in the way of a description. "He's kind of ordinary in most ways," Mrs. Moran said. "Pretty difficult to describe."

"Well," I insisted, "there has to be something. Maybe something that sounds a bit stupid but would give me a clue. If I deliver this letter to the wrong guy it'll be a wasted exercise."

Mrs. Moran hesitated, pursed her lips, hesitated some more, then burst out with something rather unusual, coming from her. "Oh!" she exclaimed, "I really don't like the man! His face is all wizened up like an old boar's testicles!"

I delivered the letter with no difficulty. There aren't many people around who fit a description like that.

Then Mrs. Moran burst out with something rather unusual...

The Killing Apology

When I was a boy in Alberta during the thirties the foothill country east of the Rocky Mountains was rich in wildlife. Everywhere you could find mule deer, elk, bear, coyote, rabbit, grouse and smaller fur-bearing animals.

Hunting was essential to the economy of the people on the land. The Blackfoot Indians and particularly the Stony Band, with whom I was most familiar, relied heavily on the deer and elk which, unlike the bison, still had abundant habitat in the foothills after European occupation of the great plains.

Even the smaller ranching operations were in such economic difficulty that wild meat took the place of beef on the table. So low was the price for slaughter-ready cattle that every possible animal had to be sold, while meat for home consumption came out of the hills.

As to whether or not the wildlife could sustain this steady harvest, the greater part of it quite illegal, we were certain in our knowledge of the hills that it could. Continuing abundance of game until long after the Second World War suggests we were correct in our belief.

It was certain that I would of necessity become a hunter of large game, but that was not in the beginning an easy development. Readily enough I had taken small game with both slingshot and firearms. But with the larger animals, particularly the deer, which I had seen in the hills since earliest memory, I had a sense of kinship which youngsters growing up in a hunting community often develop.

The deer were my friends. At the same time they were a vital source of food. I could not assume adult responsibilities without using firearms, which I had been trained to use since I came out of diapers, for the serious purpose of killing deer and other large game.

I was thirteen years old when my conflict of feeling was forced into sharp and severe focus by events. School was out at the time, and I had got work at the MacMillan ranch, a boy yet but doing a man's job in the usual way of ranch life.

In company with other members of the ranch crew I came on a buck deer. I had my rifle with me and the crew left it to me to do the shooting. I now had to be a man in hunting country, and a man I dearly wanted to be, but my eyes filled with tears, I could not shoot, and the buck got away.

The crew had no feeling for what I had gone through in that moment. We had not been especially pressed for the meat, and so the men treated the event as a huge joke, laughing about it and teasing me for days afterwards.

I was embarrassed and confused, and one day old Thomas Pedro, an outstanding hunter among the Stony Indians, came by the ranch, stopping as he did so for a meal at the cookhouse. The men made a great point of telling about the kid who got tears in his eyes and could not shoot, and my embarrassment deepened as my failure was detailed to this old Indian hunter.

I hung behind after the meal was finished while the men made their way, still having their joke at my expense, back to the bunkhouse.

But Thomas Pedro stayed behind too, and soon this old man with the creased and weathered face was standing quietly beside me. When I managed to look directly at him he asked, in a patient and gentle voice, "How was it you couldn't shoot the buck?"

"I just couldn't," I replied. "It was like he was my friend."

"Oh, I know how that is," the old man said. "I got that feeling too. But it makes you a good hunter 'cause you got a feeling for the deer. But he knows you got to hunt him for the meat. When you kill him, you 'pologize to him. You say you sorry. He knows. He hears you. Then you feel better, and you can do it easier next time. But always you say you're sorry."

It seemed strange to me to apologize to the deer after killing it, yet Thomas Pedro by that simple measure sanctioned what his calling as a hunter obliged him to do. Now he was offering this simple ritual to me, showing me how to use my sorrow to sanction what I must do.

It was not long after that when I again confronted quarry in the hills. I was alone this time, and I shot the deer, without hesitation and with a resolutely accurate shot. The kill was fast and clean. I felt the sorrow and I put words on it in my own fashion. I could not be sure that the words were necessary, yet I felt bound to say them. It seemed that I could not expect the comfort of my sorrow without fulfilling the ritual in just the way the old hunter had given it for my use.

I grew up a hunter, killing for meat or out of other necessity, always with deliberate care and always with sorrow, yet always with the ease of mind that Thomas Pedro's understanding had given me those many years before.

More About Thomas

Thomas Pedro was an old man in my earliest recollections, and after the time he helped me deal with my conflicting feelings about killing the deer, I saw more of him and learned much from and about him.

He used to borrow ammunition from me when he needed fresh meat, but always two rounds at a time, two 44-40 cartridges, never more.

One day I asked, "Thomas, why don't you take more shells at a time?"

"No," he replied. "Only need two bullets to get meat. I have to pay 'em back. I borrow too many or I buy whole box they be all gone before I could use 'em."

I learned many things from old Thomas. He showed me how to find a bear den and get the bear while he was home, how to find wolf and coyote dens while the pups were still in them and where the game went when frightened or hurt.

He taught me that to be a successful hunter you have to acknowledge the intelligence of the animals and understand the patterns in their life habits. He showed me how you must move in the environment without disturbing these patterns, how the pattern of your presence must fit in with theirs.

Through Thomas I came to appreciate how completely, in earlier days, the Indians depended for survival on killing animals, on the skills of their hunters.

Now there was another old Indian I knew, Old Sam they called him, and he wore his hair in long braids. I learned that he had earned the right to do this by serving as a warrior in battle in his youth, in the last years of the continual skirmishing between the tribes.

But Thomas Pedro did not wear braids, and this puzzled me because, of the two men, Thomas was by far the more skilled with firearms. If I had been obliged to go skirmishing anywhere it was Thomas I would have wanted with me, not old Sam.

One day I asked Thomas why he did not wear braids, and after what seemed an uncomfortable silence he said simply that he was not entitled to do so, offering no further explanation. In fact he went immediately to some quite disconnected subject, and I got a strong feeling that I should not have raised the subject.

As chance had it, the question was still on my mind one day a little later when I came on Thomas' brother Clarence Pedro, so I put the question to him, brashly, in the way of youth.

"How come Thomas can't wear braids?"

Very gruffly, Clarence said, "'Cause he never went to war."

"But," I protested, "'you know as well as I do that Thomas is ten times better than Sam with a rifle and he knows how to get around better in the hills. Why he'd be away ahead of Sam in a skirmish."

Well, I certainly triggered a lecture with that. Clarence stared at me for a while, wondering, I guess, what to say to this brash white kid, and then he went into it.

"You don't know what you're talkin' about. Long ago, Indian people run themselves and they do a good job of it. They got it organized. Each guy has what he does best and he sticks to it. He don't waste himself at something else.

"A young guy, he's good with horses. So the old men they tell him, you stick with horses. You get real good at it. And that's what he does, and he trains all the horses, trains them 'til that tribe got the best horses anywhere around. That way everybody's better off. Everybody got real good horses.

"Now Thomas, he's a hunter. When he's a little kid they see he's got it. So they help him along, teach him everything they can. Pretty soon he's better than anybody. Even when he's still a kid he's the best hunter they got.

"Now you think them old people dumb enough they're gonna send a guy like that to fight in some war where he's maybe gonna get killed?

"No, they not dumb, them old Indians. They look after that guy and they protect him. They know that some winter it's gonna be hard times, and game is gonna be scarce, and when nobody else can get game that guy's gonna get game and he's gonna keep that whole tribe alive."

Getting all that off his chest made Clarence feel better and made me feel well put in my place for asking stupid questions. But I must not have offended Clarence too badly because he then took the trouble to complete my understanding of these matters. "Okay," he said, "one way they'd use 'em, their good hunters. Maybe just a couple of 'em, you'd send 'em to find them other guys, find out how many, what they got for horses, where they got their war camp, things like that. But Thomas, they don't even use him for that. He's too good. They can't take a chance with him."

I was interested some time later to get confirmation of this practice of keeping hunters out of battle in quite another tribe. I worked for a while training horses for a Nez Perce family whose tribal homeland lay west of the mountains. The old grandmother in the family liked to tell me stories of the early days. She had been seven years old when Chief Joseph of the Nez Perce had fought his rearguard action in the mountains against the US Cavalry. The Nez Perce had developed the famous Appaloosa horse with the distinctive spotting on the rump, and the old woman recounted how the army would take the ponies from the Indians and sell them to the homesteaders for fifty cents a head for pig feed. Then the Indian youths would sneak out at night to steal back as many of the ponies as they could. All Appaloosa horses looked the same to the army, so many of them were sold and stolen back repeatedly.

To describe how bad matters became for the Nez Perce in the last days of the resistance she explained, "It got so tough we even had to send our hunters into battle."

Yes. Precious were the hunters. Precious was this old Nez Perce grandmother for telling me her stories. Precious was Clarence Pedro for pulling me up out of my ignorance about braids.

And precious was old Thomas Pedro not only for being a hunter among hunters but for all the time and patience he gave me in my youth.

Market Hunting

The majority of boys in rural Canada in the difficult years of the Depression left school on completion of the mandatory grade eight. Often a family could not afford to maintain its boys in school beyond that point, and in many cases there was little perception that further schooling had much value given the sorts of employment available in rural areas. In Alberta most boys had of necessity hired out or helped at home in ranch work of some sort and were anxious to get on with being a man. Struggling with spelling was fairly dull stuff compared to working cattle from the top side of a good saddle-horse.

The Depression was about at its worst as I approached the end of grade eight. A rancher near where my family lived sold a horse in 1936 for twenty dollars, and that twenty dollars was the only cash the ranch took in that year. You could get more for a case of eggs than you could for a grade A steer.

There was severe unemployment but no system to compare with today's unemployment insurance. It was often easier for a boy to get summer work than for a man to find anything year-round, but the summer work tended to encourage a boy to quit school in order to try his chances at finding something year-round.

The government instituted a scheme to encourage rural employment in which a payment of seven dollars and fifty cents a month was made to the rancher to hire a man and five dollars a month was provided to the man. A more generous rancher would pass his share on to the hired man as well, but many did not, and the man would work up to twelve hours a day for six days a week with chores on Sunday for the five dollars a month and his room and board.

My family lived on the edge of town in those years. My older brother had quit school on finishing grade eight, but he insisted when I finished the same grade that I should return to school in the fall and be content with what I could make from the work I would find in the summer. My father was travelling the ranching country repairing harness and my younger brother still had several years of school ahead of him.

I gave my word at the time that I would return to school, and then found work some considerable distance from home at the C-C Ranch, exercising racehorses. It was good summer work and I stayed with it until late in September, which was a poor move so far as my schooling went.

When I did get back to town I found that my father was still away on harness work, my older brother was out working on another ranch and my younger brother had scarlet fever.

Now in those years if one of the family had a disease such as mumps, scarlet fever or measles the house would be quarantined for a period of up to three weeks. A bright red notice to that effect would be posted on the door by the health authorities. For the period of the quarantine, nobody was allowed in and the children weren't allowed out. If I entered the house I would be confined and I wanted no part of that, so instead I made a little brush camp in a thicket of Saskatoon berry bushes on a creek bank near town, and from there I began attending school.

I made a little brush camp in a thicket of Saskatoon berry bushes...

It is not hard to imagine that this arrangement fell somewhere short of satisfactory. I was almost a month behind in my schoolwork, I had few clothes and doubtless was not keeping myself very clean. I probably smelled more like a polecat than like a boy fit for sitting in a stuffy schoolroom, and in the bargain I had somehow to feed myself. I took time out to hunt jackrabbits, which made catching up at school less likely. The teacher had her hands full with too many pupils already in a one room, multi-grade school, and she had no time to give me extra attention. In fact I got the distinct feeling she might be happier if I would quietly quit. When I found I could get ten cents for a jackrabbit and three cents a pound for pike at a local fox farm, I gradually began spending more time hunting rabbits and snaring pike than going to school.

I stayed in the camp well past my younger brother's quarantine, but I knew that eventually I would have to go home. Nobody was sure where I was, and they would put up with that for just so long before tracking me down and making me account for myself. At the same time I was feeling guilty because I had promised my older brother that I would stay in school and by now it was clear to me that school was out of the question.

I finally went to face my family about leaving school. My father was home by then and wanted to know just what I planned to do, so of course I said, " Get a job." Now that sounded fine but it was a long way short of realistic. Unemployment must have been running at better than fifteen percent.

I found one job for a month, for which I was paid in minor produce that I could take home to my parents but no cash.

I still had a credit at the fox farm for my later deliveries of jackrabbits and pike, and when I went to see about this I got a pleasant surprise: I had the mighty sum of five dollars and ten cents coming. Now realize that men were lucky to get five dollars a month on the government hired-man scheme, and here I had five dollars and ten cents coming from my part-time jackrabbit hunting and pike snaring.

The die was cast. I started looking for a winter hunting headquarters in the hills, and I called on my good friend Thomas Pedro to help me get started. I had been feeling very alone against the world. I had failed at school, I had broken my word to my brother and I had disappointed my family. But to Thomas Pedro I was a young hunter going about a worthy purpose, and he treated me with understanding and respect. Not only did I begin hunting for a living, I began as well to build a kind of self-respect that dropping out of school and failing to meet the expectations of my family could not erode. With Thomas Pedro's help I had found a way to be a man.

I did well. I could get from three to five dollars for a coyote, and deer meat properly killed and dressed and butchered with care to keep it clean would bring a good price provided I did not over-supply my market. Certainly the sale of deer meat brought in the bulk of my cash. As well I could still deliver such jackrabbits as came my way to the fox farm.

I was also discreet. Beyond my family only Thomas and my customers had direct evidence of my activities, and I had no fear of word spreading from these sources. So far as telling anyone else how I earned my money I would not have discussed the subject with my own shadow on a dull day.

All this presented problems for my mother. She was glad of the money I would take home from time to time, and the meat as well, but in her view you were not properly making your way in the world unless you were generating brow sweat at respectable work. People in the community would comment to her about what a good worker her boy Jim was, then follow that with, "By the way what is Wilf doing these days?" I could be seen playing baseball or hockey on weekends with other youngsters in town but was not at any time seen to be working.

My mother certainly felt the pressure of all this and one day was heard to exclaim in exasperation, "My God, Jim is always working, Dad is always working, but all Wilf does is ride around in the hills with the Indians. He's more of an Indian than the Indians themselves! How did I ever raise a boy to be like that?"

Now I could see my mother's distress, but I had found my way, and I stuck with it. Before I turned sixteen I was averaging thirty dollars a month. From then on until I enlisted in 1941 to do my share in the unpleasant business in Europe, I continued market hunting, although I also took occasional work on the ranches when extra men were needed.

I have no regrets about those years. It was a free and easy life such as a man might never experience again. In hard times I made my way, and I could hold my head up even if much of my activity was illegal. I hunted with care. I chose the bucks and dry does, never the does heavy with fawn. I dressed and butchered with care, never allowing meat to waste. I sold to customers who needed meat they could afford, and I shared meat with my fellow hunters among the Indians who in turn shared with me.

If all men would hunt as we hunted then, there would always be abundant game in the hills.

The Bow-Legged Pup
and the 25-35

During the time that I lived in my hunting camp in the hills, I would call by at my family's place whenever I would ride to town.

One day when I stopped on my way back to camp, my father called my attention to a bow-legged hound pup he had there, the last of a litter born to his prized bitch some eight months earlier.

"Take the pup with you," he instructed, "and shoot him when you get clear of the neighbourhood."

"I don't care much for shooting dogs," I complained, in what I knew was a futile protest.

"Take him and shoot him," was my father's blunt response. "I don't need him, he's no good around here and I can't sell him with his legs all bowed up like that."

So I took the big awkward pup. I tied him on a long lead rope and he bounded about on the end of it, having a happy adventure as we set off into the hills while I sat glumly on my saddle-horse thinking how much I truly did not want to shoot him.

Twenty-five miles later the pup was a little tired but still happy on the end of the lead rope, and I was not any closer to shooting him than I had been when we first set out.

As chance had it, I met Raymond Short Coat, who was out from his own hunting camp looking for game. My eyes fell on his Model 94 Winchester in .30 calibre, which used the popular 30-30 cartridge, a far superior hunting weapon to my ancient Model 73 which used the old 44-40 cartridge. Suddenly the big awkward pup and Raymond's rifle made a connection in my mind.

"Tell you what, Raymond," I said. "I'll trade you this hound for that rifle. He's good hunting stock. He'll catch you lots of coyotes."

"Wilf, you are one crazy kid," he responded. "This gun is how I get my grub. But I got another gun at camp I'll trade you."

So we set off for his camp, and the whole while I tried to get a deal on his .30-calibre weapon while persistently he made me wait to

"I'll trade you this hound for that rifle."

see this other firearm, which I assumed would be inferior to the one he was using.

I knew that now was the only chance I had to talk him out of his hunting rifle. Once we reached his camp his wife would be watching the dickering and there was no possibility of Raymond giving up the family meat rifle in that circumstance. As it turned out, Raymond stuck to his gun as it were, and on reaching his camp I still owned the awkward pup, if you could call my reluctant mission to shoot the pup a form of ownership.

Now the trade rifle turned out to be another Winchester Model 94 but in .25 calibre, using the less powerful 25-35 cartridge.

"How does it shoot?" I asked.

"Don't know," came the reply. "Never got shells for it to try it out."

Whatever I might expect of the rifle it seemed an improvement on shooting the pup, so I rode away without the pup and in possession of a new and untried firearm.

On my way to my own camp I took trails and side roads which led me by George Zarn's General Store. There I enquired of George if he had any 25-35 ammunition.

"Sure do. But can't sell it to you. Got it for Raymond Short Coat, but he hasn't picked it up yet."

So I explained that I now owned the rifle, and George sold me the ammunition.

The rifle turned out to be highly accurate within its limited range and in spite of the modest ballistics of the cartridge I soon found I could take much more game with it than with my 44-40. I quickly grew to prize the rifle far beyond its monetary worth. In the way of a boy in the middle of a difficult growing up, I valued this possession both for having come into it on my own and then for having put it to superior use.

Anxiety, however, soon clouded my delight in my new rifle.

One day some weeks later I stopped again at my parent's place, and my father asked me outright, "Did you shoot that pup?"

"No," I said.

"Why not?"

"I traded him off instead."

"What for?"

"A 25-35."

"You got it with you?"

"No. It's in camp."

"Well, bring it in. Last thing we need around here is another rifle, especially a pipsqueak like that, but we might get a few dollars for it."

Now, the rule in our family in those hard times held that whatever anyone earned at work or came by in trade could be called into the common lot. My father had the right to do with it as he saw best, and what he saw best for my new rifle was to sell it and pocket the cash.

A long time of subtle evasion followed. I would carry only my old rifle on trips to town and fend off my father's enquiries.

"You got that other rifle with you?"

"No."

"Why not?"

"Forgot."

"Well, don't forget next time."

Time passed and the evasion continued.

"Thought I told you to bring in that 25-35."

"Yeh. Well. Forgot."

"You still got it?"

"Oh, yeh. I still got it."

"Well, you bring it in."

"Okay."

I thought of offering him my 44-40 in place of the 25-35 but realized he might press the issue and confiscate both my rifles, forcing me out of the hunting business and into trying to be some rancher's hired hand again.

Time passed and my father seemed to forget about the rifle. I continued using it for illegal commercial hunting.

More time passed and the war came. I left both my rifles with Charlie Fox, an older friend of our family, and joined the Forces.

I was in England when my father finally took possession of the rifle. It seemed Charlie was at my father's place and they got to talking about going hunting, which led them to wondering where they might find some ammunition. Because of the war, ammunition was hard to come by in the stores. Suddenly Charlie remembered my rifles.

"What rifles?"

"Wilf's rifles. He left a couple of rifles and some shells when he joined up. A 25-35 and an old 44-40."

"Well, that 25-35 is mine. He got that trading off one of my pups. Let's go look."

So my father began to hunt with my rifle and even spoke proudly of its usefulness. Then one day, as inevitably he would, given the number of rifles he owned with better ballistics, he sold it.

He was a good dad, but there were things he did not understand which I had no way to explain to him either. He hurt me badly when he sold that rifle. I was a man by then, but the rifle was something solid, something I could have held in my hands and looked at later which had come out of the years of my difficult growing up, out of the time when, though still a boy, I hunted in the foothills for my livelihood and the means of my independence.

I wish he had not sold it. I would like to have it now.

II

THE WAR, BRIEFLY

Wilf enlisted in the Canadian Army in 1941. He trained in Canada, then was shipped to England in 1942 for further training and to await action. His unit went into battle following the Normandy landing and remained in action until the German surrender in 1945.

Wilf has few stories he cares to tell out of those years but some events, mostly those with a touch of humour, made good memories.

Of most significance to the rest of his life was that while based in Debert, Nova Scotia he met Vera Dunn in Truro. She was a fisherman's daughter whose father had drowned at sea. The boy from the foothills of Alberta and the girl from the fishing coves of the east coast fell in love.

On August 15, 1942 Wilf and Vera were married. Barely more than a boy when he joined up, he now went overseas to the dangers of war, leaving a loving wife in Canada waiting anxiously for his return.

Fits and Misfits

In May of 1941 I enlisted in the Canadian Army, joining the South Alberta Regiment. After a few days in which I arranged the care of my horses and stored my gear, an old friend, Jim Ryan, drove me into Calgary to a new life in military service.

In a short while we moved to Niagara-on-the-Lake in Ontario to begin training in earnest, and for most of us this was easily taken in stride. We were young and fit or could get fit quickly, we came from a variety of practical backgrounds and hard work came easily to us. Our officers and NCOs had no difficulty instilling in us a sense of pride in our unit.

We were not at full strength when we arrived in Ontario and so further men were assigned to us by the recruiting offices. We soon suspected that the best were going to the Ontario regiments while the leftovers were coming to us.

One man, on enlisting, when asked what he did for a living, replied that he made soup.

Then when asked if he was merely a kitchen helper or a fully qualified cook, he laughed and explained that to "make soup" is to to mix explosives for safe-crackers. Apparently a particular explosive, finely tuned for the job, was required to blow open a safe, and although the end use was illegal there was nothing against "making the soup" itself.

This man was soon assigned to an engineering unit.

Another man came to us because a judge had given him two choices: join the army or go to jail. I never did know for what sort of charge he was in court.

One night in the late hours, when everyone in the barrack room should have been asleep, I woke up to see this man, in the faint light available, going through another man's kit bag. I decided to watch him, intending to jump up and grab him if I saw him take anything.

Unfortunately he took too long at it and I fell asleep again. This may sound unusual but we were young, we were training hard and we slept like the dead except for such brief exceptions as I now describe.

I was now in a predicament: I did not want this man to get away with stealing but on the other hand I was too embarrassed to admit that I had fallen back to sleep while watching a thief in action.

My problem was short-lived. The man was caught thieving the next night. Barrack room justice dealt swiftly and harshly with those who stole from their comrades. This man was forced into a shower in which the water was alternated several times between cold and scalding hot. He was admitted to hospital as a result and we never saw him again.

I felt sorry for an older man — Metzik was his last name and I do not believe we ever knew his first name — who came briefly to our regiment.

He must have been close to the age limit for enlistment but he seemed even older than that. He had come to Canada from somewhere in central or eastern Europe and had been unable to learn more than the most rudimentary English. He said that his former employer had told him to try to enlist and that he would be turned down. Following this, he was told, he could keep his job. As it turned out, the army took him.

Given his age and his poor grasp of English, poor Metzik could not keep up to this boisterous lot of youngsters he had been thrown in with. In the bargain, he was too old to conform easily to regimentation in dress and daily routine. He was in trouble for some minor infraction almost daily, and was assigned most of the time to washing dishes in the camp kitchen.

Now we were in summer dress at the time — shorts and puttees and short-sleeved shirts — and we took pride in being second to none on parade. Our clothing and gear would be spotless and our boots shone brilliantly. We were young and energetic and quick and adaptable and all this spit-and-polish was no trick for us.

But for Metzik, who barely spoke English and spent most of his time washing dishes, it was all hopelessly impossible. He could not get a shine on his boots, his clothing came drab out of the wash and ironing his shirt and pants defeated him. Apart from anything else, he was too slow to get through the morning barracks routine in time to be on parade in any kind of shape. Finally, he refused to wear shorts.

His work in the kitchen had one advantage: on account of it he was often excused from parade and nobody had yet made an issue of his refusal to wear shorts.

Then one day the Regimental Sergeant Major called a parade. When the RSM called a parade, everybody had to turn out, including the kitchen staff. On an RSM parade everything had to be perfect, and we worked hard to be more than perfect. As we stood rigidly at attention not an eyelid flickered.

Now it was difficult on this parade not to crack a smile or try to sneak a glance because we all knew that at his place in the ranks old Metzik was wearing long pants and a long-sleeved shirt.

When the RSM reached this remarkable sight in the course of his inspection he let out a mighty bellow, ordering Metzik to the barracks to get on his shorts and short-sleeved shirt and return on the double. He was to be back in his place, properly dressed, before the rest of the regimental inspection was complete.

A straight face was all but impossible to maintain when Metzik returned. Indeed he had on his shorts and short-sleeved shirt, but he wore them, clumsily, over a suit of ill-fitting long woolen underwear.

Metzik was gone within the hour and we never heard of him again. I suspect he was sent back to civilian life, honourably I hope.

Gambling Man

We shipped overseas in August of 1942. We landed in Scotland, then travelled by train to the south of England to be equipped with tanks.

Along with another man, I had taken on the ship a small crown-and-anchor board. This we set up on deck, planning to make a tidy sum in the course of the twelve-day Atlantic crossing. I knew nothing about gambling but it seemed to me you could hardly lose as long as you were the one who operated the game.

And indeed we soon were making money. Word of our game got around and we looked forward to a profitable voyage.

Unfortunately, word got to the captain, who came down from the bridge in person to confiscate our equipment.

One of our comrades, Blackie, came over to console me. He explained that I'd had the right idea but that I had been too obvious. He offered no further advice at the time, however.

Now it happened that some weeks later in southern England I was ordered to drive a tank, which had developed mechanical problems but which could still travel, from our training camp to Aldershot for repairs. Blackie was provided as my co-driver.

As luck would have it, we left just before payday. Like all soldiers just before a payday, we were very nearly broke and so we crossed our fingers and hoped the repairs to the tank would be done quickly enough to let us return to our unit in time to be paid. If not, we would have to go without any money at all until the following payday.

The inevitable happened. Payday came and we were still at Aldershot. Of course everyone who belonged at Aldershot got paid and soon there were card games and dice games all over the camp.

Blackie said to me, "'I'm flat broke. Have you got any money at all?"

I replied despondently, "A measly three shillings."

He said, "Give it to me and trust me. We've got a problem to solve."

So I gave him the three shillings and he joined one of the dice games where the stakes were modest.

Soon the three shillings had grown a bit and Blackie moved to a game where rather more money was changing hands. I began to understand that more was going on than met the eye. Blackie won some and lost some but most of the time he lost the small jackpots and won the big ones. This did not happen with absolute consistency but often enough that Blackie's reserves grew at a steady pace.

Finally, when he had enough money in hand to keep both of us going until the next payday, Blackie stopped playing and we moved away from the games.

I, of course, asked for an explanation, which Blackie freely provided.

First of all, he demonstrated that he could roll any numbers he wanted with any set of dice.

Then he pointed out that even with such a talent to work with, he had also to win and lose in a pattern which would let him slowly get ahead but not arouse suspicion.

And how did he acquire these skills?

He had grown up in a gambling house. His father played poker for the house and his mother dealt blackjack. When he was a toddler the gamblers made a fuss of him and showed him little tricks. By the time he was in his teens he knew not only the little tricks but most of the big ones besides.

I learned one from him right there. I never gambled again.

A Bizarre Business

War is dreadful, visiting misery, destruction and death upon millions. At the same time, war and training for war are filled with bizarre events.

I do not much care to remember the war but when I do I tend to remember the bizarre.

After a period of training in southern England we were to move to Norfolk to a major battle training ground.

All the crews save a driver for each tank went north in a truck convoy. The small contingent of drivers, of which I was one, remained in Brighton to load the tanks on railway flatcars and then to travel north with the tanks.

The necessary string of flatcars was set on the track with a ramp at one end and planks were placed from car to car to carry the tank tracks. The plan was that the first tank would go up the ramp, then proceed to the far end of the last car in the string, followed by the second tank, which would park behind the first and so on.

Now the flatcars were just a little narrower than the outside width of the tank tracks. About an inch of tank track on each side projected over the edge of the car deck. You can imagine that this called for extremely careful driving, which is why the best drivers were in this contingent to accompany the tanks.

We brought our tanks to the railway yard and lined them up in perfect formation, facing the loading ramp at one end of the string of cars.

But now there was some hitch. The railway crew foreman explained to Lieutenant Carol, our leader, that it would be twenty minutes before we could load the tanks.

Lieutenant Carol was a young man of decent inclination. He was fair and he treated us with respect. At the same time, he could be dreadfully naive.

There was a pub nearby and Lieutenant Carol said: "All right, men. You have twenty minutes. You may go to the pub but I trust you to be back here in exactly twenty minutes."

59

We were the sort of young soldiers who gave our all in training and we were ready to give our all in war, but give us unexpected access to a pub and we would give our all to that as well. Still, we had to give it our all in exactly twenty minutes, since not one among us would violate the trust our lieutenant had placed in us.

Besides, rather much of our twenty minutes would be taken up getting to and from the pub, leaving too little time for actually drinking beer.

So off we dashed to the pub and ordered as many pints each as we thought we had time for. Then, while drinking these, we explained that we must have containers, quickly, any containers, for which we would pay whatever was asked. And, we added, don't forget to fill them with your best bitter.

So all manner of containers were rounded up, mostly the jugs and basins which were found in bedrooms lacking running water. With just enough time to get back to our tanks we departed, and as we rushed back we drank from our containers. By the time we honoured our rendezvous, the beer was finished, the containers discarded and the tank drivers drunk.

Lieutenant Carol was absolutely astounded, for this contingent of drivers had been stone sober twenty minutes ago and half that time had to be taken up travelling to and from the pub.

However, having let us go to the pub and being an honourable man, he felt he must make the best of it.

He picked out the most reliable-looking driver he could see among us and instructed him to drive on the first tank. "Now drive carefully," he emphasized, with a note of hope in his voice, as the driver boarded the tank with what appeared to us to be fairly good form under the circumstances.

Carefully would have called for a slow crawl, in low gear and with the least possible throttle, up the ramp and along the cars and over the connecting planks, with great attention to staying dead centre all the way.

Our chosen lead driver put the tank in third gear at full throttle, rattled up the ramp, then raced along the string of cars, not stopping once until he was in perfect position at the end of the last car.

It had been a breathtaking performance. Not one among the rest of us thought it possible to duplicate the feat and it now seemed unlikely we would have the opportunity to try. The train crew foreman was stunned at what he had witnessed and Lieutenant Carol appeared to be in shock.

In a hurried conference with the lieutenant, the foreman offered to arrange careful loading of the tanks. It seemed he had men with sufficient experience driving heavy equipment that the job could be done with care for both the tanks and the precious flatcars.

We were in Norfolk before Lieutenant Carol assigned us to our tanks again or, for that matter, even cared to acknowledge our existence.

Back in Canada every unit of any size had most of its own facilities and always its own canteen and bar. In England as the Allied forces gathered to further their training and prepare for major action against the enemy, many facilities, and always it seemed the canteens, had to be shared.

Some friction resulted, which occasionally led to a little brawling or other excitement.

Now the equivalent to our canteen in Canada was the Navy, Army, Air Force Institute, commonly known as the NAAFI. These were friendly coffee-shop places staffed by women who helped us remember that the world had not really turned into an all-male barrack room establishment. There were jokes about the NAAFI coffee, the NAAFI sausages and even a few about the NAAFI girls, though that was hardly fair. They worked hard to give service and be cheerful, to a pretty mixed bag of men when you got down to it.

They also had to deal with a surplus of lonely young men seeking their affection. This could be trying, but for the most part they deflected the excess of attention with tact. In the larger camps, they were often the only women within miles.

Such was the case at Norfolk where we shared the NAAFI with other units, including the Polish Armoured Division.

Now a Polish soldier had grown sweet on one of the young NAAFI women, but of course this meant nothing to the arriving crowd of young Canadians. Soon this particular lass was receiving a whole lot of additional attention, which did not escape the notice of the Polish lad. He would come in hoping to have her attention, only to find her surrounded by Canadians and trying to be courteous to everyone and do her job at the same time. With her attention so divided there was only a cheerful hello and a smile for everyone and they all had to share it as best they could.

The Polish lad could bear this no longer. He must talk with her about it. He came in one day to achieve this but she was too busy to talk with anyone.

I'm sure she would have talked with him had she foreseen the consequences, for he had brought with him a training grenade we called the thunderflash, not deadly like the real thing and incapable of throwing shrapnel, but loaded with enough explosive to train men in the use of grenades in battle.

The NAAFI was heated by a coal stove in the centre of the dining room, and fortunately there was only a small fire in it at this time. Our frustrated suitor strode to the stove, opened the door, tossed in the thunderflash and calmly walked away.

The explosive power in the thunderflash was taken up largely in shattering the stove, so the flying bits of stove and stovepipe, impressive as they were, inflicted no serious injuries.

. . .flying bits of stove and stove-pipe. . .

More awesome were the loud bang and the bursting cloud of soot which instantly reached every corner of the room, and the pandemonium as people ran into each other, all trying at the same time to go somewhere safe.

That was the most excitement we saw in our stay at Norfolk.

When the second front opened up we were still waterproofing tanks in England, so we knew we were being saved for something special. Eventually we shipped out of London in American LSTs (Landing Ships, Tank).

Each ship carried a squadron of tanks. I drove my tank onto our ship last and would therefore be the first to drive off.

We were to land on a secured beach which had been cleared of mines and tank traps. The ships would go in on the high tide, then wait for the tide to drop. Once the beach was high and dry, we would drive off our ships then form up on shore.

All the squadron commanders had entered into a wager which called for the commander whose ship unloaded last to buy drinks for all the others, and so there was considerable motivation to do a fast job of getting the tanks smoothly onto the beach.

All seemed to go well. We made our landing and waited for the tide to drop. Finally, there we sat on several miles of clear, dry beach with an LST on the sand about every hundred yards.

Our squadron commander came to remind me of the urgency of getting off quickly and then moving forward promptly so that the following tanks would not be held up by indecision on my part. I was eager and I assured him he could rely on me.

The moment the ramp was down I threw my tank into gear and rumbled forward, exhilarated to be leading our squadron ashore.

Down the ramp I went, straight into a seventeen-foot-deep shell hole full of water.

That was the only wet landing in the regiment, and it took some time to winch my tank out of there. Needless to say, our commander bought the drinks that day.

We moved up through Caen to Falaise and sprung the trap on the German 7th Army. We worked our way from Falaise to the Seine River, our next major obstacle.

When the remnants of the German army retreated they confiscated everything they could use. Short on fuel and transport, they confiscated even the farmers' horses. The road leading up through Truin was littered with dead soldiers, broken and discarded equipment and dead or crippled horses. The sight of those horses seemed more painful than all the rest. They had not declared a war, they had just got caught up in it.

When we reached the Seine we had to wait for a means of crossing the river to be devised. Briefly, though still subject to enemy fire, we had a breathing space.

There, just where we stopped, was a fine-looking bay horse, still with a saddle on but running loose and so scared he trembled. He couldn't decide which way to run.

I felt as though I had found treasure. We had this bit of time on our hands and here was a horse. I approached him and talked him down from his fear and took him by the bridle. Now I could spend a little time with him and it would be almost like home, even in the middle of this war. But even that was cut short by a quick command. "Taylor! Let go that horse and keep your head down! Anything you do that makes you look different will draw sniper fire. You know that."

We crossed the Seine on my birthday, under smoke and fire. We stopped briefly in a little village where everybody toasted us with whatever drink they had been able to keep hidden. I had never drunk enough to become experienced at it, and what with all these friendly people and it being my birthday, I soon had a little too much. Not much too much but a little too much, and so I was told to move over into the co-driver's seat.

We were clearing an orchard and I felt a little sick, so I opened the tank hatch and rode along with my head and shoulders in the open. This made us somewhat vulnerable because if the crew needed to swivel the turret, I would have to come down and close the hatch, delaying our response time.

As we rounded a corner I spotted a German soldier just thirty yards away with a bazooka aimed at us. He certainly had us if he decided to shoot, but on the instant of seeing him I waved to him. He dropped the bazooka and ran.

We all agreed that he must have thought, when I waved, that I had thrown a grenade, and this had made him more anxious to run away from the shrapnel than stay around to fire his weapon.

But that did not save me from being put on orders. I had to parade in front of the major with my hat off and the only excuse I could offer was that it had been my birthday. I caught a good lecture and a few threats about what would happen to me if I were so indiscreet again.

We worked our way up through France and into Belgium, crossing several rivers and canals.

Just outside Bruges we were held up at a canal waiting for a bridge to be put over. Advance units were engaged in furious house-to-house fighting in the village directly across from us. We had lost a close buddy of mine that morning and I was not feeling friendly toward anyone, particularly not toward the guys who were shooting at us.

Right in front of our tank a soldier from the Argyle and Sutherland Highlanders was loading a rowboat with piat bombs. He then began to row this deadly load across the canal. When he neared the middle of the canal, he came under heavy machine-gun fire, and now he rowed to beat hell. Then the firing stopped and he rowed steadily to the other shore to unload.

Then back he came for another load.

Again, out in the middle of the canal he drew fire, and soon it was evident to us that as he made the crossing he was not visible to the enemy gun position while close to either shore but was in full view for that deadly stretch in the middle of the canal.

He did not make just two trips, he made several, and every time he approached the middle of the canal he would do something different from the times before and always, out there under fire, he moved with such a burst of speed you could hardly believe one man in a loaded rowboat could do it.

We shook our heads. One trip, yes. Two trips, maybe. But several trips — and I do not remember exactly how many — impossible. Yet he had done it, for we saw him safely on shore after his last trip.

A couple of weeks later I was in a hospital getting patched up so I could go back into action, and who should walk into the ward but this same soldier who had rowed his boat in the eye of death.

"Well," I declared, glad to see him alive, "they got you too, did they?" This was more an assertion than a question.

"Oh, hell, no," he replied. "I just came in here to get my piles fixed. They got so bad I could hardly sit down. Had 'em for years and they flare up every once in a while and give me a hell of a time."

After I got out of hospital and returned to the regiment we crossed the Rhine into Germany over a huge pontoon bridge.

We went into a support position on one site where those of our tanks which were equipped with 75-mm guns were used to provide indirect fire, while the rest of us, equipped with 17-pounders, had nothing of a fighting nature to occupy us.

We were told to carry out maintenance on our tanks. Whenever our officers had no other way to occupy us we would be told to carry out maintenance on our tanks. This job would wear out pretty quickly, particularly if it happened to be the third or fourth time in a short while that we had done maintenance on our tanks.

One of the men from another troop sought me out to tell me that he had seen a small herd of deer in a nearby wood. He said he had heard that I used to hunt deer and he thought I might be interested.

I thanked him for the information and he returned to his troop. When I had some time in which I reckoned I would not be missed for a while, I went out to hunt up these deer.

This did not take long, and soon I brought down a young buck in fair condition, then dressed him out. These were small animals compared to our Alberta bred mule deer but there was enough of this buck to provide everyone with fresh deer steaks after I packed the meat back to our bivouac.

Of course I saved some steaks for the man from the other troop who had told me about the deer and these I took to him.

To my surprise he was not at all pleased. It turned out that what he had wanted was for me to take him hunting. I was to have been the guide, he was to have been the hunter.

Oh well, I thought, you can't please everybody all of the time.

Soon we were rolling forward again, into the thick of another battle. Who actually shot the little buck didn't matter much then.

The Medicine Tree

As we moved into German territory and pressed eastward, we knew the war must soon come to an end. The Russians were pressing westward and somewhere along the sprawling Allied front, the forces from the east would meet those from the west, reducing the enemy armies to isolated pockets of weakening resistance.

Even as we pressed on with the last of the fighting, battle-hardened now and more efficient, men began to think beyond the conflict and, in their thoughts at least, to disassociate themselves from the noise and the clamour and the senselessness of war.

For me this process had begun with the terrified saddle-horse back at the Seine. After that I thought more and more of home, of horses and old friends, of the foothills and the call of the loon and the yelping howl of a coyote at night.

Even the short hunt in which I brought fresh deer meat to camp seemed like a step away from the war and toward the real life which I had set aside for the duration of this terrible business.

Long ago on the western plains and in the foothills a warrior would make a ritual with his young son.

He would take the boy to some secluded place where he would tie a young and supple sapling into a knot. As the sapling grew the knot would form a heavy head and when eventually the tree was cut down, the head, with a section of the stem for a handle, made a warclub.

Sometimes the warrior would split a short section of the stem of a young tree, then place a stone more long than wide through the opening. Over the next several years the stem would grow stronger, closing up tightly on the stone. When cut, the stem with its tightly secured stone made a formidable weapon in the hands of a young, strong man.

Neither the warrior nor the boy would return to the secluded place where the warclub grew until it was time for the boy's first sundance, and the rituals through which he would become a man and a warrior himself. Then together they would go there to cut the young tree and return with the weapon.

There is a story that once long ago a great warrior, much respected among his friends and widely feared by his enemies, brought his young son to Spitzee Crossing on the Highwood River, the place we call High River today, to set a warclub. The warrior selected a well-shaped stone, then split a section of the stem of a strong, straight sapling, placing the stone carefully in the opening. "When we come here again," he told his son, "you will have the finest of warclubs."

But when the boy was ready for his first sundance and came with his father to fetch his club, he was dismayed to see that instead of growing fast around the stone to secure it, the tree had separated and grown into two strong trunks.

The youth was dismayed and he turned on his father. "You made it the wrong way and now I have no warclub," he cried. "You have failed me!"

"No," the old warrior replied. "This tree will grow to be a great medicine tree. It will grow to the sky and the clouds will be its leaves and whoever comes here to pause beneath the tree will be filled with peace."

I heard variations on this story, and part of the myth had to do with how, from High River, you could see the great expanse of the foothills and the great mountains beyond reaching to the sky, often with billowing thunderheads rising into the blue above. And indeed, if you paused to look westward to this most powerful of landscapes, a great sense of peace would come over you and truly you paused then beneath the medicine tree.

And now, in Germany, the war was winding down.

We were in a farmyard just south of Oldenburg. Our troop was together, standing about drinking coffee and thinking and talking of home and what a man might want to do first.

I was half listening to the talk but much of my mind was far away when someone caught my attention with the question we were all trying to consider. "Wilf, what are you going to do when it's over?"

I thought for a moment, then said, "I'm going to pause beneath the medicine tree." Then, knowing that would not mean anything by itself but not wanting to explain it, I added, "It's just an old Indian story. Kind of complicated to explain."

Nobody pressed me on the point and the question moved to someone else.

III

AFTER THE WAR

This was a difficult period in which Wilf carried a burden of disappointment. It begins with his return from overseas in 1945 and ends in 1950 as he concludes that his opportunity to earn a living for a growing family in the foothill country is too insecure.

For the most part, Wilf remembers an event and tells a story about it for its humour or its human interest or for what it tells of animal life.

In this interval, Wilf tells the story of his disappointment. For many years, he mentioned it to no one and, apart from telling it here, he does not dwell upon it.

With that story told, Wilf goes on to recount some happier events.

A Difficult Return

Returning from overseas at the end of the war, I faced a problem shared by millions of service people: I had gone into service barely out of boyhood with only the Great Depression of the thirties for an experience of life's opportunities. I came out of the service substantially matured and hoping to anchor some substance into my future but without much certainty as to how that would be done.

In addition, I had met and married Vera in Halifax on the way overseas and visited with her on my way home after the war. Shortly she would join me in Alberta. I was not a boy any longer, free to roam the hills. I was a man with a family soon to care for.

As did many others, I supposed, naïvely, that my country's goodwill toward its returning service men and women would help me, in the common meaning of the phrase, to make something of myself. My hope was reinforced when I learned, through meagre counselling offered on discharge, that through the Veteran's Land Act I might acquire property.

While settling the great plains, the Canadian Government had surveyed virtually the whole of the prairies and much of the foothills into sections, tracts of land a mile square, containing 640 acres.

Long before I was born the whole of the plains had been taken up, and in the foothills country rural society consisted mostly of two classes of people: the cattle ranchers, in possession of large acreages and generally prosperous, and the rest, who got what work they could as hired hands or tradespeople. These might, at most, come by enough land on which to build a home and keep a cow and a few chickens to help feed a family.

Most of the girls in the landless families sought work in the towns after finishing a limited rural schooling; many of the boys grew up to move about in search of work as hired men, living in bunkhouses.

A few of the more determined and able young men would become year-round steady hands on the larger ranches. For these men there was some possibility of marriage and a modest house provided by the ranch, a distinct improvement on a single man's bunkhouse existence.

When the lands were laid out to be granted to the arriving settlers, two sections in every township, Sections 11 and 29, were set aside for school purposes. As matters turned out the rural school system did not use these, so the school sections, as they were known, were the only lands, by the end of the Second War, still held by the government.

If the government was to assist returning service people to acquire land, these school sections had to be available. However, in most cases, these sections had been leased to neighbouring ranchers as additional grazing land for their cattle. The ranchers were not in the least interested in giving up these grazing leases to make way for returning veterans.

The government compromised: no land would be used for settling veterans unless the predominant part of the tract could be brought into cultivation. In addition, the rancher would be compensated for improvements such as fencing.

Having travelled my part of the foothills extensively by saddle-horse, I knew the land well. Particularly, I knew who owned what sections and which were still held by government and in these cases which ranches held the grazing leases.

I applied for the west half of a school section in which the bulk of the land was in wild hay and amenable to cultivation, with only the northeast corner in rough land suitable only for grazing.

The road providing access to the property cut through this corner of rough land.

The property was fenced on three sides by adjoining ranches but not on the side adjoining the ranch which held the lease. This rancher did not graze his own cattle on the land but sub-leased it, by informal arrangement, to yet another rancher.

I expected to be notified of a time for the land to be inspected by a Veterans Land Act (VLA) representative so that I could be present during the inspection and explain how I planned to use the land. I understood that both the applicant and the lease-holding rancher were to be present at all inspections.

The first indication that something might be amiss came in a chance encounter with another rancher, Jim Sauley, some weeks after I had filed the application. I met him on the road and we stopped to talk. He asked me why I had applied for the rough land in the north half of the school section. I explained that I had, in fact, applied for the west half, which contained the usable land. He responded with the usual oh, I see, and then explained briefly that he had met the VLA man, along with the rancher who held the lease and a third unidentified man, on what he assumed was the inspection trip. They had been looking at the northeast corner of the section.

I attached little importance to this apparent confusion at the time, assuming that the VLA representative would have referred to the application and the map, discovered the error and proceeded to the west half. I so firmly expected to receive the land that already I had purchased the horses I would support on the property, using it as a base for an outfitting operation. My mind was not ready to register a signal of something gone wrong.

Then the blow landed. I got a letter from the VLA inspector advising that my application was disallowed because the land I had applied for was not suitable for cultivation and, further, there was no appeal from this decision.

The letter, with abrupt finality, destroyed all the plans I had made since learning of the Veterans Land Act settlement plan and identifying this particular half-section as available land. I had no experience in dealing with government and in my bewildered frame of mind could think of no way to salvage anything of my hopes.

A few days later and still bewildered, I chanced on Raymond Short Coat in the hills. We gave our horses rein enough to graze while we talked. Soon I told Raymond of my disappointment.

Raymond, it turned out, had witnessed the inspection.

He had been hunting coyotes that day, horseback with two hounds on long leashes, and had gone by only yards from the road where the inspection party had been standing, looking out over the rough northwest corner of the section.

Unlike Jim Sauley, who had stopped only briefly, Raymond had seen a vehicle arrive, watched three men emerge, looked on while considerable pointing and arm waving had ensued, then watched the party drive away.

The entire proceeding, including the brief stop by Jim Sauley as he had driven by, took no more than twenty minutes by the sound of it.

Suddenly, facts which I had long known and the information that Jim and Raymond provided came together in my mind to convince me that I was not simply the victim of a sorry misunderstanding, I had been deliberately and blatantly cheated.

The rancher who held the lease was a heavy-drinking man and a bit of bad luck had put my hopes into his hands to be disposed of as he chose.

With some guesswork, a picture took shape. The VLA representative, unable to reach me by telephone but wanting to set up the inspection, had telephoned the rancher. Could he contact Wilf Taylor and could all three meet at the ranch and proceed to the inspection?

Of course he could. Men were easily found who would pass themselves off as Wilf Taylor or anyone else for a ten-dollar bill and a few drinks of whiskey.

And then a few drinks of whiskey for the inspector when he shows up, a quick drive to view the rough land in the northeast corner of the section and it's all over in minutes, never mind that the land the real Wilf Taylor applied for is actually the west half and a forty-minute walk from the nearest point on the road.

Even the guesswork was later confirmed.

No longer was I bewildered, I was plain angry and I went to the Royal Canadian Mounted Police officer in Nanton expecting to get help in exposing the lies which had been used against me.

Not only did I fail to get help but in a short and harsh exchange with the police officer my situation went from bad to worse.

Relying on Raymond Short Coat's account of the inspection, I explained the deception I was convinced had occurred.

Immediately I was upbraided for presuming to accuse an established rancher of wrongdoing.

Did I realize how serious that was, to make a false accusation? Raymond Short Coat? So who's Raymond Short Coat? You don't expect anyone to take an Indian's word against a respected rancher, do you?

In an outbreak of frustration and anger I said, "All right, I'll get the truth out of the bastard my own way!"

"Oh. How do you plan to do that?"

"Well hell, I'll *force* it out of him!"

"You'll use force, will you? Well, just you remember that you have stated to me your intention to use force. On the basis of that I am going to secure from the magistrate an order binding you over for two years to keep the peace. You get in so much as a fistfight in an alley and you'll land in jail. Now get out of here and stay out of trouble."

Looking back after many years experience in how government bureaucracies work and with a better sense of how the legal system can be used to redress unfair treatment, I am sure there were ways in which I could have exposed the fraudulence of that rancher and the incompetence of the VLA inspector, but within the limits of my knowledge then I had nowhere to turn. I had been cheated by a greedy ranch owner and the system of law and justice from which I had sought help had served only to further entrench the injustice.

At such a point a man either lives with his bitterness until he can direct his hopes and hard work to other objectives or he throws everything away in an act of revenge which, while it might give him some sense of justice done, will as surely mess up his life beyond repair.

I went from the RCMP office to the bar at the Nanton Auditorium Hotel. I ordered a beer and sat alone at a table to sip it while I tried to fume my way to a decision about which direction I would choose. There is no doubt a swift and violent squaring of accounts appealed more, in the frustration of the moment, than any other.

The bartender interrupted my black and vile brooding. "Guy out in the lobby wants to talk to you."

"If he wants to talk to me, he can come in here."

"This guy never comes in a bar."

"That right," I said, and sat a while longer until my curiosity got the better of me. Then I stood up, put a ten-dollar bill under my glass of beer and headed for the lobby, muttering to myself about seeing now if the world was so goddamn mean someone would even steal the ten dollars from my table.

The man waiting for me in the lobby turned out to be Tommy Farrell, Superintendent of Burns Ranches. It was with this outfit that I had left some horses on enlisting in the army, older horses

I put a ten dollar bill under my glass of beer...

which I had not expected to be of enough use to have troubled to fetch them when I had arrived back in the country.

Tommy Farrell came straight to the point in a friendly but efficient manner. "Wilf, I just want to welcome you home and tell you two things. First, the ponies you left at the ranch are still there and the old mare has had a foal every year, so you've got some good young stock there as well. You should come to fetch them. Second, there's a job for you at the ranch any time you want it. Not pressing you about it, you understand, but it's waiting for you if you should decide you want it."

I thanked him, but I was stuck for much else to say. I wasn't prepared, at that moment, for ordinary decency. But I did put one question. "How did you know I was here?"

"Raymond Short Coat told me." With that he left, and I stood a while in the hotel lobby, staring out through the large window onto the street, trying to get the bad and the good into perspective in my mind.

The superintendent of the largest ranch in Alberta had taken the trouble to breed my old mare to the ranch stallion every year so I'd own some young stock when I came home. Now, on the word of an Indian, whose word the police officer discounted completely, he had come to give me a few positive things to think about when I most needed something fresh in my head.

I was not ready then to take up the job offer but I left the hotel lobby by way of the door to the street, not back to the bar. I thought briefly, as I left, about my ten-dollar bill under the part glass of beer but said to myself, the hell with it.

There followed the most difficult period of my life, lasting fully two years.

I did not immediately take up the offer to work for Burns Ranches. I had been too long counting on running my own place to want to drop into the role, however secure, of year-round hired hand.

Yet clearly I must make a living. Vera was due to arrive west within days.

A friend, Sid Young, had bought a piece of land known as the Dixon quarter which had a modest house on it. He did not need the house and through his generosity this would be our first home together. I reckoned I could get by well enough breaking horses for surrounding ranches, contract haying and fencing and taking enough meat out of the hills to meet our own needs with perhaps some extra to sell.

I could also do some horse trading for extra cash now and again, but clearly I could not use the string of heavy packhorses I had been gathering, so I rounded these up and sold them to the fox farm. It was a bitter way to sell off the remnants of my dream of a place of my own, but it was the only fast way to recover some cash and be rid of the horses.

On the heels of that Vera arrived. With an old Model A Ford I had bought for a few dollars and kept running with ingenuity I went into Calgary to meet her and fetch her home to the borrowed house on the Dixon quarter.

Not then nor for forty years afterwards did I tell Vera about applying for and being refused the half-section of land. I had expected to surprise her on her arrival with land of our own on which to begin our married life, and I could see no use whatever in telling her now of how we had been cheated out of that opportunity.

There was a barn and the necessary corrals at the place, so I began bringing in unbroken horses, a few at a time, to break and train for use in ranch work.

Running cattle in the foothills called for men on horseback, a few at some seasons, many at others. A ranch could hire enough reasonably useful riders to get the work done but had to provide for each rider several well-broken, reliably gentle and decently trained horses.

Only one working cowboy out of many had the skills and the inclination to break a range-raised horse to carry a man in the saddle, respond to the rein, work cattle and to give up, for all practical purposes, the natural desire of the half-wild horse to turn any occasion under the saddle into a bucking contest.

It followed that those few men with the skills and inclination to break horses could make the better part of a living at the work provided they did a consistently good job. *Reliably gentle* and *decently trained* meant just that, and if you turned horses back to the ranches still half-wild, you would soon lose the trade.

Now roughly speaking there were two extremes to the individual style of breaking horses: a slow and patient approach on the one hand, a fast and rough approach on the other.

The patient horse breaker took a long time in the preliminary stages and avoided, as much as possible, a bucking contest and other confrontations of sheer will and physical force.

The rougher man hurried the horse through the earlier sessions and aimed to do most of the training from the saddle. He expected to buck the horse out a few times in the process. Resistance on the part of the horse at any stage would be met with tough discipline, and clearly there was opportunity for mean treatment.

Either way you break a ranch horse, the horse needs many days under the saddle to complete the training and build in the essential reliability. A man will work with a few horses at a time, which means extra long hours in the saddle, long days in the hills alone with the horse and lots of time to think about other matters.

In the long days at my disposal in those two years I could not keep out of my mind the brooding, smouldering thoughts of how I had been cheated of my hope for a piece of land on returning from military service.

I went into the hills with a rifle in a saddle scabbard because, of course, we needed the meat. You could not buy store meat on what a man earned breaking horses. But I would ride in the hills above the land out of which I had hoped to make a place of my own, and never far from the land of the rancher who had prevented my getting it. As persistently as the smouldering anger ate at my soul, I was drawn to ride where a confrontation could most easily happen. Somewhere below the level of deliberate, conscious intent, the rifle may not have been only for meat.

And where I rode, that rancher's breeding cattle ranged. Through the crucial months of early summer when next year's calf crop depended on every breeding cow receiving a bull in her heat, I quietly herded the cows away from the bulls. This was excellent training for the horses I was breaking, and it played hell with next spring's calf crop.

I broke the horses in a rougher fashion than I need have done, although I turned each horse back to its owner reliably broken and thoroughly disciplined, probably more disciplined than necessary. In my anger I had to pick a fight where I could, and the horses I was breaking were the handiest living creature for the purpose.

Now a man can waste his time in a bad rut getting nowhere for a long time without having the wit to see who he's hurting most. The best thing then is for someone to whom he might listen to tell him plainly he's going nowhere and in danger of sliding backwards in the bargain. I was fortunate, after fully two years in my bad rut, to be confronted with some essential home truths by one of the few people, given my frame of mind, whom I would have heard out.

Frequently I stopped by at the Ryan Ranch, only three miles from

the Dixon quarter, to chat with Mrs. Ryan. She was a good neighbour and always wanted to know how we were managing.

One day she said to me, after we had talked a while. "Listen, I've
got a letter here I want to send to Pat. She's working at the Brazil
Ranch. That horse needs some miles on him by the looks of him.
Will you take the letter?"

I agreed, and the next day I left early from home, telling Vera I
might or might not be back by nightfall since it was fifty miles round
trip to the Brazil Ranch.

I arrived at the ranchhouse in the late morning and delivered the
letter, then went to the barn to feed my horse and wait for the lunch
bell to ring. I was pleased when I arrived at the barn to find Clarence Pedro. I had not realized that he was working at the Brazil
Ranch, so seeing him came as a pleasant surprise, and soon he had
drawn me into a discussion which had the earmarks of being quite
deliberate. I got the sense that he might even have been waiting
there for me to arrive.

He asked casually about some of our mutual friends around the
district and I offered what I could tell him.

Then he asked, "You see anything much of that outfit down by
Section 29?"

I said, "No. I don't go around that way much."

"Yeh," Clarence replied. "I wouldn't go around them people
much myself. But that's not the way I heard it, Wilf. What I heard
is you been spendin' a lotta your time ridin' the ridges down that
way with a rifle under your leg."

I was looking down at the ground by this time, and anyway Clarence did not seem to need confirmation on the point. I said nothing
and soon he continued. "Wilf, you keep that up and one day you
gonna get a chance to do something, and you maybe not gonna be
able to stop youself. Then you gonna hurt a lotta people, not just
youself. You right when you want to do something about how you
was cheated, but you do it and you gonna lose.

"Sure you was cheated. So was the whole Stony Band. Our people
was all living off the land in the foothills and the mountains when
the reserves was made. It was the only place left after the buffalo
was gone. The government never set any land to one side for us
'cause we was still makin' out on our own. Now there ain't enough
left open in the foothills for us to get by the old way and we got no
reserve, no land to settle on and raise some stock. You know about
that. All we do is work around from one ranch to another and
sometimes stay with a relation at Morley if the band there'll let us.

"But we got no home, and there ain't no use us tryin' to straighten things out by takin' the law into our own hands, like they say. Now we all your friends, and we know how you feel, but you got to get away from what you doin'.."

Once Clarence got going there was no stopping him, and I was not about to try. He took another breath and pitched a new argument. "Now," he said, "you mostly breakin' horses these days. Maybe you breakin' horses just so you can hang around down that way.

"Well, you not cut out to break horses. Guys who break horses steady, after a while they ain't got the patience anymore, and they start to get mean. Wilf, you not meant to be like that, but you goin' to get like that if you don't look out.

"You and Thomas, you both the same. You got a feeling for animals. You guys even pray over 'em when you got to kill 'em. I know all about that. Might be best if you just go away someplace in the bush for a while, some place where there's lotsa animals.

"But whatever, you got to get outa hangin' around down that way where you can't get it outa your mind what happened."

The lunch bell finally stopped old Clarence, but in any case he had about finished. He said only one thing later, after we had eaten lunch at the cookhouse with the crew and I was setting off for the ride home.

He came to see me off and he said, "Sorry if I spoke out of turn, but we all pretty worried about you. Whatever you do, we all on your side."

"It wasn't out of turn," I answered. Then I mounted up, said goodbye and left.

I still had the feeling that Clarence had been waiting for me, that he'd known I was coming and now I began to wonder what was so important about the letter to Pat that it couldn't have taken the time to go through the post office.

When I arrived home I told Vera I was going to take a job at the Burns Ranch, that we needed something more reliable than deer meat and breaking horses.

I Poach a Few Ducks —
Entirely by Mistake

While the major event of my return from the war was my bitter disappointment over the settlement land, more than a few amusing incidents occurred which stand out in my memory. I'll go back to the beginning of that time to tell about these.

When I first returned my parents and my brother Don were living in Calgary. I did not think it proper to cut and run for the hills on my first day back, so for a few days I visited about in Calgary.

Now every bar in the city was filled with returned soldiers, drinking free beer and swapping stories. I had seen a little action and been wounded a couple of times but the last thing I wanted to do was talk about it. I wished more than anything to go back to where a man could find a horse and perhaps hunt for some meat and otherwise get back to a proper way of life.

Don, younger than me by five years and who by his youth had, thankfully, missed the war, sensed I was at a loss and asked if there was anything in particular I would like to do.

I thought about that, and since we were now into the fall I said, "Sure. Let's go duck hunting."

Don said, "Gee, Wilf, I dunno. It's getting late, and they're all gone south, or they're so spooky you can't get near 'em."

"I don't care," I replied. "All I want to do is shoot at a couple and watch 'em fly away. It doesn't really matter whether we get any or not. Just like to go out there and smell the swamp and hear 'em quackin' around. Just sort of for old times sake, you know."

We had time enough for me to buy a hunting licence, and well before daylight the next morning we took two shotguns and drove into the countryside in my younger brother's old Chrysler.

Once into duck pond country we drove along about five miles an hour with the windows down, listening for ducks and smelling the yellowing leaves and old grass in the rich fall air.

Now sitting in a duck blind in the dark before the dawn and listening to the ducks organize themselves for their morning flight is an experience I particularly cherish. If you're lucky, when they fly you'll get one chance to take a few ducks home for the pot, and the rest will wing on south.

Soon I heard ducks, so we took the next road that turned in the direction of the sound. We drove without lights down a rutted, grassy road, stopping every hundred yards or so to verify with our ears the presence somewhere ahead of the pondful of ducks.

Finally we could tell by the volume of sound and the strength of the pond smells that we were close. We parked the car and sneaked forward to the water's edge.

In a whisper, I asked Don, "Where are we?"

"Damned if I know," he replied.

As dawn broke the ducks lifted off, and they flew right down our shotgun barrels. Soon we were out of shells and began picking up our ducks. It had been incredibly easy, practically made to order.

Then Don said, "There's something damned wrong here."

I said, "Not really, they're just glad to see me back."

"I don't mean the damn ducks," he replied, in a grim voice.

As we started to climb up from the water's edge Don said, "I figured so. Look!"

By the side of the road, next to Don's car, stood a six-foot-square sign saying Bird Sanctuary — No Shooting or Molesting Birds.

As we quickly drove away I knew we would wait a long time to experience bird shooting to equal what we had just enjoyed. I felt sorry for my friends who had found nothing better to do than sit in the bars and talk about a distant war.

By the side of the road stood a six foot square sign . . .

The Thirty-Mile Horse Race

The stampede, now more commonly called the rodeo, is perhaps the better known of the ranch country events involving cowboys and horses. But horse racing, in fact, occurred more frequently throughout the west.

Racing took many forms, from the spur-of-the-moment dash in which one cowboy undertook to demonstrate the superiority of his mount over that of a companion, to professionally organized races with horses bred for the purpose at established tracks with pari-mutuel betting.

In earlier days, racing was often a competition between the larger ranches, which competed at first with range-bred stock-horses but eventually with carefully bred thoroughbreds raised on the side, as it were, to defend the reputation of the ranch in local competition.

A wide range of race conditions prevailed, usually defined by type of horse, distance run, nature of track and prize money offered.

In the early days in the west, ranches would work together to gather cattle from jointly used open range in an early summer round-up, in which the calves would be tallied and branded. At the start of the work the chuckwagons would race from the rendezvous point for the choicest springs and campsites, laying the foundation for the modern-day chuckwagon races at the Calgary Stampede.

As with many entertainments, horse racing had been curtailed by the war in the first half of the 1940s, but with the end of the war and the return of many young cowboys in 1945, racing enthusiasts cast about for new and better events to sponsor.

In early 1946 the Western Riding Club of Calgary announced that it would hold a thirty-mile marathon race on the 24th of May to start and finish at the Paradise Grove stampede grounds near Midnapore, Alberta.

Any horse could be entered, stock saddles must be used and the combined weight of saddle and rider must be no less than two hundred pounds.

A first prize of five hundred dollars was offered. To put that in perspective, most cowboys would be lucky to earn that much on the range in six months, while a good horse for this sort of race could be purchased for thirty-five dollars, even, with luck, for as little as fifteen dollars.

A good horse for this sort of race, which called for incredible endurance as well as speed, would be sired by a thoroughbred stud bred to a heavier built stock-horse mare with the staying power needed for long days working cattle on the open range.

Inevitably, the combination of good prize money and a long distance created the danger that cowboys would push their horses beyond reasonable limits. A willing horse is easily run to death by a rider eager to cover distance but insensitive to the animal beneath the saddle.

A conscientious rider would pace his or her horse, not pressing furiously in the early stages, in order to have strength left in the crucial final sprint for the finish line.

The five-hundred-dollar first prize drew in forty-three starters, Wilf Taylor of Nanton among them.

When the race was announced I had thirteen or fourteen horses, but no one of them suitable for the race, so I began scouting for a mount.

I approached Allie Streeter, a good horseman and rancher, about a horse he owned which I had observed at work and which I believed could be conditioned and carefully ridden for a good performance over a thirty-mile course.

He was not impressed with my proposal.

"Wilf," he said, "if you want a saddle-horse I'll sell him to you. But to run him to death in a race like that, never. You and I know that getting a good day's work done with a horse is what counts, not who can run a horse fastest over thirty miles."

I was a little horrified that Allie could think like that about me. I had every intention of taking care in the race and only winning if I could do so without hurting my horse. But Allie's comment certainly made me resolve again to take scrupulous care of any horse I might ride in the race.

I bought an Appaloosa bronc from another rancher, Ernest Blake, for fifteen dollars and my solemn promise that I would not bring that horse back under any circumstances.

I soon found out why the promise was part of the deal. I rode this bronc around the hills for most of a week and every time she bucked, which was too damned often for my liking, she got rid of me. So finally I got rid of her. I sold her to Allie Streeter for bucking stock, and she then took up the chore of bucking off rodeo riders, which she seemed undoubtedly to enjoy. Rodeo horses, generally speaking, live a good life. They are well fed and cared for, and all they must do in return is buck like mad for eight seconds each time they come out of the chute, which is seldom more than a few times a week.

Now I was back to square one and with little chance of success in the race for two reasons: first, I had no suitable horse, and second, time in which to condition a horse was running out.

I had a tough little pony in my bunch. His mother was a Shetland-Arab cross, and he'd been sired by a thoroughbred. If he'd had a little more size to go with his toughness he'd have been ideal. As it was I decided to use him, but again resolved to take good care of him throughout the race.

Now this pony was a little spoiled. When he saw you approaching with a saddle to put on his back, he'd start bucking in his stall. As you put a foot in the stirrup to swing onto his back, he would try to catch you with what we called a cow-kick, a forward and sideways swipe with his near hind leg.

I liked to ride him. Sure, he bucked often but he gave you an honest day's work in the bargain, and if you were careless at the end of the day and dropped a rein, he'd drop his head and buck for a hundred yards.

I rode him steadily now to get him into the best condition I could before the race, and I rode him to Calgary to give him a final workout.

The course laid out began at Paradise Grove, proceeded up a steep grade for six hundred yards through an open field, then along a gravelled road for a little over a mile. After that the course went through a gate into the Sarcee Indian Reserve to follow wagon-rutted trails in a rambling course which came back to the same gate. The final lap of the course returned along the gravel road and down the open slope to the starting point at Paradise Grove.

The stampede grounds lie on flat ground surrounded by open hills in the sort of natural amphitheatre often chosen for race tracks and stampede grounds in ranch country, where the construction of bleachers is out of the question. People arriving in cars and pickup trucks would park not only around the arena area but wherever on the surrounding slopes a parking place could be reached. Press reports at the time claim a crowd of ten thousand people witnessed the race, arriving in vehicles bearing licence plates from such distant places as British Columbia, Montana, Saskatchewan, Washington State and California. Two American horses ran in the race, both out of Washington State.

The day was warm and sunny and all the horses leapt out eagerly at the starting gun.

I kept my pony in check after the first short burst and trotted him up the all-too-steep first six hundred yards. All the other riders took the hill at pretty much a dead run, and when I reached the top, half the contestants were out of sight.

Now I was riding the smallest horse in the race but he had to carry the required two hundred pounds like all the others. I asked him to keep up a steady pace but less than he could have given in the early miles, in order to save his strength for the later stages.

I was about ten miles out when I began to pass other riders whose horses were showing fatigue from being pushed too hard in the early miles.

At about twenty miles out I overtook a rider on a large bay horse. Coming up from behind I could see the horse was foundered. With my own horse in a heavy sweat I thought of Allie's words, run him to death.

I passed many riders after that, their horses not holding up so well as my pony, and I made up my mind that at any point other horses overtook us, I would take that as a signal that my pony had done his best and I would drop out.

The last control post lay just three and a half miles from the finish line. After the first fifteen contestants had gone through, the judges advised the remainder to dismount and walk their horses in since they had no chance of finishing in the money.

I was in that first fifteen, and while I was no longer passing other riders, neither, up to this point, had I been passed since I began overtaking others at around the ten-mile point.

At the twenty-eight mile point Clem Gardner, an old rancher on a stout thoroughbred built more on stock-horse than racing lines, passed me riding hard. He was in hot pursuit of Floyd Haynes, a young cowboy from the High River country who had been holding the lead for some while on a big half-bred horse.

At the twenty-nine mile point I pulled up my pony, dismounted and walked the last mile in.

Clem Gardner did not quite catch Floyd Hanes. They reached the finish line together, well ahead of anyone else, but the old rancher came in a bare second behind the younger cowboy.

The winning time on the race was reported at one hour, forty-one minutes and eighteen and two-fifth seconds. This was a phenomenal pace and so far as anyone connected with the race could establish, a record throughout the Canadian and American west. It must be said, of course, that such races have been held from time to time throughout much of North American cattle country with no central record keeping. But record or not, it was an incredible pace and I admired my pony considerably for how well he had held up to it.

The horse which had set the pace for much of the race died within half a mile of the finish line. In a state of exhaustion, the horse stumbled on a loose stone and died from hemorrhaging after the fall. Although there was no mention of it in press reports at the time, rumours were about that eight horses altogether had died.

I stayed in Calgary for a week to rest my pony before riding back to Nanton, and I had a good chance to talk with other riders who had been in the race. I came away leaning a good deal more to Allie Streeter's view of this sort of horse racing: if you want to kill a horse, you can take him out and shoot him, you don't have to go to the trouble of running him to death.

There was much public protest about the race and no more of the sort was held in our part of the west, a good thing in my newly conditioned view.

I Bet on My Milk Cow
and Win

In the years immediately after the war, rodeos were still mainly a local event and most contestants were home-grown ranch boys who longed to demonstrate their bronc-riding or calf-roping skills before a crowd of spectators. Often there would be a young woman in the stands whom the young cowboy particularly desired to impress. It was later that the rodeo circuit became dominated by professional riders and ropers, leaving the home-grown boy with little chance at placing in the money.

Now when we still lived on the Dixon quarter and our first baby, Joanne, had newly arrived, I scouted around for a milk cow. With luck I was able to buy a cross-bred cow with some Jersey in her. She was what we called high-strung — that is to say, somewhat nervous — but very gentle and needing always to be handled with tender loving care to keep her milk production up.

One day while I was bringing my gentle cow in from the pasture I decided to ride her home. This was an imposition which many gentle milk cows would put up with, and many a farm or ranch hand, tired at the end of the day, would rather ride even a cow than walk.

I got the surprise of my life. My gentle cow had no intention of tolerating this indignity. She fired up as though she had gunpowder in her cylinders, and I was soon getting up off the ground with considerable respect for her skills as a bucking-cow. I was also hard pressed to explain to Vera why we had very little milk that evening.

A few days later a young neighbour came by to ask me if I could do his chores for a few days because he wanted a little time off to take in a couple of local rodeos. Always ready to help a fellow young man in pursuit of this particular brand of foolishness, I readily agreed.

Then I asked him, "What are you going to enter in?"

"Well," he said, thoughtfully, "I reckon I might go for calf-roping and bronc-riding. Maybe I'll try bull-riding, too."

Now bull-riding as a rodeo event had undergone a significant recent development which made it a lot more serious than it had been before the war. Brahma bulls with mean horns and a big hump at the shoulders—twice as hard to ride and more likely than ever to maim a man after he got bucked off—had been taken into use.

I said, "Calf-roping and bronc-riding I can see but you should stay away from bull-riding. I don't think you're cut out for bull-riding."

He was somewhat taken aback. "What do you mean, I'm not cut out for bull-riding? Hell, I've got about as good a chance as anyone else around these parts to ride any old bull. I'd sure like a chance to show you you're wrong about that."

At this point I said casually, "Listen, I bet you couldn't even ride my old milk cow." While saying this I indicated with a gesture of my hand our primary producer of dairy product, which happened to be standing nearby in the corral.

He said indignantly, "You gotta be kidding!"

I challenged him. "Betcha ten dollars."

"You got a bet," he shot back.

So we led the gentle old cow alongside a gate and ran a piece of hard-twist lariat rope around her girth. My friend climbed the gate, dropped onto the cow, took a grip on the rope and said, "Turn this old girl loose."

I did, promptly, and this old girl bucked with a sure and swift spinning motion seldom seen outside a rodeo arena, handily dumping my friend into the accumulated manure of the corral enclosure.

I won the ten dollars.

Again I got the frosty treatment in the house that evening because there was no milk.

The following week my young friend took second money in the bull-riding at the rodeo.

"...you couldn't even ride my old milk cow."

I Get Two Spooky Cows
for a Day's Work

Bill Hay, an old Scotsman and a good friend and very much a right sort of guy, used to farm down on the flats about seven miles from Nanton. Now Bill had got his start up in the hills, and when he got the land down on the flats he would trail his cattle up into the hills for the summer, then feed them on the lower ground during the winter.

One fall we got an early blizzard. There was a mean north wind up and snow was blowing so badly you couldn't see your hand if you stretched your arm out straight. Nothing that lived could move.

Finally the wind began to die down and the snow slowed, but everywhere there were deep drifts and you could only tell where the roads were if there happened to be a fence alongside.

As it happened the telephone line into the Dixon quarter had survived the storm and Bill cranked up our signal.

"That you, Wilf?"

"This is me, Bill."

"Say, listen, I was moving my cows down when this storm hit and I lost a couple of those wild cows in the brush. They headed in there and I couldn't get 'em out. Had to leave 'em behind so I could get the rest of the cows home safe. They must be in bad trouble by now, Wilf. Could you go out and hunt 'em up and shoot 'em? They're so damn wild I can't do much with 'em and I can't stand to think of 'em sufferin'. I hate to just shoot 'em but I can't think what else to do."

"Fine," I agreed. "I'll head out of here right now."

I had a strong, well-fed team in the barn which I hooked up to the sleigh, then loaded some oat sheaves onto the rack. I undid the belly bands on the harness so the horses wouldn't kick them apart if they got floundering in deep snow. I said to Vera, "I'm going to try feeding those mossy-horned cows. I'll only shoot them if I got no other choice."

Only a few hours out I came on the cows. They were holed up in dense brush, and they were spooky all right, the kind of range cows that spend their lives with the instincts of wild animals.

But also they were acutely hungry. I broke out just enough of the oat sheaves to get their interest, then broke trail for them back to the sleigh. There I gave them a little more feed, then turned my rig and started back, slowly, in my sleigh tracks. The cows followed and every little while I would give them a bit more to eat. By this process, late in the day, I had these two wild cows secure in my corral and filling up on yet more sheaves of oats.

I telephoned Bill. "Got your cows here," I said, then explained what I had done. "You can pick 'em up whenever you're ready," I added.

He was so mightily relieved that the cows were safe and hadn't starved to death during the blizzard that he declared emphatically, "Them are your cows now, Wilf. Any man got the guts to go out in this weather and work that hard to save 'em, they're his!"

So I got two wild cows for a day's work in tough weather. Not bad, especially in those times.

A Novel Way to Break an Axe

During the winter of 1948 I hired out on a slashing job to earn some much-needed cash.

This was a government-sponsored job, clearing land for a dam project at Spray Lake in Banff National Park, and the snow was about four feet deep. You had to slash and pile the timber and you were paid $125 for each acre of land cleared.

In the strange and devious ways of government, it had been decreed that this work must be done entirely by hand, that is to say without power tools or machinery of any sort, in order to create the most hours of labour possible. I was glad no one had thought of us chewing the trees down with our teeth as I'm sure the politicians would have gone for it.

Most of the men worked in pairs but I preferred to work alone. I was felling the light timber with a very sharp double-bitted axe and after a little trial and error I discovered a rapid way to get the tree off the stump.

I would make a deep V notch in the usual way of making the undercut, but on starting the back cut I found that a very sharp blow with a quick lift on the axe handle while the blade was still buried in the wood had such a levering effect that the stem of the tree would snap from the stump and, in exceptionally short time, I would have the tree on the ground.

One very cold morning I was practising my cut-'em-fast procedure and on my swift back cut with the quick levering action, the handle of the axe broke deep in the eye of the axe head.

I took the axe to camp to get a new one.

The foreman, Curley Peters, inspected the axe, then said, "It's impossible to break an axe like this. How did you do it?"

"Don't know," I said.

Some four years later I took charge of a district in Yoho National Park. When I was introduced to my crew, who should be there as the trail crew boss but Curley Peters.

He looked at me with considerable puzzlement and then said, "I've seen you before somewhere."

I laughed and said, "Spray Lake."

His face brightened with recognition. "You're the guy who broke the axe. How in hell did you break that axe?"

"You just have to be strong," I offered.

"No," he said, with assurance. "You did something different with that axe. I sent it to the factory. The handle was broken but the steel was split, too. They tested at the factory to repeat that break and they couldn't do it."

I had not realized the steel had split but I did recall that, with this particular tree, I had misjudged the lean and the tree, on snapping free of the stump, had fallen back onto the axe instead of forward over the undercut. The pressure generated had been exceptional, more than the steel of the axe could stand.

I didn't offer the explanation to Curley because it seemed a little far-fetched, even to me. In any case, I had long since given up this novel way to fall timber and break axes.

Some People Don't Know
Wild Meat Even When They're
Eating It

There have always been people who don't like eating wild meat — some on principle, some on taste and some, I think, just because they like to hear themselves expounding on the subject.

I arrived at a small ranch one time, the sort which depended on wild meat on the table in order to conserve ranch beef for selling, just as the rancher had taken a mule deer buck in prime condition, along the road at the edge of a field of hay.

I helped him to dress out the deer and that evening cut the meat, some into steaks which could be cooked up for a feed of fresh meat but the greater part into pieces suitable for canning. Home freezers were not around in those days, and what could not be eaten fresh within a few days had to be canned or consigned to a salt barrel.

The rancher's wife asked me to stay over to the next day in order to share in the feast of fresh meat, and of course I accepted. A good feed of fresh venison is not something I avoid if I have any choice in the matter.

A huge meal went into preparation the next day. Fresh vegetables from the ranch garden were gathered in quantity, milk fresh from the morning's milking was brought to the table, butter churned from cream separated from earlier milkings was laid on the table and the rich aroma of fresh meat well peppered in the frying pan filled the kitchen.

About ten minutes before the meal was to be served a neighbour couple arrived. Now the lady of this couple objected to deer being killed for domestic consumption. The prosperity of her own ranch was such that she could afford to stand on this high ground and, as it happened, she had seen the evidence of the kill which had provided the main fare of the feast which we were about to enjoy.

"I just cannot abide it," she declared. "People just go about shooting deer any time they want. They have no conscience. I never eat

93

deer meat, not even in the season. It's all so brutal. The poor things. Can you imagine, just yesterday someone shot a deer right beside the road."

Now our hostess had a problem. In rural society, if unexpected people arrive just as a meal is about to be served, extra places are laid at the table, unobtrusively, and the visitors sit down for the meal. But here the newly arrived lady disclaimed ever eating deer meat and denigrated taking deer meat for home consumption while the only meat available to put on the table was freshly killed deer meat, meat from the very kill which she was now vigorously denouncing.

With the sort of cool aplomb often possessed by hard-working rural women, our hostess spread the table with good meat, vegetables fresh from the garden, home-baked bread, butter, milk and a boat of splendid, rich pan gravy to pour liberally over everything.

Her guest, who so detested the abominable practice of killing mule deer, pitched in with the rest of us. She had not one, not two, but in fact three good helpings of this splendid ranch beef that she was offered. At the same time, she could not understand why our host kept doubling over with laughter, the cause of which he was so bad-mannered as not to disclose.

Much later, this lady confided to me that our host that day was the rudest man she had ever met.

An Active Companion in a Confined Space

One July I had a hay camp set up where I was cutting and stacking hay on a contract for one of the foothills ranches.

I had come by a well-worn jeep of the sort sold off as military surplus after the war, and in this somewhat cramped vehicle I was returning to my camp one evening about eleven o'clock with a man who worked for me in the hay camp.

The little-used rural road we followed entered a coulee some miles from the camp and for about six miles there was no way off the road because of the narrow walls of the coulee.

Just as we started into the coulee a large band of mule deer began crossing the road ahead of us. I stopped the jeep to avoid running into the deer and, in the light from the headlamps of the jeep, began counting deer. I was curious to know how many deer were running in this particular band.

My companion, with no warning, picked up a .22-calibre rifle which happened to be in the vehicle and shot one of the deer.

Now we were using deer meat in the camp and I had no aversion to this activity except that the circumstances this late night were not favourable. The first rule when poaching deer meat is to arrange matters so as not to be caught doing it, and we were on a road we couldn't get away from for six more miles and on which other traffic could be expected.

Well, what's done is done, so I got out, grabbed the deer and threw it into the back of the jeep. By this time we could see headlights approaching.

These old jeeps at best could do about forty-five miles per hour on a down grade and this road was in poor shape. I reckoned we would be pounding along for most of fifteen minutes before I could leave the road to get out of sight in the bush.

Then it turned out that the deer had not been killed with the .22-calibre bullet, only stunned. He came to life in the back of the jeep, although not with enough strength to leap out.

What he could do was thrash about with his hooves. The driver's seat was solid enough, but the passenger seat my companion occupied hinged forward to allow easy access to the space behind the seats now occupied by the deer. In the fray, the sharp flying hooves of the deer pounded a tattoo on the back of my friend's head which was, by now, crammed up hard against the windshield.

On this particular occasion I sided with the mule deer, but I was much too busy trying to keep the jeep on the road to enjoy the event.

I doubt if that man ever shot another mule deer, which is probably just as well.

...the sharp flying hooves of the deer...

An End to Market Hunting

Alberta after the war was not the same as Alberta in the Hungry Thirties. There was more money around and ranches which had been poor before had some measure of affluence now.

There were also more people about in the foothills country, many of them young people with no experience of the hard times.

Attitudes had changed but were by no means consistent. On the one hand, many people who once had used meat from the hills now spoke unfavourably of poaching. What had once been an honourable though illegal lifestyle now perhaps was no longer honourable. On the other hand, some who did poach seemed not to understand the fundamental ethic which had once governed the activity.

One day as I worked in the field, a young neighbour came by to ask me if I could use some meat.

"Sure," I replied.

"I came on this bunch of deer," he said, "and I kind of got carried away. I killed four of 'em, so I got meat to spare. You understand how it is."

I said I would make good use of some of the meat but that, no, I didn't understand because I never killed more meat than I could use at a time.

The following winter I was bringing in some badly needed cash by hunting coyotes for the pelts.

I staked down a cowhide on a sidehill as bait, and every morning and evening I would take up a stand on the opposite side of the draw. Sitting with a large boulder at my back I had some protection from the wind and my outline was so well obscured that no coyote approaching the cowhide ever sensed my presence. This was a very productive setup. The distance across the draw did not exceed a hundred and fifty yards, and with a rested shot I couldn't miss. I was making good money in coyote pelts.

One morning in February I took up my stand in the last of the dark, then waited for daybreak. It was the time of the year when the whiskeyjacks were gathering nest material and the mule deer does were heavy with fawn. Only a young buck or a distinctly dry doe would be a fair meat animal at this time of year. You would kill very selectively and then only if you had urgent need of the food.

A small band of deer, perhaps seven in all, were gathered in the willows in the bottom of the draw and I watched them as I waited.

Soon a coyote came toward the bait, and I rested my rifle on my mitts, which I had placed on a small rock. This fully rested shot assured me of the accuracy I would need to take the coyote in a swift kill, without damaging the pelt. I waited a while longer for the coyote to turn to my advantage for the shot.

Suddenly the coyote spooked and ran off. Something clearly had gone wrong. I had not spooked the coyote, nor could the deer have spooked the coyote.

Then down the draw came two men on horseback, charging through the deep snow toward the deer. The deer bounded from the willows to escape but were impeded by the deep snow. In their poor condition in late winter and heavy with fawn they could not outpace the barn-fed horses. The two men opened fire, shooting indiscriminately. Some deer went down, others struggled away badly wounded. These the men chased down to finish off with further wildly directed volleys of fire.

Undetected, not fifty yards away, I watched this slaughter. It entered my mind that if these men were to see me they might want to get rid of a witness; but on the other hand, I had a rifle in a rested position and, unlike the deer, I was not defenceless. I stayed on my stand.

These men made a poor and messy job of cleaning and dressing the slain deer, then skidded the carcasses up to the road with their horses.

After they left I sat a long time thinking, sick at heart. On the face of it, these men were poachers and I was a poacher. But the event I had witnessed had been criminally cruel and wasteful. The understood ethic of killing selectively, of killing carefully, of taking what you could use and no more had been utterly set aside.

One of these men was a local rancher, the other a farmer from down on the flats. Both were respected men. I thought of turning them in but realized at once the futility of that. Apart from the absurdity of one poacher turning in another, these were prominent citizens who could lie their way out of anything. Besides, come spring when the blood and the mess would be discovered, I would be a more likely suspect than either of them.

I took a long time going home, trying to clear my mind. When I got to the house I said to Vera, "Get ready to go out. We're going visiting."

"Where?" she asked.

"One of the neighbours. They got some extra meat. I reckon to pick up a hundred pounds or so."

"But you can't do that! You can't just walk up to someone and say I hear you have some fresh meat and I'll take some steaks and oh yes, throw in a few roasts as well."

"The hell I can't. Just get ready to go." While Vera got herself together I harnessed my work team and hitched them to the sleigh.

When we arrived at the neighbouring ranch there was a scramble going on to get the meat hidden away in a shed and generally tidy up the evidence. The rancher felt caught in the act and hurriedly said, "Ernie and I just happened on a nice buck. Would you like some meat?"

I said, "You guys are busy, so I'll just pick out a couple of pieces when we're ready to leave."

We stayed for a visit of the sort which needed no explanation in rural Alberta in those years. Anybody could stop by anywhere without invitation just to talk for a while or take a meal.

When we left I went alone to the shed where the meat had been cached. I took several roasts and made a point of taking five hearts. I wrapped this meat in a piece of canvas I had brought along and placed it on the rack on the sleigh.

On the way home Vera asked, "What did you take for meat?"

"About fifty pounds of good roast," I replied.

"Wilf, that's not fair," she protested. "That's most of their buck, and the best meat besides."

"Take a look," I suggested.

Vera uncovered the meat and saw the five hearts.

"Oh," she said.

"Yes," I said. "The bastards killed a whole bunch, mostly does heavy in fawn. For what it's worth, now they know that I know what kind of a kill that was."

That was the end of market hunting. I still shot deer for our own use, bucks or dry does in good condition, but never a pound to sell.

There were times when we were desperately short of cash, and I knew prosperity was only a rifle shot away.

However, I had come to a time when my own ethic about taking meat from the hills had to tighten up if only to disassociate myself from the behaviour of others who did not understand that dependence on the wildlife called for respect for the wildlife as well.

The Last Straw

I had given up market hunting, but I was still short on cash, and with a young family to feed I turned to a legal way of harvesting wildlife. I applied for and was granted a trapline stretching from Longview to west of Fort McLeod.

The price for weasels was strong and there were plenty of weasels. I set out one day with nine hundred weasel traps and a barrel of bait. It took me five days to set all my traps. I made sets in every creek bridge and culvert in every road allowance within the perimeter of my line.

No sooner had I set all my traps than I started checking the line for trapped fur. With luck I would get back my investment in traps and have some money to help support the family besides.

Unfortunately, I had not taken into account the predilection of some of the farm families throughout the area to regard even the road allowances as their private property. Not only was the trapped fur stolen from my traps, but the traps themselves were being stolen. Of the 900 traps I had set out, I recovered 350 after the first check of the line.

It was not that anyone really needed my fur or my traps. As hard as farm life might have been, these were the people who had the good fortune of being established on the land. They cried mighty hard to the government whenever farm income fell short, but still one or more among them, it was clear, would steal from a man with no land, trying his best to make a living by what work he could get and a little trapping in the winter months.

Now I can't say if my traps and my fur were being taken by a number of people haphazardly or by one person deliberately travelling behind me to benefit from my work. In my experience most rural people are honest, but some are not.

It was common in those years to hear white people speak badly of the Indians, to accuse them of theft and general dishonesty. Never did Indian people steal from me, and many times in my boyhood they helped me to make my living in the hills.

It was the white people who stole from me. Nine hundred traps was a big investment in those cash-short days with a young family coming on. With over half the traps stolen and any fur I might have harvested gone besides, I could only lift what remained of my traps and give up the enterprise.

Instead of bringing in a few dollars I was now out the cost of the traps and the bait. It may not sound like much now but it was a hell of a setback at the time and it certainly helped me make up my mind that I must look for a more reliable way to support a family than patching a living together in the foothills without land of my own.

IV

PARKS, WILDLIFE & FORESTRY

This period covers the years from 1950, when Wilf first joined the National Parks Service, until 1965, when he went to a forestry school to improve his qualifications.

During this period Wilf worked mainly for three employers: the National Parks Service, the Alberta Forest Service and the Alberta Game Branch. In times between these main employments, he occasionally took shorter related employments such as big-game guiding.

In these employments, the wilderness environment, the relationship with the people who worked or visited in the bush and the experiences with animals remained much the same.

By now Wilf and Vera had the first three of their six children: Joanne, a few months over three; Charles (Chuck), coming up two; and Hugh, coming up to four months.

The disappointments of the early years after the war recede now into the background as Wilf enjoys combining security of income for his family with the outdoor life so essential to his own happiness.

During this period, the family is joined by the remaining three children: Bruce, born in February 1953; Lynn, born in November 1954; and Karen, born in October, 1957.

Into the Parks Service

In the late forties and early fifties Canada's National Parks Service expanded to better manage the National Parks, which were coming under pressure from rapidly increasing public use.

Banff and Jasper National Parks were not far from the foothill country and I had a fair grasp of the sort of terrain which lay within their boundaries.

Also, in those years, horses were used for travel and transport of supplies in the back-country of the parks. Unless you wanted to be a "town" warden and spend all your time parading your uniform in Banff or along the highway, you had to work with horses.

In fact, at that time there was no better preparation for work in the back country of the parks than a thorough apprenticeship in ranch work — which I had.

As well, I had a young family coming on, and I knew I should try to land work with more stability and future in it than came with even the better jobs in ranching.

So it happened that in early 1950 I submitted an application to the service for employment as a park warden at the basic entry level. Of course I didn't let myself count much on the success of it, and in the spring of the year I was camped out on the far reaches of the Bar U ranch on a contract to cut building logs.

One day the young cowboy who was breaking horses for the ranch showed up in my camp to deliver a letter. Since I was seventeen miles out from the home ranch, this horse and rider had been given a thirty-five mile round trip for the purpose. I thought this must be quite a letter.

Indeed it was. Mr. Frank Bryant, Chief Warden of Banff National Park, requested that I travel to Banff to meet with him at my earliest convenience.

It is remarkable how quickly everything moved after that.

I went to Banff and was hired at once as a Park Warden. However, the snow in the back country district to which I was assigned would be too deep for horse travel for another two months, so I had to find provisional accommodation in the town.

Back at the Bar U ranch headquarters I had a small travel trailer of the sort you could tow behind a heavy car or light truck. This I could park in the warden's bunkhouse yard in Banff, and although it would be crowded, Vera and I and the children could manage in it. I had no cash reserves and renting in the townsite was out of the question.

Also I had no vehicle with which to tow the trailer to Banff, but I thought I could find a friend in Nanton who would help with this.

I went to Nanton and approached a man I knew who was in the trucking business in a small way. I asked him what he would charge to tow my trailer from the ranch to Banff.

"Two-hundred and seventy-five dollars," he replied.

"Oh," I said. Then I said the equivalent of "see you around" and went on my way. Two-hundred and seventy-five dollars was a hell of a lot of money in 1950 and several times what the trip was worth. You could buy second-hand the kind of trailer I owned with that sort of money and have some left over. Everything else aside, I didn't have anything like that much money.

I proceeded down the street and soon met an old Stony Indian, King Bear Paw, grandson of Chief King Bear Paw who, legend has it, placed the taboo on the Lost Lemon Mine.

The story goes that prospectors in the early days had discovered gold on the east slope of the Rockies, but ill fortune fell upon the prospectors, and knowledge of the location passed with them. (At this writing, a modern day geologist believes he has located the mineralization which the prospectors had come across and a minor gold rush may be in the making, but we won't hold our breath waiting for it.)

At any rate, the other part of the story, less well known outside the district, is that some Stony Indians knew the location, but the Chief saw nothing but trouble coming from exploitation of the prospect, so he forbade his tribespeople, under penalty of death, to travel the area or to disclose the location.

The story also has it that the father of my friend King Bear Paw was the last Stony to know the location, although this is not something which I ever undertook to verify with King. King spent most of his summers with generous grubstakes from white businessmen who hoped he would find them the Lost Lemon Mine. It was a profitable business for King, and I doubted if he ever looked anywhere near where the prospect was known by his father to occur, but this is

something else which I did not ever quite have the courage to enquire about. King was my friend, and I thought the subject might be
sensitive.

But on this day King's prospecting ventures were not uppermost
in my mind.

King was a big, powerfully built man and he had a big heavy car.
If for no other reason, he had to have a big heavy car because he
couldn't get into a smaller one. This car was equipped with an eight-
cylinder motor and a trailer hitch. I invited King to have coffee with
me in a local cafe and approached him about moving my trailer to
Banff.

The critical question was, "How much?"

King smiled. "I need an excuse to go to Morley," he said. "You
buy the gas."

So we drove to the Bar U, hitched up the trailer and headed for
Banff. On the way through Calgary I asked King, "Do you like Chinese food?"

"Don't know," he replied. "Never tried it."

Now I knew a Chinese cafe which offered all you could eat for a
fixed price, rather like a smorgasbord. As it turned out, King found
he liked Chinese food, and he all but ate the place out if its supplies.
I was pleased to have found something I could do for my huge
friend to partly compensate him for his trouble on my behalf.

When we arrived at Banff King stayed with me until the trailer
was set up and levelled.

Then I tried again. "King, you have to let me pay you something
for this trip."

"No," he said, "I think this is gonna be a good job for you. I
think maybe you belong here in this park work."

I wasn't quite sure what that had to do with whether or not I
should pay him for making the trip, but I had one more possibility.
King had earlier shown an interest in an old .22-calibre repeating
rifle which I had stowed away in the trailer.

I fetched this and said, "Here. I'm making you this present."

Now that was different. King could donate his time and trouble to
my cause, and I could make him a present. He took the rifle with
obvious delight.

Then he left, and I set about my new life as a Park Warden.

In fact, as it turned out, this was the beginning of a series of
related employments. With minor breaks, I worked in succession in
the park, then for the Alberta Forest Service and finally for the
Alberta Game Branch.

Out of these years I carry memories of working with horses, some good and some intractable; of the travelling public, some strange indeed; of a collection of bush characters, good and bad; and of many encounters with wildlife.

"Here. I'm making you this present."

Minor Embarrassments

Now it did not escape me that there was something anomalous in my new career, examined against the background of my earlier days.

I had, in fact, jumped clean over the fence. Having once been a poacher myself, I now must be on the lookout for poachers as well as persons otherwise breaking the rules in the park.

This, in fact, didn't disturb my conscience in the least. What did from time to time give me an anxious moment was the possibility of my past activities coming to the attention of my present employers.

On one occasion I was sent down to Calgary on behalf of the Parks Service to conduct several bits of business, some of which had to do with park violations, and I had to appear in court. It followed that I must wear my uniform.

The work in Calgary took longer than expected, and I was obliged to stay over a weekend. To pass the time, I drove to Nanton.

I visited about a little, and as the supper hour approached I proceeded to the more popular of the less splendid but also less costly cafes on the main street, with the intention of having something to eat.

Now as I walked toward the cafe, out came Big Jim, a local rancher and very good friend from earlier days. When he'd had to conserve his beef for market I had sometimes sold him deer meat.

It took him a moment to recognize me in the smartly pressed uniform, and when he did, he could hardly believe his eyes.

"Wilf!" he cried. "What the hell are you doing?"

I hurriedly explained that these days I worked as a warden in the park and I was just in town for a short visit.

"You! You are a warden in the park?" he all but shouted in his astonishment.

"That's right," I said, as quietly as I could because I feared our exchange might be drawing attention along the street.

"Well I'll be damned!" he further exclaimed. "You? Well, I never thought . . . say, do you remember the time . . . ?"

Big Jim just couldn't get over it. Between bursts of uncontrollable laughter he blurted out as best he could his memories of this or that exploit of which he had, unfortunately, rather more knowledge than most. He had been a good customer, and only good customers knew in any detail the feats by which I had secured the meat I sold them.

Now a crowd was gathering, but Big Jim paid the audience no mind. I, on the other hand, was painfully conscious of the audience. I could think of no more certain way to have my history leaking up to Banff than to have it thoroughly aired on the main street of Nanton.

I had to do something quickly and so, giving up on the idea of having supper, I said to Jim, "Let's go have a beer." I don't much care for beer parlours, and I liked even less going into one in this uniform, but something had to be done.

Jim accepted, and as we left the gathering crowd dispersed. In a quiet corner of the parlour as we sipped our beer I tried to explain to Jim how times had changed and that perhaps it was better not to draw attention to earlier days.

Jim would never intentionally say anything to hurt a man's career, but he could see only the funny side of this entire situation. Even my squirming embarrassment only added to the humour.

Fortunately his loud laughter ebbed and we talked more quietly in our secluded corner. Further, I knew that once he was not in my company he would say nothing more on the subject. The joke was strictly between the two of us; it was only that it was such a good joke that out on the street there had been a real danger of some of the more damaging parts of it being overheard.

There was another occasion when I cut abruptly into a conversation building around an incident out of the past, but to understand my apprehension in this instance we have to go back to the beginning.

A number of years ago, another ranch hand, Shelly Wilson, and I were gathering poles with which to build a new corral for one of the foothills ranches.

We had cut the poles and needed to skid them down to the corral site, so we loaded a gentle workhorse into the back of a pickup truck and drove up to the timber.

Just as we were backing the horse down the ramp from the truck box, a buck deer appeared at the edge of the open, saw us and sped into the timber.

Shelly wanted the buck and I had a light rifle adequate at short ranges, so I took this and together we started scouting about through the aspen patches to see if we could locate the buck and get a shot.

We came through a patch of aspen trees into another open stretch and the only deer we could see was a good four hundred yards away. I couldn't count on making an accurate shot with my light rifle at that distance, but Shelly seemed unaware of this limitation.

"Shoot him!" he said, urgently.

"Where?" I asked, facetiously.

"Head or neck," he urged.

Now, when I don't seriously want a particular animal I will often shoot over it to frighten it off. This way, the animal is conditioned to be more afraid and quicker to take flight on another occasion, with an increased chance for survival.

So I aimed high over the buck and fired a shot, but damned if he didn't drop on the spot. We hurried over to find I had hit him behind the ear in what had to be the fluke shot of the year and then some. We dressed him out and Shelly made good use of the meat. End of story, you would think.

But years later, along with a biologist who happened to be my supervisor at the time, I set up a game-checking station in the foothill country during hunting season. We pulled a trailer with two rooms in it across a bush road much used by hunters. While one of us would take a shift in the front end of the unit, the other could catch some sleep in the room at the back.

We would work together during the day, I would work the evening shift to midnight at which time my supervisor would take over, and I would go to sleep in the back.

I had just settled into bed one midnight when in came a party of hunters, fresh from the bar by the sound of them. They were on their way into an area where they would make a rough camp and then hunt at daybreak.

I heard a familiar voice enquiring of my supervisor, "You know Wilf Taylor? Believe he works with you guys now."

"Yes, I know Wilf," came the reply.

"Hey," the voice went on. "You should'a been with us one time. That Wilf, he shot a deer so far away you could hardly tell what it was without a pair of binoculars. Got 'im right back of the ear, too. He's a great shot, that Wilf. He used to..."

I barrelled out of my bunk and reached for my trousers. I knew that voice and I interrupted with a loud bellow from the back room,

"Shelly, if you don't get the hell on the road, you're going to miss the morning hunt!"

"Oh, hi, Wilf."

"Hi, yourself."

After a little more conversation, which I controlled with great determination, Shelly and his companions continued toward their hunting grounds, and I went back to bed.

I Didn't Hunt as Much
as Before

Not only did I not hunt the way I once had, I hunted much less than before, apart from employment-related hunting such as controlling elk populations in the park.

In one instance I joined a friend at his request to hunt deer, when again my new position became a factor. I was working with the Alberta Game Branch at the time.

This friend, Vic, had a quarter-section of land just west of Coleman, and he asked if I would help him sell it.

We went to look at the quarter-section, and I saw it was growing a prolific stand of young Douglas fir trees, ranging up to fifteen feet in height. The trees were well formed, and if ever I saw a huge crop of Christmas trees, this was it.

I said, "Vic, don't sell this quarter. Cut Christmas trees from it."

"Christmas trees?' he queried. "I'd have a tree for everyone in Coleman and still wouldn't make a dent in it." He thought this was a great joke and I had a hard time getting him to stop laughing long enough to listen.

"No, no!" I said, impatiently. "I don't mean a few trees to supply Coleman. I mean ten or fifteen thousand trees to ship to the States. There's a good demand, and over in the Kootenays they're shipping them out by the boxcar load."

I had a little time to spare so we cut a hell of pile of trees and shipped them off.

Then Vic said, "Let's go deer hunting. There's a lot of pressure on them now and they've moved back some, but I know a place where there's lots. But it's pretty thick bush. You seldom see more than forty feet away, and that's in the clearings."

So we went to this place and hunted in separate directions for several hours. I was not particularly keen to shoot a deer at the time, so I mainly just wandered about.

Then I heard Vic shoot and made my way out to the road to wait for him. After about an hour he arrived back at the truck and I asked him what he had shot.

"I shot at a buck and missed," he said.

Now that seemed strange to me. Vic was a good shot, and any shot in this bush was going to be at short range.

I was still puzzled the next day, so I went back into this piece of bush on my own, and sure enough someone had dragged a deer out to the road and hauled it away.

I sat by the roadside for a long while trying to figure matters out. If it was Vic, why had he excluded me from the kill? Maybe Vic had missed and another hunter had come in later and made a kill. Could I ask Vic outright? Not very well, because I didn't want to put him on the spot.

On a hunch I drove to Vic's parents' place, where his mother invited me in for a cup of coffee.

After we had chatted a while, I asked, "Did Vic leave any meat for me by any chance?"

"Yes," she said, "he did. But I guess he didn't quite know how to give it to you."

Now if Vic didn't know how to give me a share of the meat and he had not acknowledged having killed a deer to start with, there was more here than met the eye, as it were.

I went to Vic and asked him outright, "Why in hell didn't you tell me about shooting that deer?"

"Well, Wilf, I didn't want to put you on the spot with something you wouldn't want to know. And I thought you might feel that you'd have to pinch me, and that wouldn't be very pleasant for you."

"Let's have the story, Vic."

"Okay. I was working my way along in that thick brush, and suddenly just across a little clearing I saw this big buck looking at me. Mostly I could see his head and his big rack of antlers. He was standing in some low brush, and there was more higher brush behind him.

"I was going to make a head shot at that range, but then I thought, no, I'll take him in the chest, and I'll have the rack to mount for the Fish & Game Club contest.

"So I shot and, damnit, there was a doe standing across in front of him, but you couldn't see her for the brush. I killed the doe, and the buck got away."

Of course he'd felt a fool for the mistake he'd made, as understandable as it was, and besides he had no idea how I would have to deal with it in view of my responsibilities as a warden. So he came out to the road, gave me the story about missing a buck, then went back later on his own to bring out the meat so it would not be wasted.

It can happen to the most conscientious hunter. Case closed.

I enjoyed hunting pheasants and ducks in the season. Although my days were busy with road checks and patrols, I could often slip out in the evening and pick up a few birds.

Now success hunting pheasants and ducks requires the help of a good dog and I had one, although in the beginning I almost sent him off for incompetence.

My younger brother liked dogs and sometimes would show up at shows featuring hunting dogs. One time a couple of dogs got loose, with the result that a springer spaniel got bred by a labrador retriever. The owner of the female was furious but my brother asked the breeder if he would save one of the pups for him.

"Okay," came the gruff reply, "although I'm damned if I know why you'd want it. I'll destroy the rest. I breed registered dogs, not cross-bred mongrels."

The pup turned out to look like just about any other black labrador, except that perhaps he had some of the set of the springer about him. My brother and my dad undertook to train him, but after a while he seemed to be too much dog to stay in town where my brother lived, and so he was handed on to us so he could live in the country.

My boys at the time were nine, twelve and fourteen years old, and of course the dog and the boys took to each other immediately. Seldom did you see the dog without the boys or the boys without the dog.

There was usually good pheasant hunting along the little-used country roads near where we lived, so one evening I decided to take the dog hunting, but he seemed no good at the job at all. I would be walking in the rough in the roadside ditch where the pheasants would be, but the dog would stay up on the easy travelling on the road.

At this rate I figured I could hunt just as well without the dog, so one evening at supper I said, "Major's got to go."

Now I had three horrified boys on my hands demanding to know why.

"Because he won't hunt," I said, and I explained his dismal performance.

I would be walking in the rough in the roadside ditch . . . but the dog would stay up on the easy travelling . . .

"Sure he hunts!" they all cried together.

"Show me," I said.

So we took a 410 shotgun and headed out for birds.

I picked out a road I thought should produce results and got out with the dog. Then I explained to the boys that I could never get him to go into the rough and hunt.

"That's not how you do it, Dad," one of them said.

"Yeh," another said. "You turn him loose on the road, then you follow behind him in the car."

So I followed instructions, but it seemed a strange way to hunt birds. I didn't even get a shot at the first two he flushed because I hadn't got onto the system and was taken by surprise.

The dog's method was to trot down the middle of the road until he smelled a bird. He would not go into the rough until he had picked up the scent of a bird.

Immediately on picking up the scent he would wag his stubby tail to let you know he was onto something, and promptly he'd flush a bird. As long as you were fast enough with the shotgun, you'd get all the birds the law allowed.

I hunted with this dog until he got too old to move, and often he amazed me.

Once I shot a rooster which went down in a field of three-foot-high sweet clover.

Major was with Vera a quarter of a mile away, and I called him. When he arrived I pointed into the field and said, "Hunt!"

He was somewhat puzzled as this was not the usual way to proceed, but finally he figured he'd got the plan and went into the sweet clover. Soon he came out and put a rooster in my hand.

"Well done, Major," I said, just before the rooster flew off. The dog had gone hunting all right and had grabbed a live bird. So I explained matters to him again, and this time when he went into the clover he came back with the rooster I had shot.

On another trip working down a road I saw another hunter with a black labrador working toward me. When we met, we stopped to talk, but both dogs continued to hunt.

"I feed that dog the best dog food I can buy, but I swear every year he gets stupider," the other man complained.

Just then a rooster flushed from practically beneath our feet. Both dogs had known it was there. Not too stupid, I thought, but refrained from saying anything.

One evening after I had been checking hunters all day, I went out to get a few roosters for myself.

As I worked my way down a road with Major I noticed a car parked farther along. I was just close enough to see that several people were in the car, and one was watching me with binoculars. When you work for the Game Branch, this can be a little disconcerting, but I kept on hunting.

I soon had my limit, and a little later the car drove up. One man got out and said, "I'd like to buy that dog."

"Can't sell him," I said. "My family wouldn't let me come home again if I sold that dog."

Then they explained that they had come over from Creston and hunted for four days without seeing a rooster, and here they had watched me get a limit in less than half an hour.

So I took these fellows hunting with Major, and soon they all had a limit. They left full of praise for my old hunting dog, the one, I constantly remembered, that I had threatened to send off because he wouldn't hunt.

He was a pampered old softy in the winter months. He'd lie so close to the stove in cold weather that he would singe his hide, but in November with ice forming along the edges of the sloughs he'd jump into the water at the crack of a shotgun and stay there until he found the duck you had shot.

Now Major did not only go out with me, he spent many hours afield with our three boys.

Many hunters move out on the sloughs and begin "pushing the clock," that is, they don't wait for legal shooting light before taking some ducks. They do this because often all the ducks leave at legal light, and they come away empty-handed. It's a hard practice to suppress, and as long it remains low-key and not blatantly out of hand most wardens overlook it.

I stopped by a local sporting goods store one day to buy some shotgun shells, and after I had made my purchase the store owner hemmed and hawed a bit, obviously with something on his mind.

Finally, he said, "Been meanin' to talk to you. You know sometimes when you're out on the slough early it's hard to tell when you can start to shoot. Sometimes some of the guys get a few ducks in the water, but they don't try to pick 'em up right away."

"Oh, I understand," I said. "I know how that happens. It's not something I'd get very concerned about."

"Well," he went on. "Thing is, your boys got that damned good dog and sometimes when the guys go to gather up their ducks, the ducks are gone."

"Oh," I said, "I see. Well, I'm glad you mentioned that to me." We exchanged a few comments about the weather and I left.

I could picture it. There would be my boys and old Major crouched in the bushes at the edge of the slough. A shot would ring out and the duck would splash into the water. Old Major would be given a quiet tap to let him know what was expected of him, and he would slip out without a sound and fetch in the duck.

I had a little talk with the boys. I didn't accuse them of anything, I only explained that there was this problem of the disappearing ducks.

The problem did not occur again after my little talk.

A Motley Lot of Horses

In the years when I worked in the Parks Service horses were used to pack gear and supplies into the back country and to transport employees and their families.

Unfortunately, the people who bought the horses often knew little of what to look for in saddle and pack stock. Also, not everyone who used the animals afterwards had much experience with horses, and poor handling of any horse leads to a spoiled animal, reluctant and given to bad habits like bucking, kicking and biting.

If the horse gets away with this sort of behaviour for some time it can take fairly rough discipline to make the animal reliably useful again. I preferred not to have to discipline a horse with anyone else present for fear that someone not knowledgeable would view the event as brutal.

When the time came that I was to take over the district at the head of the Red Deer River, I had to make do with some less-than-well-behaved saddle and packhorses.

I had Mike, a young half-bred bay gelding with a rough gait and a reputation for bucking. He had also been known to rear up, lose his balance and go over backwards. This is not a common problem, but there are horses given to it, and it is dangerous for whoever happens to be in the saddle at the time.

I had Nellie, a cream-coloured mare. She was a fast walker with a comfortable, easy gait, but she had long since learned how to travel in hobbles. When you camp at the end of the day you turn your horses loose to graze, each with its front feet held together with a hobbling device which lets the horse move about to graze but prevents the horse deserting the expedition. But some horses, and Nellie was one of them, develop a special gait with the hobbles that covers ground in a hurry. So when you camped, you had to keep one eye on Nellie all the time, and when she'd got enough to eat you had to tether her immediately.

I had Clipper, a thirteen-hundred-pound packhorse who delighted in chasing after bear and often gave a pack a fairly hard pounding in the course of it.

I had Peggy, a gentle little cayuse that was easy to catch whenever you wanted to use her. I decided she would be a good horse for Vera.

With these horses I had to pack supplies into the district cabin and then take in my family as well. At this time we had three small children.

Marty, a senior ranger, was to turn the district over to me, and so he and I made a first trip in, riding two horses with as much gear and supplies as possible packed on the others.

We packed out of Lake Louise and up the Pipestone River to what we called the Little Pipestone cabin. I rode Mike and Marty rode Nellie.

Now Mike was well enough behaved that day but, as I said, he had a rough gait, so the next day I put a pack on him and rode one of the other horses.

For side packs I put eggs in cardboard cartons into the pack boxes, then surrounded these with oats. Given reasonable behaviour on the part of the horse, this would be sufficient protection for the eggs. For a top pack I loaded on a fifty-pound sack of potatoes and my horse-shoeing equipment, then tied everything down with a diamond hitch.

The trail was sufficiently narrow that with Marty riding in the lead and me bringing up the rear, we could let the packhorses travel loose in between.

Unfortunately, just a mile or so from the summit in an unguarded moment, Marty let Mike crowd past him, and the big horse could not resist the new freedom. He started to buck.

He smashed one pack box into a tree, which didn't do the pack box any good, but also the impact loosened the rigging enough that the whole outfit rolled around his girth, ending up under his belly.

When Mike bucked he would bring his hind feet up close under his belly as he gathered himself for the next jump. If you were riding him you would swear he was trying to kick your feet out of the stirrups.

On this occasion he got his feet caught in the pack outfit, went over sideways off the trail and down a short steep bank.

I immediately caught the other horses and tethered them to the handiest trees. Marty had gone ahead to see where Mike had come to rest, and now he came back down the trail to report that Mike was in a heap and unable to get up.

"I do not care," I said, "if Mike is in hell."

Now I don't much care to beat a horse when he is down, as it were, but on the other hand I did not want a repeat of this performance. I cut a stick stout enough to cause the required discomfort but not stout enough to do any physical damage and took considerable advantage of Mike's helpless condition.

When I judged he'd got the connection between his bucking and what I was now doing to him, I undid the pack rigging and led him up to the trail to tether him to a tree.

Marty and I got down on our hands and knees and prospected through the moss and grass and rocks for potatoes, precious horseshoe nails, shoeing tools and scrambled eggs.

Then I patched the damaged pack box, and we re-packed Mike. Never again did he buck under a pack, although he gave me a contest one more time when I was riding him.

This other event took place when I was out with Mike clearing trail.

Shortly after I joined the Parks Service, I bought a brand-new roping saddle. This was a beautiful saddle, and even the fact that it was new was exceptional, since in all the years I had spent polishing saddle leather with the seat of my pants, it was rare that the saddle was even close to being new.

This beautiful new saddle had cost me two months' wages, and there was not a scratch or a blemish on it anywhere.

This was the saddle I had strapped on Mike when we went out clearing trail.

Now I carried in one hand a full-length double-bitted axe, and I had only a hackamore on Mike, not a bridle, so I could more readily tether him when I would dismount to cut through trees which had fallen over the trail or clean a few limbs from trees beside the trail.

When I would remount, I would put my foot in the stirrup and grasp the saddle-horn with one hand to pull myself aboard while I would continue to hold the axe in my other hand.

This procedure had been working well until Mike finally decided to take advantage of me as I swung into the saddle. Just as I had swung into the seat, but before I was settled, he ducked his head and started to buck. In the commotion, my axe struck the leather covering on the saddle-horn.

I was not happy about the bucking, but I was furious about the nick in the leather on my new saddle.

When you ride a horse who persists in bucking out of sheer bloody mindedness, you can often stop him if you strike him on the shoulders with a heavy quirt or supple stick just as he lands. Do this each time he starts to buck and there's a good chance you'll soon break him of the habit altogether.

I had no quirt or stick, but I did have the axe. Once I was settled enough in the saddle to know Mike was not going to buck me off, I shook the axe out until I had it by just the end of the handle. Making sure that the flat of the axe-head, not the blade, would strike him I swung the axe across before me to strike him once on each shoulder.

Immediately he stopped bucking. As I rode him back to the cabin at the head of the Red Deer River, I inspected the nick in the leather on my saddle-horn, which I knew I must simply get used to as there was no way to repair it so it would not be visible.

Mike exhibited a little tenderness about the shoulders for a few days, but he never bucked again. In fact, Mike became a thoroughly reliable trail horse and I grew very fond of him.

As I mentioned earlier, the people who bought the horses were not the ones who had to use them. I have noticed over the years that this problem afflicts governments and large companies to a considerable degree. Since the people who must use the gear do not have the authority to purchase it, the gear is often to some extent unsuitable for its intended purposes.

At one time in Calgary the rodeo stock contractors started to sell off some of their older and less suitable horses.

Now the job of a rodeo horse is to buck with such determination that within eight seconds out of the chute he will have dumped all but the best of riders.

Rodeo riders insist that the horse does just that. The points given for the ride depend not only on the cowboy's skill in staying on board but also on the fury with which the horse bucks. No rider wants to come out on a pansy because even if he earns full points, the horse will earn so little as to keep the total well out of the money. Not uncommonly, a rider drawing a horse which does not buck well will ask for a re-ride on a better horse.

So as horses get older or lose their enthusiasm for bucking, the contractor who owns the horses and earns his living by supplying good bucking stock to the rodeos sells them off.

Now you can imagine the delight of the stock contractors in Calgary when, with rather more than usual stock to get rid of, the purchasing agents from the Parks Service, who barely knew a horse from an ox-cart, showed up in town looking for horses. Several stock-truck loads of these rodeo rejects came into the park for the wardens to use as packhorses.

I had dealings with only two of this lot.

One I called Big George, and he was aggressive. If you were not watching him constantly with a wary eye he would charge at you with his front feet reaching out to strike. He had hooves on him the size of pie plates.

The other I called Badger, and he was a very gentle horse to handle, but if anything at all went wrong, regardless of where you were, he would come unstuck and spread gear from the pack outfit all over the place.

One of the commonest hazards in packing with a string of horses along a timbered trail is the lowly little yellowjacket, that builds a nest not in a tree but in a small cavity in the ground in loose soil near the surface.

For reasons unknown, such yellowjacket nests are occasionally located immediately beside the packhorse trail, but of course you never see them, you only find out about them after all hell has broken loose in your pack string.

When you come along with your string of horses the first few get by unscathed. By about the fifth horse past the nest, the yellowjackets are buzzing about furiously, and the rest of the horses get thoroughly stung.

Now there were some lakes known as the Red Deer Lakes which were located within convenient hiking distance from one of the main roads through the park. They were a very popular fishing spot, but they lacked sufficient spawning grounds, so occasionally the park would stock them with fresh fingerlings.

It so happened then that one day another park employee, Jack Bloomquist, and I were packing into these lakes with a tankful of fingerlings on each side of six packhorses.

We had come over the summit of the trail and were heading along a creek down toward the lakes when the major event of the day occurred. Most of the horses got by the nest, but just as old Badger got there the yellowjackets struck in force. The rest of the packhorses hurried along the trail to get out of the way, but Badger started bucking with all his rodeo experience evident in every jump.

He did not hit any trees and he did not fall down, and for a while I thought the packs were going to make it. But Badger was too much, even for the well-tied diamond hitch. Half his load of fingerlings went into the creek and the other half up the bank on the high side.

Although this creek reached the lake, there were minor waterfalls along a steep part of the stream course which would prevent fish coming up from the lake, although we supposed our fingerlings would have no trouble making the journey down. We took the remaining pack loads on to the lakes and released them.

It was several years later that one of my brothers hiked into the Red Deer Lakes and was surprised to find excellent fishing in a small stream about four miles from the lakes. Since fish could not come upstream from the lakes, he and his party were considerably puzzled as to how they could have got there.

Half his load of fingerlings went into the creek . . .

The Visiting Public

There were many interesting animals in the parks and the hunting country where I worked.

Often, it seemed, the visiting public were the strangest animals of all. A great number were quite out of their element, having come from a city to camp or view nature or ski or hunt. More recently, the enthusiasm among young people to be knowledgeable about backpacking and camping has brought some well-clothed and well-equipped visitors into the bush, but in the fifties your run-of-the-mill person out of the city was uninformed to say the least.

Skiers frequently went through remote timbered areas to reach less used slopes without a light axe and matches or the means of making a snow shelter. People would drive the bush roads in back country without a shovel in the trunk.

Once I drove down a little-used bush road and realized someone must be travelling ahead of me. Timber which had fallen over the road through a windfall area was freshly cut off as close to the light end of the stem as possible, leaving a good deal of it still on the road but creating just enough room to squeeze around. Anything which lay close enough to the ground to drive over with a bit of a bump was still intact. The road was a mess, in fact, and I spent some time with a saw and axe cleaning it up.

When I had finished I drove to the end of the road to speak to whoever must be responsible. I came on a man sitting in his parked car and suggested he had not been a very good woodsman.

"Well," he said, defensively, "I did my best."

Whereupon he showed me the only instrument he had with him to cut windfalls out of the way: a hacksaw with about a ten-inch blade.

When I was stationed near Radium in Kootenay Park a car carrying a state licence came into the warden station yard.

A well dressed woman in what I judged to be her early thirties got out of the car and I went over to meet her.

124

"Are you the warden?" she asked, in tone of voice which suggested she was not happy.

"Yes," I replied.

"Well, where does someone go to file a complaint around here?"

"You could write to Ottawa," I offered, "or you could write the Park Superintendent. Or you could just tell me."

"Well, you seem to be a nice boy, so I'll tell you. I stopped at a campground near Banff and a man swore at me. I think he was in charge of the campground."

Tactfully, I asked her the circumstances. Apparently she had wanted to light a fire, so she placed some of the uncut rounds of wood which the park supplied into one of the designated campfire pits. She then struck a match and held it to the wood. Now the uncut rounds were perhaps six inches in diameter, and of course she went through most of her matches before realizing that her technique was not going to get her fire going.

It seems at that point the campground attendant arrived, and she said she was not having any success making a fire with the wood which had been supplied.

Perhaps he had already had a long day, but in any case he did the unforgiveable in park service; he proceeded to observe that any stupid bitch ought to have enough sense to cut some kindling and walked away, leaving her none the wiser but with very hurt feelings.

The poor woman simply did not know what kindling was or how you made it.

I fetched an axe and split some kindling from a round of wood which happened to be nearby, then showed her how to pile it together with some fine twigs and bits to first catch the flame from the match.

"I see," she said thoughtfully, then went away in a much improved frame of mind.

———————————   ———————————

Banff, Yoho and Kootenay Parks all straddle main highways linking Alberta and British Columbia.

Many stretches of the road receive very heavy snowfalls in winter, and we constantly looked out for people in trouble, their cars stuck in the snow. The few people who carried warm clothing, including good footwear and, of course, a few basic tools were not a worry to us. However, the many travellers in dress shoes and light clothing and no equipment at all could be at great risk in short order in a heavy storm and were very much on our minds.

Our grader operator out of Field was clearing the highway on one occasion near Wapiti Lake just after we had received four feet of new snow.

He passed a large mound on the side of the road which looked somewhat out of place. On glancing back for a second look, our operator saw that some of the mound of snow was falling away to reveal part of a car. Quickly he stopped his machine, then walked back to brush vigorously at the snow, hoping as he did so that the covering of snow had provided sufficient insulation to keep the occupant at least safe if not comfortable.

In the car was a worried man from Alabama whose observation on opening his car door was, "It sure do snow hereabouts, don't it?"

At Marble Canyon it was not uncommon to receive about four inches of fresh snow every night, and the daily routine all winter began with two hours of shovelling snow around the station.

We had a barrier on the road to stop traffic when the roads were no longer passable, but even then some drivers would crash the barrier and then need help to get out of the trouble into which they had driven themselves.

With the snow every night the ploughs had to work every day. By February the snow would be very deep on both sides of the highway, and anyone going off the road would literally bury their vehicle.

One evening about seven o'clock a man came into the yard at the station on foot to explain that his car was in the ditch a short way out on the highway. He wondered where he could get a tow truck to pull it out.

I explained that this was not practical since the nearest tow truck was fifty miles away, but that I would call the snowplough operator at Hawk Creek.

The operator soon arrived and we went to the site. I did the necessary shovelling, by any reckoning the hardest work required in this rescue, to get a tow line safely attached to the bottom side of the vehicle frame.

Then the plough operator started up his winch and, with ease, the car came back out of the snow and onto the road. The rescue accomplished, I brought the traveller and the plough operator back to the station for a meal.

Now this man turned out to be a salesman for a line of fine Cowichan sweaters, the sort which are hand-knit from heavy homespun wool yarn. A good Cowichan sweater is a splendid winter garment and fine in appearance as well. Most people would be delighted to own one.

So in his gratitude, the salesman gave the snowplough operator a sweater and then another one to Vera since she had fed him a large, hot supper.

Then he turned to me and said, "I know that since you are a public servant, you are not allowed to accept a gift."

And I was the bloke who did all the hard work!

Not more than a few days later another man walked into the station at about the same time in the evening. He had gone off the road into the snowbank, virtually burying his car. Only with great difficulty had he crawled out a window and got back to the highway to walk to the station.

When he knocked Vera opened the door and at once he said, "May I talk to Wilf, please?"

I recognized the man as our office clerk from Radium, and I urged him to come in at once.

"I must talk to you first," he said, anxiously.

I was puzzled by this behaviour, but stepped out into the night and closed the door behind me. Apart from the squirrels, we were alone, but he spoke in such a whisper you would think the squirrels were going to tell on him. He described how badly he had got the government vehicle into the snowbank and how badly he needed me to help him get it out.

His predicament sounded routine enough to me, so I started up my truck and proceeded to the site. Indeed, he'd done a good job. You couldn't even see the car from the road, and it would need hours of snow shovelling to get it out. I suggested he come back to the station for the night and we would tackle this job in the morning.

Immediately he became further agitated and began whispering again. "Wilf, I have the park payroll in the car. I have to get that money to Radium tonight."

I tried to convince him that the money was as safe where it was as it would be in the bank, but to no avail. The responsibility for the money was too much for him to bear.

So again I called Hawk Creek and again out came the heavy equipment. With some shovelling to get a safe purchase on the vehicle frame, we winched him out.

As he got in his car to start it up and leave I thanked him for being so conscientious about my paycheque.

Hurriedly, he shushed me and reverted to his whisper. He was dreadfully worried that I might give away his awesome secret.

So far as I know, the squirrels never told on him.

_____   _____

Sometimes the end of the story is not so fortunate.

I was up to Mount Norquay Lodge one time to visit and found the manager was not having a particularly cheerful day.

I asked him what was wrong.

"Skiers," he replied, with disgust. "Skiing is a disease, and I'd rather have cancer. One day they'll find a cure for cancer but, by Harry, they'll never find a cure for skiing!"

Well, I had to agree that with some of the people coming into the park to ski, he had a point. You could put up all possible signs to direct people to safe trails and slopes and other signs to keep people away from danger, but in spite of all this, people would manage to get into grief.

A young woman ventured into rugged terrain along Marble Canyon. She lost control and fell into the top pool. The water there is only twelve feet deep but the current is so swift and turbulent that we could not get a seventy-pound hook to the bottom.

The whole current then drops through a steep, narrow falls and then over a lesser falls of fifty feet or so. Having fallen into the top pool, the young woman had hardly had a chance.

We stretched a net across the river at the bottom of the canyon. We had to tend the net constantly to clear it of debris.

Bob, the Chief Warden from Radium, and I were cleaning out this net one day in miserably cold weather. We wore mackinaw jackets and hip waders, and between the cold air and the cold water we were not on a picnic.

Bob, with his teeth chattering, turned to me to make a general observation on people who go on holidays.

"You know," he said, "I've figured something out."

"Oh, yes," I replied, without anticipating any particular reply. I'd figured a few things out myself over the years. It was not an unusual event.

"Yeh," he said, dryly. "When some people go on a holiday, they go to the bank and take out their money, but they put their brains in the bank for safekeeping. That's why they do some of this dumb stuff we get to deal with."

Bob spoke from thirty years of experience in the parks. I had no cause to dispute his observations.

Sometimes the misunderstanding of a visitor could be exploited to lighten the day.

From time to time we had to reduce the elk herd in the park, since with no hunting and little predation the animals would soon multiply to numbers far beyond the capacity of the range to support them. The consequence of that would be undernourished and diseased animals with a periodic heavy winter die-off. The parks service had long concluded it was better to take out enough animals from time to time — while the animals taken were fit to be used — to keep the herd healthy.

Our job in the park was to kill the elk with carefully placed head or neck shots, then paunch them out. After that the carcasses were trucked to a slaughterhouse for final processing. The parks service distributed the meat to people who had need of it, so it was in no sense wasted.

On one occasion I was sent along with Jack Rae, the park blacksmith as it happened, to kill a small herd which had holed up near the highway in heavy timber.

I chose to wear my badge and warden hat, while Jack went in regular gear which in no respect identified him as a park employee.

When we located these elk they were in the heavy timber not far from the highway. We did not want to shoot them in the timber as it would have been impossible to get them out afterwards to load on the truck.

I said to Jack, "I'll go circle around behind them and fire a couple of shots to scare them out. When they come out on the road allowance, you shoot as many as you can."

So that is what I did, and everything went according to plan. I got behind the elk, fired the necessary shots and heard the elk move on through the timber toward the highway.

But I heard no shots from Jack. Even after a long interval I still heard no shots.

I followed the elk tracks then, and when I came out on the highway I could see they had crossed just where we had expected. Now they were across the highway climbing the hill toward a golf course, one result we had hoped to avoid.

I also saw Jack standing by the truck engaged in a heated argument with a tourist who had parked his car nearby.

When I approached, the tourist saw my badge and warden hat and immediately declared, "This man is hunting elk in the park! I want to make a citizen's arrest."

". . . I want to make a citizen's arrest."

I said, "Well, that's very good of you. I'll take care of him. There's no need for you to interrupt your holiday over this park poacher."

Then the tourist said, with evident relief, "I'm sure glad you came along. I don't know if I could have handled a big guy like this by myself."

The tourist went happily on his way, but it was a long time before Jack could see any humour in the situation.

Even the visiting hunter, one sort you would expect to better under-stand the outdoor world and the wildlife, sometimes exhibited a little gullibility.

I once helped staff a checking station in good game country. Hun-ter success was high and we had a steady lot of animals to check.

We would ask the hunters as they went through on their way to hunt to please save the lower jaw of any animal they shot and, un-less they were planning to have the head mounted, to leave the jaw with us on their way out. From these we could obtain valuable in-formation about the age and other characteristics of the harvested animals and better manage the game herds.

Most often the hunters simply brought back the whole heads and left these with us since this saved them the trouble of separating the jaw. Of course we spent considerable time on this task, but we were glad to do it for the useful information we gained.

One morning I faced a pile of elk and deer heads about four feet high, and as I worked my way through, cutting out the jaws and recording information on a report sheet, a party of three hunters drove up and got out of their vehicle.

"Where are the elk?" one of them asked, and something in his manner and that of his party suggested they might like to talk for some time about where the elk might be.

Since I was well occupied and wanted to get on with my task I replied, without interrupting my work, "Up the road about a quar-ter of a mile." Of course I had not the least idea, except in a very general sense, but I thought that sounded convincing enough to get these hunters on their way.

Well, off they went and damned if about five minutes later I didn't hear a shot.

Back down the road soon came two of the hunters in the vehicle. They jumped out on arriving to declare, "Our buddy got that one. Where's another one?"

I explained, in my most diplomatic manner, that it was only fair of me to give away the location of one elk to a party of hunters and that they must locate the next one on their own.

In any case, the odds against repeating my success were so over-whelming that I thought it better to quit while everyone thought I was the wisest man in the woods.

Perhaps the most touching moment with a visitor from distant places came when we were in the cabin in a district called the Leanchoil.

Some previous warden's wife had planted lilac bushes, and in the early summer when the blossom was on with its strong and evocative fragrance a young American woman knocked on our door.

Her request was simple. She was on her honeymoon trip and she had grown homesick for the garden in her parents' yard back in the States.

Could she, she asked, please just smell our lilac flowers?

I doubt if we ever granted a more simple favour yet gave more pleasure.

Oldtimers

Working in the parks and in the game and forest service for the Province of Alberta carried with it the blessing of meeting some very interesting oldtimers.

When we moved into the Leanchoil district in Yoho Park such neighbours as we had came to call, and we in turn visited them.

The last to come around was old Charlie Lawrence, a trapper who had come into the Beaverfoot River basin in 1919 and was still there in 1952.

He was pushing sixty years of age and about as tough as they come. He had a main cabin and the odd trap cabin, but he spent a good deal of his time on the trail, camping out where night found him.

He worked for the BC Forest Service in the summer and trapped in the winter. His trapline lay just outside the park, extending southward toward Kootenay Park. At that time there were no roads into the area, and you lived on what the land had to offer, supplemented by what you could bring in on your back or with packhorses.

Charlie was a bit silent, rough-talking when he did speak and very set in his ways. Most people were a little afraid of attempting anything in the way of a friendly overture with him, much less an attempt at practical humour.

I came out of the bush onto the bank of the Beaverfoot River one day just as Charlie was about to cross from the opposite side. The Beaverfoot was one of those streams which is more a large creek than a river and a wind-fallen tree could span it, offering a provisional bridge.

Such a tree lay across it here, and as Charlie stepped onto the light end to cross, I stepped up on the stump end and began jumping up and down, creating considerable motion at Charlie's end.

Charlie calmly settled the corks of his boots into the bark and stood fast.

Then he said, in a dry voice, "Whenever you're done playing."

I asked, "Charlie, did you ever fall in this river?"

"Hundreds of times. And it's not much fun, dumping a guy, you know."

Well, I didn't dump him and hadn't really thought I would, and we stopped after he crossed for the sort of brief exchange of words which passed for conversation with Charlie. He was a resourceful and fiercely independent old woodsman, and I mightily respected him.

When he worked for the forest service in the summer months he could be considerably irked by regulations. One regulation required that all personnel when travelling in the bush must carry a small two-way radio so they might call for help if they got in any sort of trouble. Charlie regarded this as totally unnecessary in his case, but his supervisor insisted. Charlie acquiesced. He carried the radio but lightened his load by leaving the batteries behind.

One day the BC Forest Service ranger came into our station to tell me that someone had called for help on the forest service radio frequency but had gone off the air before giving identification. The radio operator had then called, in turn, everyone known to carry a radio. With one exception, all confirmed they were in no distress.

The one exception was old Charlie. The operator could not raise Charlie. Could it be that Charlie was in trouble, had made the initial call but now was not able to respond to the operator's attempt to reach him?

I was about to say, first, that Charlie was highly unlikely to be in distress and, second, that Charlie could not have made the call or responded to the operator because Charlie did not carry batteries for his radio.

Then I thought better of that because while Charlie had trusted me with the knowledge that he did not carry the batteries (don't need the goddamned radio anyway, had been his expression), he obviously did not share this information with the forest service for whom he worked. Who was I to pass on his secrets?

So off I went into the mountains and finally located the old bush-rat. I got a scorching lecture for thinking for a moment that he could be in any sort of difficulty, but I sensed also that he was genuinely pleased that I thought enough of him to go out looking for him in the first place.

In the area in which he trapped there were a number of mineral showings. These of course attracted prospectors whom Charlie resented, and none more than the city types who would not cut trail for themselves but would make liberal use of the trails which Charlie maintained.

On one occasion a party consisting of an inexperienced prospector, the woman who had backed him with a grubstake and a young boy set out to backpack into the headwaters of the Beaverfoot River. It seems the woman, whose money supported the prospecting venture, wanted to see for herself the ground which offered riches in return for her financial backing.

Late in the day heavy rain began falling and the party decided to camp. As city folk often do, they camped right astride the trail. Once off in the woods themselves, they rarely can imagine that anyone else might be out there as well.

After many attempts in the pouring rain the woman and the boy got a fire going, right on the trail.

About eight o'clock in the evening, as they sat one on each side of the fire trying their best to dry out the next pieces of wood to go on the fire, Charlie, tramping down the trail, emerged out of the dark.

He did not stop, he did not speak. He calmly walked up to the fire, stepped over it without a glance sideways at anyone, and walked on down the trail to disappear in the gloom.

As soon as daylight arrived this party broke camp and hurried to our station to report that there was a wild man out there in the woods. I knew from their account of the event that it was only old Charlie who had hiked through their camp, but I am sure they thought they had seen Bigfoot himself.

I am sure they thought they had seen Bigfoot himself.

Few people knew what a splendid person lived inside Charlie's tough shell. He never went out to town without bringing back some treat or other for our children and they, of course, thought he was wonderful. He had few friends, but those few had the undying loyalty of an almost possessive old eccentric.

Also in the district at Leanchoil I had an old Norwegian, John, for a lookout man. He had been a gold prospector in his youth and he really knew his way around in the mountains. He taught me a good deal of what I know about how and where to prospect.

In those years we would take a lookout man into his lookout tower and camp on horseback. We would carry in his supplies at the same time on however many packhorses that required. During the season we would check on him occasionally and re-supply him with a packhorse load of goods. He was, of course, in radio contact with us at all times.

One season John insisted on taking his old border collie bitch to the tower camp for company. Unknown to John, she had enjoyed a love affair with some nondescript dog before departure and produced a litter of pups following arrival in the camp. John had no use for the pups, and in the ordinary course of such matters the pups would have been destroyed. But not with old John, and so I packed more dog food into John's camp that summer than I packed grub for John himself.

John, like many an oldtimer in the bush, could be taciturn and stringently practical.

Once along the banks of the Ice River I showed him a deposit of beautiful blue sodalite.

He said, dismissively, "I doesn't see any gold."

On another occasion John came by as I was sighting in a heavy bear rifle in .405 calibre. You could tell by looking at the cartridge that this rifle on firing would deliver a substantial recoil into your shoulder.

I enquired, "You like to try it out?" Most outdoorsmen like the opportunity to take a shot with a rifle, whatever the circumstances.

John grunted, "I doesn't want a sore arm."

John's lookout tower had a good view of the Chancellor Peak campground. This was one of the campgrounds beside the highway which were provided for the use of the travelling public. This particular campground was only a few minutes' drive from our station.

Most of the time campfires were allowed and firewood was provided for the purpose. However, during the dry season fires were prohibited and signs were posted to this effect.

With his powerful binoculars, John could not only look into the campground, he could give the location of a particular camp and a description of the people making use of it.

If he saw someone fetching wood to make a fire he would call me on the radio and give me the location and description of the party. I would jump into my vehicle and drive to the campground.

When I arrived I would not look around at anyone else but go directly to the party preparing to make fire, often arriving on the scene just as the match was being struck. Then I would say that fires are not allowed just now, didn't you see the sign, and leave the party dumbstruck as to how I knew with such precise timing what they were about to do.

John, like many an old Scandinavian who had immigrated to Canada and gone into back country, had a passion for snuff, almost invariably the brand known as Copenhagen.

One time when I had loaded the packhorses with John's supplies and was about to head out on the trail to his tower, Vera dashed out the door of our cabin to tell me I had forgotten John's snuff. She then handed me the ten-tin roll of his much loved fix.

Rather than undo a pack to put the snuff with the rest of his supplies I rolled it into my slicker and tied it behind the cantle on my saddle.

When I arrived at the tower I unpacked the horses, placing the pack boxes on the steps of John's little cabin. At the same time, he came down from the tower to carry his goods into the cabin and stow everything away in his simple cupboards.

As he emptied the last pack box and went into the cabin with the last of his supplies, he called back with a note of urgency in his voice, "Wilf, where is me Copenhagen?"

"Golly, John," I replied, "I must have forgotten."

For the only time I ever remember, old John got a stiff upper lip, and he said, solemnly, "I walk off de mountain."

It didn't take me long to remember where I had stashed his Copenhagen.

John was a good tower man. He would stay up in the tower day and night if there were thunder storms and plot the location of every lightning strike. He was seldom less than impeccably accurate.

When we were at the head of the Red Deer River I decided to build a pack shed in order to store equipment and supplies out of the weather. The office in town sent out Lloyd, an old retired ranger who had been raised in lumbering country, to help with this undertaking.

We felled the trees, cut the logs to length, peeled them, then skidded them to the building site with one of the horses.

Then we started to build and in twenty days we had the walls up to the plate log, the last log before the roof structure goes on.

The days were growing short and I knew we must get out soon or we would be snowed in for the winter. I decided we would leave the building at this stage and let the logs dry a little more over the winter, then put the roof on in the spring.

I was sitting on the plate log when I made this decision, and I passed it on to Lloyd, adding, "We've done pretty well, don't you figure? We've worked less than a month, and here we are with a new building that just needs a roof and we'll be using it."

Lloyd snorted, "Less than a month! Why, my God Wilf, when I was a kid we logged with horses and oxen and when we moved to a new site everyone slept out the first night and by the second night we had the cookhouse, bunkhouse and stables up and it was all done with crosscut saws and axes! This piddly-ass little shed we got here wouldn't a' taken half a day."

Lloyd was a good logger, but he was about to meet something that was a little out of his line.

He was sleeping in a tent in front of our cabin, and when he had first arrived Vera had told him that she would leave the front door open in case a grizzly bear came in the night and bothered him.

He had laughed at that and said he'd been in the bush all his life and hadn't seen a grizzly bear.

I explained that on patrol in the district I had seen a number of grizzlies, but he merely grinned and asked, in a skeptical voice, "Where are they?"

Now all summer I had been receiving complaints about a large sow grizzly with a two-year-old cub that had been challenging people on the trail, forcing them to make a wide circle into the bush to get around. Some of the stories suggested the cub may have been the more aggressive of the two.

I had spent several days trying to run this pair down, but of course I did not want to shoot any bear until I could be certain it was the right one and that it was likely to cause serious trouble.

The night before we were to set out from the cabin at the head of the Red Deer River, one of our packhorses, Clipper, started chasing something about in the pasture. We all headed for the cabin porch to see what was up. In the fading evening light we saw a big sow grizzly with a beautiful two-year-old cub carrying splendid colour on his hide.

The bears headed for the fence, easily going under it. Lloyd was very excited and not a little afraid, I think, when the bears stopped about twenty yards in front of the cabin.

I felt certain that these were the bears about which I had been getting reports, and I thought I had better use the opportunity. I fetched my .270 rifle, loaded it and prepared to shoot.

Lloyd said, urgently, "Don't shoot!"

I asked, "Why not?"

"You might miss, and I don't think them bears are cowards. Suppose you miss and I'm out there sleeping in the tent tonight when they come back?"

I explained that I had wasted a lot of time out looking for these bears and I might never get another opportunity.

But Lloyd was both very worried and adamant. Finally he said, "We have to leave in the morning, and I won't help you dispose of the bears."

The old sow was still standing there, peering at us and everything around her. I decided to let well enough alone, and I did enough shouting and hollering to persuade the bear to take her cub and go on her way. It was the cub that turned last to leave, having stared about him with a defiant indifference.

I got no reports of the pair the next year. Undoubtedly they separated, as the sow already was overdue to have another cub, and I assumed the coming three-year-old moved farther back into the mountains once on his own.

I was glad afterwards that Lloyd had persuaded me not to shoot.

———————————————   ———————————————

One time when I was in Calgary I looked about for a light-calibre pistol to carry in back country when I did not want to be encumbered with a rifle but nonetheless wanted some firepower.

I found a pistol for sale which had come into Canada in parts in a gasoline tank and had been reassembled afterwards. Due to the nature of its arrival in the country, the owner had not attempted to register it.

I thought it would do, but first I went to the police to enquire if I would be able to register it.

The answer was no dice. The police knew who owned it and would be picking it up along with the people involved as soon as they completed an investigation then underway. I got the distinct impression that more was under investigation than the pistol.

However, the corporal I talked with told me of another pistol he thought I might buy for a good price at, of all places, a bake shop on 17th Avenue. I went there and approached the owner about the pistol, which he gladly sold me. He said the police had been suggesting to him that he had no need of it and should sell it.

I believe this was one of the first Sturm Ruger .22-calibre pistols to come into Canada. I supposed it was a good pistol, but it did not fit my hand and practise as I might I could not shoot accurately with it. Not being humble enough to admit to any shortcomings on my own part, I blamed the pistol for the lack of accuracy.

One day I was working the phone line on the Ice River road, clearing out saplings and branches which would interfere with the wire if left to grow another season. Close to noon I drove to a new cabin we had built by the river to cook and eat my lunch. This cabin sat at the end of the road and at that point a bridge had been built in anticipation of a further road across the river at some time in the future.

As I was making lunch an old prospector by the name of Pete happened to come across the bridge. I added a few more ingredients to the mix in the pan and invited him for lunch.

Now when I had emptied my pack on the cabin table, this new Ruger pistol was among the odds and ends.

I noticed Pete staring at it, and I asked, "What do you think of my new pistol?"

"I thought I knew guns," he said, "but I never saw a pistol like that before."

"Would you like to shoot it?"

"Sure. Like to try any new gun."

So after we had eaten our lunch I made a blaze on a tree about the size of a quarter and paced off thirty yards. It is not uncommon to have a little target competition on meeting another firearm buff in the woods, and I looked forward to this small entertainment. I handed old Pete the pistol.

Pete took three quick shots and damned if they didn't land into the blaze so close together they were touching each other.

I hadn't said anything to Pete about taking a turn myself, so now

I just said to him, "Shoots good, eh?" and put the pistol back in my pack.

A year or so later I told this story to an outfitter friend of mine, and he laughed a good laugh. Then he said, "Old Pete must be pushing seventy if he isn't past it and you bet he's a good shot. But his wife is better. Now she can really shoot."

It turned out that for long years past this old couple would sit in their rocking chairs on the porch of their cabin every evening and, for entertainment, shoot with their pistols at tin cans set in a row on the top rail of their yard fence.

I'm glad I didn't take a turn at shooting that day at the Ice River cabin. I liked to think of myself as a good competitive shot but clearly I would have been out of my league.

We were stationed one time at a place called Lynx Creek. My supervisor was the ranger at Castle District. His name was John, and he had an assistant there whose name was also John so we knew them as Young John and Old John.

One day while I was working with Young John he explained to me that Old John had a strange habit. On the nights when his wife did not wish to respond to Old John's amorous approaches, Old John would go out in the night and play his bagpipes. This, it seemed, was Old John's equivalent of taking a cold shower. He did not, of course, have a shower, so naturally he needed some other device. Still, the story seemed a little improbable but Young John insisted it was the case. Old John would go out into the pasture and play his bagpipes with the elk, the deer and his horses for an audience.

I treated this story with some skepticism until late one night at about two in the morning our bush-line telephone rang. (We strung telephone wire from tree to tree along backroads and trails to provide elementary communication between cabins in the remote regions of the district.)

It was Old John's wife on the phone, and she said Old John wanted Wilf to hear his bagpipes.

So there we sat, out in the bush, from two to three o'clock in the morning, with our ears tuned to the telephone, listening to Old John play all the Scottish marching tunes on his bagpipes.

The fidelity over the wire strung from tree to tree wasn't great, but the anguish of Old John's unrequited passions certainly came through loud and clear.

I was glad it was his problem, not mine.

We had a warden in Banff, Jack was his name, whose nature it was to tell tall stories. He would set about telling you a story which was certainly a huge lie, but then he would work hard to convince you it was the truth, and in the process he would convince himself that it was the truth. Of course at that stage it became almost unfair not to believe him, and in any case his stories were harmless.

One summer during a wet spell I came into town for supplies, and the office asked me if I would go to help Jack move his gear out of his cabin. It seemed the power company's dam upstream was about to break, and while we could not save the park cabin we could save Jack's furnishings and other personal belongings if we acted quickly.

Now the water was rising when I arrived at the cabin, and Jack was scurrying about in a fit of confusion. Haste was obviously the order of the day, so I quickly loaded onto my light truck all the furniture and belongings in sight. I did not go into the dank cellar beneath the cabin which passed for a basement. Jack was not paying it any attention, and in any case it was half full of water, so I assumed there was nothing in it worth getting wet to save. I can verify there was nothing of value left in the cabin itself.

The power company was responsible for losses and these had to be determined largely from statements made to the board which was struck to assess damages. I went to Jack's cabin a week after the dam burst and it was buried to the ridgepole in gravel. Any evidence about lost contents was buried with the cabin, so the board had no choice but to take Jack's word on the subject.

Well, would you believe that Jack lost a whole houseful of furniture and four hundred dollars' worth of bottled fruit in the basement besides, which he had put down himself at great labour?

I wouldn't believe it, but the board did. It was the best flood Jack ever had.

Greenhorns

Not all the people I knew or worked with in the parks were oldtimers, well-seasoned and knowledgeable.

Some were young and short on knowledge of such matters as how to pack and otherwise work with horses. Often because they knew so little they were unable to imagine how much there was to know.

One such was Dusty, a young Irishman and green as Irish grass, who, when asked if he could pack, said sure. He thought they meant backpacking as in a small pack on his own back, not that of a horse.

In truth the young lad hardly knew how to put a saddle on a horse.

Early in 1951 Vera and the children and I packed into our main cabin at the head of the Red Deer River. Grass for the horses was still in short supply at this higher elevation so we decided to travel down the trail to a lower location along the river, known as Scotch Camp. There was plenty of work to be done here on the lower trails, plus sufficient grass for the horses and a couple of good cabins we could use. We brought with us enough camp outfit to be comfortable for two or three weeks.

Now our closest neighbour so far as we knew was twenty-three miles away on the Panther River with ten to twenty feet of snow in the pass between us, so I was considerably surprised one evening to hear a knock on the door.

I was more surprised when I opened it to find Dusty standing there in soaking wet clothes.

"Where did you come from?" I asked, astonished.

So Dusty told us his story.

He had been assigned temporarily to the Clearwater District, far away on the other side of the Red Deer River.

He had gone to the Ya Ha Tinda Ranch, a main headquarters where horses were kept, to get his saddle and pack animals and had set out on the trail from there.

Two old hands at the ranch, Neal and Mickey, had packed his horses for him, then advised him to go over Clearwater Summit to

143

get into his district since this was the lower pass and there would be less snow.

Once out of sight, however, Dusty had struck for the shorter route through the much higher Divide Creek Pass. This trail went by not far from Scotch Camp on the opposite side of the river.

Within a mile of the summit he had encountered snow to depths of twenty feet. At first he had tried to break trail by forcing his horses into the snow. Then, being young and strong as a bull, he had dismounted and attempted to break trail on foot. Unfortunately, he had managed only to tire himself out.

Finally realizing the route might be impossible, he had led his horses back out of the snow, then attempted to remount his saddle-horse. But the big, raw-boned, half-broken pinto the men at the ranch had given him to ride by this time wanted no part of the caper and had promptly dumped Dusty into the brush beside the trail.

Dusty then had led his horses back down the trail until he was just across from Scotch Camp. There he had stripped the packs off, letting gear fall where it may. He could no longer even catch his reluctant saddle-horse, so he had walked to the river, stripped off most of his clothing and swum across. He had intended to get into Scotch Camp for shelter and to use the telephone to ring up the office in town. He wanted to tell the people there he had quit and that they could send someone else to fetch the horses and gear.

We gave Dusty a hot meal and dry clothes, and after he had eaten I persuaded him to come with me across the river to get his horses and gear.

We crossed on two of my horses and soon I had caught all his horses and repacked them. Dusty had tied a rope around his saddle-horse's neck with a slip knot, contrary to an absolute rule when taking in lead or tethering a horse. The horse had stepped several times on the trailing shank, tightening the knot, and by the time I caught up to him, he could hardly breathe. The knot was so tight, I had to cut the rope with a knife to get it off.

By dark we still had not found all the halters, but we had to leave to get back across the river. When I did find the remaining halters the next day they had been well chewed by rodents.

Once back in the cabin, Dusty insisted on calling our Chief Warden, Frank Bryant.

Dusty told Frank all his troubles and then said at the end of his tale of woe, "I guess I just can't do it."

But Frank, one of the finest men I have ever worked for, was a gentleman, and he believed in encouraging young men to believe in themselves. He would have none of Dusty quitting, and he asked him to put me on the phone.

I could not add much more to describe the problem than was already evident from what Dusty had said—at least I could not and keep a straight face. On the surface of it, Dusty was the problem but you could hardly come out and say that.

More accurately, the problem was that the parks service had hired a man without that long apprenticeship in handling horses and getting about in the bush that was essential to the work at hand. This was no fault of Dusty's. He was a stout lad and intelligent and the worst that could be said of him was that he didn't care much to be told how to do something, he preferred to find it out for himself by trial and error, a not uncommon route to excellence.

At any rate, Frank asked me if I could somehow get Dusty and his outfit into the Clearwater, not only because he believed it was right to encourage Dusty to persevere but also because fire season was coming and he had no one to send in his stead.

The next morning we set about our task, and our first problem was that the big pinto had bucked Dusty off so many times Dusty no longer wanted to try to ride him.

So I ran him into the corral and strapped my saddle on him to try him out and see if I could discover the problem. He was a tall horse, running close to sixteen hands, and I had to stretch to get a foot in the stirrup in order to mount up. In such a case a horse has you at an initial disadvantage due to the difficulty of climbing up so far just to get on top. But the big horse was not troubled by the procedure, and once in the saddle I took him out of the corral, along the trail for half a mile and back again. He was not broken to neck rein but apart from that he seemed a reasonable horse.

Back in the corral I persuaded Dusty to mount up and take him for a short turn while I could watch. If the horse fired up I might see what Dusty did that upset him.

To my absolute astonishment, Dusty walked over to the horse, took the reins and the saddle-horn in both hands, then in one mighty jump leaped clear up over the horse's back to land with a wallop in the saddle.

Before Dusty could find the stirrups with his feet, the horse took a mighty jump of his own, dumping Dusty in the mud. It all happened in a split second and it was abundantly clear why.

So I explained patiently to Dusty that a first rule with horses is that when a horse has learned to have something done a certain way, you do not vary the routine.

For the convenience of training horses in such a way that others may use them with no surprises for horse or rider, certain routines have become standard.

All cowboys approach to mount on the horse's left side. Always, the cowboy puts his left foot into the stirrup, then with his right hand on the saddle-horn he draws himself up, placing his right leg over the horse and settling into the saddle in a smooth movement.

When you go into a stall to lead out a horse tethered to the manger rail, you always go in on the horse's left side, and you start talking to him well before you enter the stall so he knows you are approaching and will not be taken by surprise.

Now there are, of course, many gentle old horses with whom you can do any strange thing you like and they won't mind at all, but with half-broken colts and any horse with whom you have not had a long-standing acquaintance, do not deliver surprises. Stay with widely accepted procedures and avoid sudden movements.

Once more I persuaded Dusty to mount up and this time he did so in the time-honoured fashion. This perfectly satisfied the big pinto and off they went together for an uneventful short ride.

So now we could get on with breaking trail to the Clearwater District.

Leading our packhorses, nine in all and wearing only halters, we rode across the river and onto the trail to the Divide Creek Pass. This was the pass which Dusty had been advised to avoid because of the deep snow but since he was now here, not miles away at the Clearwater Summit where he should have been, I reckoned it was easier to break our way through the snow than go the distance to the other trail.

When we reached the snow we released our packhorses, herding them onto the trail ahead. They pushed their way into the mushy spring snow, sometimes one leading, sometimes another, and slowly we made progress.

It was a long and tiring day for the horses, but finally we got through and out of the snow on the other side. Then we turned about and travelled back on our broken trail. Very late in the afternoon we returned across the river to Scotch Camp.

The next day I showed Dusty how properly to set a pack saddle on a horse, how to balance the pack, what sort of gear to put in the pack boxes on each side of the horse and what sort to put on top across the horse's back. Then I showed him how to use his lash ropes to secure the pack and what hitches to use. We were a long time packing up, for I had to have him do the work as well as show him how. It would have been much faster if I had packed while he watched, but there was little chance he would remember much from that.

It soon became evident that however much he might remember, it would do him little immediate good. He resisted being told how to do something and, I suspected, once off on his own would do it his own way and end up in trouble.

Dusty, in fact, was one of those stout and intelligent young men who could become skilled at virtually any craft or calling but who have within them a stubborn streak which compels them to disregard advice and instruction, then learn everything through a difficult process of trial and error. Many good men are made that way, and Dusty was one of them, but their trails are often strewn with avoidable debris.

Now when Vera and the children and I had packed in for the season to the head of the Red Deer River, we had got ourselves and all we needed to the camp in one trip with five horses.

It was only after I had agreed to help move Dusty into his camp that I began to realize how large an undertaking it would be. It took altogether twenty-eight packhorse loads and several trips from Ya Ha Tinda Ranch to the camp.

Although it grew tedious, the task was not without its lighter moments.

Dusty had an old packhorse he called Santa Claus. Now, old Santa was a good horse, but every once in a while he would come unstuck and try to dump his pack. However, he bucked straight ahead like a thirsty kangaroo going for water and did not hurt much gear because he would not leave the trail nor go far from the other horses.

Once I put a couple of loaded boxes on him as side packs, then put a fifty-pound bag of flour on top, rolled up in a piece of canvas. The ends of the rolled canvas stuck out on each side and my plan was that as old Santa Claus went along the brushier parts of the trail the canvas would take the punishment from the brush and the flour sack would come through intact.

In a narrow trail through brush and timber it is practical to let your packhorses loose on the trail with one rider in the lead and another bringing up the rear. However, each rider must not let a packhorse get by, neither to go ahead on the trail at the lead, nor back down the trail at the rear, particularly not any horse prone to bucking. The room and the freedom is usually more than the horse can stand and the bucking contest is on.

I preferred to have Dusty ride ahead because bringing up the rear I could keep an eye on the entire pack string and have some chance to spot trouble before it started.

So off we went with Dusty up front and Santa immediately behind him. I had told Dusty emphatically not to let Santa get by, but sure enough it happened, and once out in front with enough room, Santa set to bucking. The pounding was too much for the sack of flour. Every time the horse hit the ground more flour would escape to puff out of the ends of the roll of canvas as they flapped up and down in time with the horse. Of course what Santa had started for the fun of it he now did in earnest, as the flapping canvas and the puffs of flour scared the wits out of him.

. . .every time the horse hit the ground more flour would escape. . .

I hadn't a chance to get by the pack string and Dusty as well in time to catch the old horse before he would play himself out, so I stayed where I was and enjoyed a good laugh at the sight. By the time he quit we had lost a lot of flour, but everything else came through in good shape.

On another trip I found waiting for us at Ya Ha Tinda a set of cupboards which the carpenter in town had made up for another camp but which Dusty persuaded us should be installed at Clearwater Cabin. I shook my head a little at this but said nothing. I had come to realize that when Dusty proposed to go into the bush, everything including the kitchen sink was going to go with him.

I suggested to Dusty that he take the cupboards apart, then pack them flat, one on each side of a gentle horse. He could then re-assemble them at the Clearwater. Neal and Mickey agreed with this and offered to help take the cupboards apart, but Dusty would have none of it. He wanted them packed as they were.

Reluctantly, I secured the cupboards with a basket hitch onto a gentle horse we called Buck.

I said to Dusty, "You'll have to lead Buck. We can't take a chance on him getting off to the side of the trail and hitting a tree with this oversized pack. Whatever you do, don't let go of him. I'll fetch up the rear with the rest of the packhorses."

We made our way for a few miles and I began to think this was going to be a quiet trip. But Dusty and Tom, the big pinto colt, had never learned to trust each other and besides, whoever had cut trail along here had done a poor job of it.

Dusty rode by a long stump beside the trail, and when Buck came by the stump, the cupboard on that side bumped the stump lightly, making a loud, hollow bang.

This noise startled Tom, he jumped, Dusty started fighting with him and matters grew steadily worse.

If Dusty had just dropped the halter shank and attended to his own horse I believe everything might have turned out all right. With luck Buck would have stayed on the trail until Tom settled down. But I had told Dusty that he must never let go of Buck, so he hung on.

Now Dusty, on board Tom, was charging back and forth through second-growth pine with Buck in tow. After the pack had struck about twenty trees the basket ropes broke and the cupboard doors came open, and it looked as though a small airplane was flying through the timber about four to five feet off the ground.

I could not do anything but enjoy the show. By the time it was over Buck had got rid of the remains of the cupboards and got loose from Dusty as well, and was heading down the trail for Scotch Camp, dragging his lash rope.

I waited patiently while Dusty gathered up his broken cupboards and took the pieces down so he could pack them flat on another horse.

Then we started for Scotch Camp with Dusty well out in front and not talking.

On the way there is a place called Terral Creek Flats. It was a good camping place with corrals and plenty of grass for horses and was used from time to time by outfitters and other travellers.

When we broke out of the timber at this spot I saw that the outfitters, Ray Lagace and Jimmy Simpson, were camped there with a crew. They had been gathering horses.

Tethered to a tree was our horse Buck.

By this time we had been packing back and forth for long enough that everyone in the district who spent time on the trails knew us, and it was customary to stop to pass the time of day. Dusty ignored the whole outfit and rode on through. He did not even recognize our own horse tethered there.

I stopped and after some small talk I went over and untied Buck. "Okay, where's the lash rope?" I asked.

All the gathered hands looked blank, and one replied, "He didn't have one."

I took that in good humour with a chuckle but said, "Look, Dusty might be green, but I'm not. This horse dragged a lash rope down the bank to these flats, and I know damned well he couldn't untie it. So let's have the lash rope." A good lash rope that belongs to the park is a nice find any day but we still needed it.

So Ray Lagace said, "Wilf, you tell us what you had packed on him, and we'll see about the lash rope."

So I told the story and everybody had a good laugh. Then two more of the crew came riding in from the Scotch Camp direction to ask, "Wilf, what's the matter with Dusty? We met him on the trail, and he wouldn't even speak to us!"

So I told the story again briefly, then collected my lash rope, which had come out of hiding, and went on my way.

Once I had helped Dusty get all his gear into camp I had to leave him to make out as best he could because I had a district of my own to look after. Still, stories kept reaching us all summer of the problems he was having with his horses. On one occasion his entire string showed up at Ya Ha Tinda Ranch with their gear torn to pieces.

As you can imagine, Dusty became discouraged, and his time with the parks service was short, which was unfortunate all around. Dusty was a good man and eager but he was pushed too soon into working with horses and carrying responsibility in back country. It's true he resisted advice and guidance, but with patience this could have been overcome. If he'd had the chance to work with an experienced warden for a couple of years before taking on his own district, he would have been a great asset to the parks service.

During the winter months in Banff Park we would make snowshoe and ski patrols into our districts. We would shovel snow off cabin roofs and trail bridges, check snow levels and generally show the flag to the few travellers who would venture into the back country in winter.

Highway patrols were made out of Banff and Field, since most of the activity in the parks during the winter was concentrated along the roads. I preferred the back country patrols to the highways.

Local residents had a prank they would play on an unpopular warden. These fellows knew that if a warden saw snowshoe tracks coming out of the woods onto the highway, he then was obliged to backtrack the trail to see if whoever had been in the woods had been up to no good.

So every once in a while some energetic lad would board the train in Banff or Field with his snowshoes and backpack.

As the train slowed down on one of the steeper grades in the park, the lad would jump off into the snow, snowshoe in a wide circle to come out on the Trans Canada Highway, then hitch a ride into town.

The next day the warden would see the tracks and have to backtrack the trail. After five or six miles the unfortunate warden would arrive at the railway track only to have to snowshoe all the way back to his vehicle.

Meanwhile, back in the snooker hall in town everybody was a having a good laugh. What made the prank more onerous to the warden was knowing, most times that he set out on such a trail, how his trip was going to turn out.

As I said, I preferred back country patrols but went on a bad one once with a young man who was good on skis but not at much else.

It was a long patrol requiring a number of days on the trail, and another warden had been slated to go along with a young casual worker from Banff.

This warden refused to go but would give no reason, and this put the Chief Warden on the spot. Refusal of duty was grounds for dismissal, but the warden in question was a valued employee.

I defused the situation by volunteering to go. The Chief Warden, relieved that he could ease out of dealing with the other's refusal, accepted my offer.

I had a touch of something akin to flu at the time, but I thought I could sweat it off on the trail. I also bought a bottle of rum and tucked it in my pack, thinking that if I couldn't get rid of whatever ailed me, I could at least feel better in my sleeping bag at night.

Now I was a snowshoe man, and although I could see that people who travelled well on skis made better time, I had not up to then used skis, and I felt more secure sticking with my snowshoes when a variety of tasks had to be carried out while wearing them.

However my young companion was a skier, and he refused to travel on snowshoes, so we went to stores and drew skis.

We were driven to Lake Louise, where we set out under sixty-five-pound packs, skiing up the Banff to Jasper Highway, which at that time of year was wearing a good seven feet of snow.

Fifteen miles up the road we reached a snug little warden cabin called the Waldorf to stay for the night. We shovelled snow out of the way to get into the cabin, then got a fire going and warmed the place up.

I planned on having something to eat, then getting into my sleeping bag to see what the rum would do for my ailment. However no sooner were we well settled in than the warden from Saskatchewan Crossing, Bill Black, and his wife Dorothy came skiing up the trail in our tracks. They were returning from holidays to their district.

Well, my rum bottle wasn't as big as it had appeared earlier, but we had some cheery hot drinks and a great visit with plenty of tall tales. The next morning Bill and Dorothy left ahead of us, so we would have a broken trail to travel on for so far as their route and ours coincided. We had work to do, so of course we would not travel as quickly.

We skied up to the Mosquito Creek construction camp and set up in a small cabin. Here we had to remove the snow from the roofs of the larger buildings where the span could not carry the weight of a full winter's snow.

The two-person technique we used for this called for the use of a length of nine-gauge wire. With one person working at each end of the building, the wire is held taut and worked down through the snow at the ridge until it reaches the roof.

Then with a sawing motion the wire is worked down the roof, as close as possible to the shingles, to the eaves.

If the job has been done carefully, the whole load of snow slides off in one go when the wire reaches the eaves. Both workers are well out of the way at the ends of the building.

Sometimes the wire will work its way up in the snow as you bring it toward the eaves. When this happens the snow may be prevented from sliding by the wedge of snow, with its thick edge at the eaves, still bound to the roof.

In this event, one person must work along the eaves with a shovel to clear out as much of this wedge of stuck snow as possible, in order to undermine the wire-separated slab. The other person should stand well back since as the slab breaks loose there is a risk that the person working along the eaves will be unable to get out of the way.

We cleared several roofs successfully but then, on a roof approaching a hundred feet in length, the snow refused to slide.

It fell to me to work along the eaves, undermining the slab of snow. When I was about halfway along the slab broke loose. I threw myself toward the building to get into the protection of the eaves but the snow caught me, rolling me outward. When the avalanche was over, I was buried upright in the snow, fortunately with my head exposed. But my skis had got crossed and I could not move.

Now was the time when I needed my companion, who had kept out of the way in case of such an accident. But he only peered cautiously around the building. Not immediately seeing me he did not stop to look further. He panicked and skied off down the trail heading for town.

I shouted with all the voice I had, knowing that if I could not stop him I'd be dead before anyone else could reach me.

Fortunately he heard me and returned, and clumsily, while I directed him, he got me out. I resolved to take extra care from then on, for clearly I could not count on help in a bad situation from this character.

We finished our work there that day and went into the cabin to dry our clothes and make a meal. I think I could have dried out from the heat of pure exasperation.

I was early into bed and slept well for the first part of the night. Sometime close to midnight I got up to fix the fire but then found I could not go easily back to sleep.

In those years I smoked a little and carried a tin of tobacco with cigarette papers. I had left these on a bench near my bed earlier and now I reached out to pick up the tin. It was as dark as the inside of a black cow in the cabin, and I could not find the tin on the bench, so I gave the bench a whack to make the tin rattle enough that I could tell where it sat.

A frightened voice in the dark said, "Wilf?"

I did not answer, and after a while he said, "Wilf, I think there's something getting at our skis."

I said no more, pretending to be so soundly asleep as not to hear him and waited to see if he would screw up the courage to get out of bed and check around to see if everything was all right. He didn't.

The next day we skied back to Louise but immediately set out for my cabin at the head of the Red Deer River. The journey took three days and my apprehensions about my companion did not lessen.

At night he would sit in the cabin telling stories about slides and avalanches until he had himself scared half to death.

Out on the trail he would ski far ahead in the safe places, complaining how slow I was, but the moment we came to danger he would find some excuse to hang back and have me go ahead.

When we had to ski over an open area with slide potential or cross the ice on a lake or river which might be weak in places, he would not go out first into possible danger.

When we had done the work at the Red Deer River cabin we left for a cabin we called the Little Pipestone because it lay by the banks of the stream of the same name. I was getting more skilled on my skis but was far from expert. Coming down from the summit toward the Little Pipestone I crashed against a tree, striking my ear, which hurt with a searing pain that did not ease in the hours after the accident.

We arrived at the cabin with enough daylight left to get the snow off the roof. I lit a fire, then told my companion to go on the roof to do the short job of shovelling. In the meantime, I skied with a bucket out to an opening in the ice about forty feet away to fetch water.

These openings in the ice occurred where the current was too swift for the ice to form. The water would be only about a foot deep, but the snow hole down to the water was a good five to six feet deep. If all went well you would approach the edge of the hole with caution, then lower your bucket with a short rope into the stream. After it had filled you would draw it up and back away from the edge of the snow hole.

Things did not always go well because the snow around the hole could be unstable. This time it was, and it gave way. I flipped over and found myself hanging upside down from my skis with my head about two feet above the water.

I shouted for help, and since I was only forty feet from the cabin and my predicament could easily be seen from the roof, I thought surely the guy will help this time. But not a chance. Finally I reached up, undid my fastenings, fell in the water and got to my feet. I crawled up out of the hole with a bucket of water, resecured my skis and proceeded to the cabin, roaring mad.

I flipped over and found myself hanging upside down from my skis . . .

In a fury, I dressed down this useless excuse for a man and made him the solemn promise that if just one more time he failed to help me when I needed him I would bury him under the ice.

The following morning both my ear and my temper were giving me trouble. I took the lead on the way out and never stopped nor spoke all the way to Lake Louise.

Our transport was there waiting, and I offered no account of how the trip had gone. Our driver sensed there had been trouble but also that it was not something to ask about.

In Banff I went directly to the doctor, who ordered me to bed. My eardrum had perforated and infection had begun.

The next morning Vera phoned to say I would not be in to work as I had been admitted to hospital.

Frank Bryant, our Chief Warden, came up to the hospital shortly to see me. He asked what the trouble was and how was the trip. He asked both questions together and anxiously.

"Well," I said, "you could always ask that guy who went with me."

"I did and he said he didn't know. I asked him how the hell he could be out there with a guy who goes straight into hospital and not know, but that man never gives a clear answer to anything."

I said, "That's not all he doesn't do, but I don't want to go into it.

Let's just say we made the trip, and we got the work done, and I banged into a tree and hurt my ear which is why I'm in hospital."

"That's all?"

"That's all except the next time, if he's my choice I'd rather go alone."

There was a term used around the park to describe a particularly useless and parasitic sort of person. The term was "ski bum."

I think I had met one.

When I worked as a trapper for the Alberta Game Branch, I also worked in game checking stations and on other related duties.

One day the supervising warden, Dennis, called me in to tell me he had a new employee with no previous experience in the wildlife area coming in to work in enforcement, and I was to work with this person to show him the ropes. After some initial instruction, I was to leave enforcement tasks to the new man and point out to him afterwards in private any errors he might have made.

That seemed reasonable, but then the supervisor said, "I should tell you that this guy's application was signed by the Minister of Lands and Forests and that his sister works for the Director. I think he's been sent to spy on me."

Now that was another kettle of fish. I will approach the task of training a greenhorn with an open mind although it can be trying at the best of times. But here we have a guy who got the job through very high connections. If he is bright and wants to learn, things may work out. If he turns out to be indifferent and lazy, what do you do with him? If he got in through high connections, we probably could not get him out.

I said, "I'll give it my best shot."

So the young man came to work. Louis was his name and he had little previous experience in anything, much less game law enforcement.

To my considerable relief, right from the start he was keen to learn, intelligent and likeable and certainly easy to get along with. He made a few mistakes but nothing of any consequence and he took my guidance with good grace.

Within a couple of weeks we had become good friends and on the way back to town after a busy day in the field Louis asked, "Do you know how I got this job?"

"No," I said. "No idea."

"Well, Willmore signed my application, and my sister works for Rocky. Dennis thinks I'm here to spy on him."

Now I had it from both sides, and you have to agree, the stories jibed. No discrepancies at all.

Only on one occasion did Louis miss what he should have seen as an obvious infraction.

Louis was still new on the job as we went into the fall duck season. We would stop cars along likely roads, and if the party was hunting, Louis would check their guns and hunting licenses while I would weigh their birds, take a sample of breast feathers and, if the hunter agreed, clip a wing tip. Our biologists could glean useful information from the samples, and the weight records were a good indication of the adequacy of feed and other habitat requirements.

As part of his enforcement duties, Louis would also look at the birds for compliance with limits and other aspects of the regulations.

Not long before Louis came to work the government had declared full protection for canvasback ducks for a two-year period.

One day we stopped a party of hunters from Calgary with about twelve ducks in the trunk of their car.

As I progressed through this pile of birds I came on two with their heads removed. These were canvasbacks, and the heads had been removed to make identification more difficult.

I completed my data sheets, then handed the two canvasbacks to Louis, who was chatting away with the hunters as amiably as old friends.

Louis failed to pick up on what he had in his hands or why I had passed them to him. He turned them over a couple of times, said nice ducks and handed them to the hunter, who was quaking in his boots.

When I put the day sheets in front of Dennis, our supervising warden, he scanned down the pages and stopped at the entry on the canvasbacks.

"Where are they?" he asked.

"Where are what?" asked Louis.

"The canvasbacks, you dummy."

"Calgary by now," I interjected.

"Oh my God," said Louis, appropriately embarrassed as he realized why I had handed him two of the ducks.

Dennis was fair and did not make a big issue of it, and Louis never missed an illegal bird again.

On another occasion Louis got taken in by a flimsy story.

It was illegal to carry a loaded firearm in a vehicle or to shoot from a vehicle.

We drove into a field, where the crop was down in swath rows, to find a car coming toward us. While one occupant drove the vehicle, the other was shooting out the window.

The shooting stopped but the car had to stop in front of us because we blocked the opening into the field.

I stayed out of this because it was strictly enforcement. Louis went over to the car and talked a while with the occupants.

Then Louis came back and said, "It's all right. We can let them pass."

So I moved our vehicle and the car drove out of the field.

"Why was it all right?" I asked.

"They live around here. They were just scaring the ducks off the swath rows."

"Louis," I asked, "how well do you know the prefix numbers on Alberta licence plates?"

"I don't," he replied. "Never gave it much thought, I guess."

"Well, it would be a good time to start. There are several series of prefix numbers that are issued in Calgary, another group in Edmonton and so on. Then out here in the rural areas there might be only one series in a district. It's handy to know the series in your district, and because of where we work, it helps to be able to identify a Calgary plate as well."

Louis was very silent, and I left him to mull it over for a minute, then I said, gently, "That car came from Calgary."

I never knew Louis to be taken in by a weak story again. After that, he treated with great skepticism any yarn which purported to justify an apparent infraction of the game laws.

After about a year, Dennis and Louis came to trust each other and enjoy a good working relationship, although I know that Dennis could never accept the way the young man got the job.

I did not accept that either, but because of it I was particularly glad that Louis had turned out well. If he had been useless, we would have been stuck with him.

A Random Zoo

When you live in the bush you have a good deal of daily experience with a variety of wildlife. Your relationship with animals is considerably different from that experienced, for example, by the seasonal hunter from town.

Much of your experience is pure pleasure, such as when you watch a pair of grizzly bear cubs play rough and tumble in a mountain river to cool off on a hot summer day while the old sow stands vigilantly by.

Other times there is regret for what you must do, such as when you are assigned to trap the excess beaver in a series of ponds where the feed is too little to support their numbers or they are disrupting farming activity in the district.

Some animals such as squirrels are around you everywhere and occasionally they are made pets.

One early season I had a forest development crew working in central Alberta. We built weirs in small streams which could be used to accurately measure water flow, we cut trail and sometimes we planted out seedlings.

One day the crew felled a tree without seeing that it contained a squirrel's nest. The nest landed directly in a small stream, dumping the young ones in the water. The crew members jumped in the water at once in an attempt to save them. Most of the squirrels were swept away but two were saved. These were each put inside a crew member's shirt to dry and warm up. One died but the other came through.

Now making a pet of a wild animal is seldom a good idea, but often it happens through just such an accident as had befallen our squirrel. This squirrel now proceeded to have the run of the camp.

At mealtimes he would run around the table by jumping from shoulder to shoulder of the assembled crew, often taking a little nibble at an ear on the way by. He was fed abundantly, although much of what he got was probably not the best squirrel food.

One day the crew went to town to have a break from the steady round of camp life and took in a movie at the local theatre. The squirrel came with the crew, of course, travelling, as he was accustomed to do, in a warm jacket pocket.

Part way through the movie, as the crew and the rest of the audience were engrossed in the film, the squirrel escaped from his lair and bounded down the rows of seats, jumping from shoulder to shoulder and taking little nibbles at ears as he went by.

The show in the audience soon had more attention than the show on the screen.

The crew got busy at once pursuing the squirrel. They could tell his movements by the trail of startled cries and general commotion which wound down through the audience.

Once they got near him and he recognized them, he soon came back to the safety of his pocket.

Other small animals are almost invariably regarded as a nuisance to be disposed of if they get into your cabin or other camp buildings.

Perhaps the commonest of these is the bush rat or pack rat as he is most often called. He is a little larger than the common brown rat and lives just about anywhere he can find some protection from the elements to assemble his nest. He gathers a remarkable pile of trash at the nest site, mostly bits of sticks and other forest debris, but if he settles near a cabin where people live he is not beyond packing home any small item of their belongings that he can carry.

Now, the pack rat is not popular for two main reasons. First, he has a large scent gland which gives off a strong, unpleasant odour. In short, he stinks. Second, he likes nothing better than to move into a vacant cabin or the attic of an occupied dwelling to make his messy home.

The warden house at Leanchoil was about thirty years old and had been condemned, but since the government in its ponderous ways had not yet replaced it, we had to live in it.

Vera was using a gasoline-powered washing machine set in a back room which we used as a general utility area. The floor was rotten in places, and one leg of the washing machine went through the floor. To solve the immediate problem I simply moved the washing machine to a stronger part of the floor.

Of course I intended to patch the hole — soon, as I told Vera.

But of course I was busy. There were always jobs out in the park more important on any given day than the hole in the floor, so it tended to stay there.

One night Vera shook me awake and said, "Wake up! There's something in the house!"

I listened and soon I heard the tell-tale thump, thump, thump of a particular small animal running across the floor.

I laughed. "That's just a pack rat."

"What are you going to do?"

"Nothing."

"Oh, yes, you are! That pack rat has to go."

"Okay," I said, "I'll tell you what you do. You listen very carefully, and if he comes in the bedroom you jump up quickly and close the door and then we can catch him."

I thought with luck that might be the end of the matter, but indeed the pack rat came into the bedroom and Vera heard him. She jumped up and closed the door all right, but she was on the other side of it. The pack rat and I now shared the bedroom.

She jumped over and closed the door all right, but she was on the other side of it.

So I caught the pack rat and put him outside, and we went back to bed.

The next morning there was a pile of leaves and twigs and debris in our front room, and if you paid attention you could pick up the slight smell of pack rat, which would grow stronger with prolonged occupancy.

I had important work to do that morning out in the park, but Vera was having none of that. Today the government would wait until I had fixed that hole in the floor.

There are no animals about which more stories have been told than the wolverine. The largest of the weasel family, the wolverine is incredibly strong for its size and known to twist apart and destroy traps designed for much larger animals. An adult male weighs about thirty pounds.

It will raid the traps on a trapline and tear into a trapper's well-built cache building and will stand its ground against much larger predators when contesting possession of a kill.

When we went into Banff we heard a good deal about wolverine, and they had broken into our headquarters cabin on two occasions.

I decided to take an aggressive position with any wolverine showing up in the vicinity of our camp at the head of the Red Deer River but saw none there during the summer. I did see one female with three young but at such a distance out from the camp that I did not regard her as any threat.

The following winter I snowshoed into the camp to shovel snow from the roof and do a general winter patrol.

While travelling out on the ice of a frozen lake I saw a wolverine coming toward me. He was a great distance off, and I spotted him well before he saw me. I took off my substantial pack, then sat down in front of it to break my outline, and waited quietly to see how close the wolverine might approach and what he would do on discovering my presence.

He came along in his one-sided lope until he was fifty yards away. At that point he spotted me, spun about and started to run off.

Now wolves and coyotes have great running stamina and can maintain a swift pace until long out of sight. They may stop occasionally to check on your movements, but it will be little more than a glance back from the relaxed stance out of which they can again take up their swift and tireless departure.

This wolverine behaved quite differently. He ran as fast as he could in his loping gait but within fifty yards would be winded. Then he would stop and spin about to face me, snarling and ready to fight.

After he had caught his breath sufficiently, he would run another fifty yards then again spin about, prepared to make a ferocious defence.

He left the lake, then crossed a long snow-covered slope a half mile away, and I had to use my binoculars to watch him. Even at that distance, as long as he was running from perceived danger he stopped at the end of each run to offer his defiance while he caught his breath.

When I reached the camp I shovelled the snow off the roof, shovelled trenches out from each window to let light in the cabin and of course cleared an access trench to the door.

About nine in the evening I was sitting at the table reading by the light of a trapper's bitch, a wick soaked in oil and lit. It's called a bitch because it throws a poor light and it smokes a good deal.

I looked up momentarily from my book. Cabin tables are always set by windows and there in the dark, on the other side of the glass and with his face illuminated by my feeble light, was a wolverine, staring in.

I kept still, and for a moment or two we shared a mutual curiosity and probably a pretty surprised look as well. Then I made a slight movement and he was gone.

We often had to deal with animals which had become too used to one or another of the few settlements in the parks. The animals would lose fear and become a hazard in the townsite. Sometimes there was no choice but to shoot the animal, other times we could live-trap it. Sometimes then it could be released at a great distance out, in the hope that it would not return. Other times we would ship the animal to a distant zoo, where accommodation was now improving from the old bare cages to something approaching comfortable surroundings.

That spring the crew live-trapped a wolverine near Banff, and arrangements were made to donate it to the Glasgow zoo.

We had the animal in a large cage made to live-trap bear, so he had some room to move around. He accepted food and water, and apart from providing these we stayed away to minimize his stress.

We were assured he would have good quarters in the zoo, and since we could only destroy him here it seemed a good move. However, to get him to Glasgow we knew we had to put him in a smaller shipping crate.

This the carpenters made up. Then came the problem of transferring the wolverine from the large cage to the small crate.

We moved the crate up to the bear trap door, then opened this just enough to match the opening in the crate.

Our wolverine, Joe we now called him, would not approach the crate. He retreated to the farthest corner of the bear cage, crouched down and growled.

We contrived a soft snare that would not hurt him and tied this to the end of a pole. This we then tried to slip over his head but he was so swift that before we could close the loop, he would claw it off with his back feet.

Still we persisted and finally got better at what we were trying to do. Eventually we got the snare over his head and tightened it, with one hind foot caught in it as well. This would not have held him long, because with his incredible strength he would have torn his way out of it, but we had him for just long enough to transfer him to the shipping crate and close the door.

As the shipping crate door shut behind him he whirled around to challenge us. Then, seeing his defeat, he looked about him. The only thing in the crate was a feeding tray. He grabbed it up at once and tore it into little pieces.

A week later we received reports that the longshoremen in Montreal were astounded at the ferocity of a wolverine in transit to the Glasgow zoo. We just hoped that when he got into more spacious quarters in the zoo he would cool down and make himself at home. It still seemed a better choice than to have destroyed him.

In the wild, animals regularly come to grief from a variety of causes. Sometimes injuries will heal, but very often even a minor injury will lead to death due to infection or the inability to hunt.

Sometimes an injured or obviously sick animal will be discovered by someone, and most often the local game officer is called to deal with the problem.

I returned home from the field one day when I worked as a trapper for the game branch to find a message asking me to phone the office.

When I called, the game officer, Lou, answered. "Wilf," he asked, "what's a mink worth?"

"About twenty-five dollars."

"Well, come on over. We have twenty-five dollars for you."

When I arrived at the office I found two wardens, an RCMP officer and a local rancher gathered around.

I asked, "Where is this mink?"

They indicated a plastic garbage can with the lid tied down. I reached for the cord to undo it.

The police officer jumped up and declared, "Don't untie that in here!"

"Why not?"

"We think it may have rabies."

"Well what about me? You guys don't want me to deal with it in here close to you, but you think it's all right if I take it outside and deal with it myself. Suppose *I* get rabies?"

"But Wilf, you're an expert at these things."

"Hah! You pikers!"

The trouble was, we had a habit of playing pranks on each other and now I was not sure how to proceed. At any rate I carried the garbage can out to my vehicle, then went back in and asked for the story. It is always important to get the story before you try to deal with the animal.

It seems this mink had been chasing the rancher's children around the ranchhouse, and on the second pass the rancher popped the garbage can over the mink as it came around a corner.

That sort of story is not uncommon. An ordinarily wild animal which normally will avoid people will sometimes lose fear and become aggressive toward people and other animals when it is not well, especially in the case of rabies.

Any wild animal should be treated cautiously if exhibiting totally uncharacteristic behaviour, and mink do not usually chase kids around houses.

Yet it still sat in the back of my mind that these guys might be setting me up. That garbage can might contain nothing more serious than somebody's old cat, yet indeed it could be a rabid mink.

I decided I could not take a chance, but I indicated nothing of what I had in mind to the present company.

I left and drove to the local veterinarian for advice. I told him all I knew, including the propensity of my friends to perpetrate practical jokes, and we discussed the matter at some length, from time to time lifting the garbage can and moving it gently around while we listened to the noises from within. The noises from within did not help much, but they did not sound like somebody's old cat.

Finally, the vet recommended that we drill a small hole in the lid and insert a generous amount of ether into the can, which we did. When the animal must certainly have been dead, we took off the lid.

It was a mink all right, but it had not had rabies. It had tangled with a porcupine and its mouth was packed with quills. It could not have lived more than a few days and in utter misery. That it had shown aggression to the children was a measure of its distress.

I never did tell my friends how I got the mink out of the garbage can.

When I was a game branch trapper I was often called out by local farmers whose chickenhouses had been raided by a lynx.

Now a lynx likes chickens, but apart from that it is about as dangerous as your grandmother.

Early one Sunday morning I received such a call and left rather hurriedly in my pickup truck, taking the boys and our old dog with me.

On arrival at the farmhouse I confirmed what had happened, and it seemed likely the lynx would still be nearby in a wooded area. I turned the old dog loose. He made a few circles to pick up scent, and sure enough within a few minutes he had the lynx up a tree not far from the house.

Now I realized that in my hurry to get to the farm while the lynx was still in the vicinity I had left much of my essential equipment in my other vehicle and must borrow an item or two from the farm.

I asked the farmer's wife for an old washtub. There was always an old washtub in a farm household and soon she brought me one. It was just the right size.

Next I had my boy Chuck, who was fourteen at the time, climb the tree to effect the next step in capturing the lynx. He climbed until he was close to the lynx. Then he took a couple of photographs of the animal with his box camera, and after that he shook the branches with such vigour that the lynx could not hang on, and down it came.

As the lynx landed safely on the ground I quickly dropped the washtub over him and sat on it.

The farmer and his wife were amazed. "Why don't you just shoot him and be done with it?" the farmer asked.

"No need for that," I replied. "We'll take him miles away out in the bush and turn him loose. You got a crate of any kind, like an old pig crate?" If a pig must be transported for any reason, putting the pig in a crate to start with makes the task much easier. Pigs are notoriously uncooperative about being transported. As with the old washtub, most farms had an old pig crate.

Soon the farmer produced the pig crate, and we carefully transferred the lynx from under the washtub to the crate. Then we loaded the crate into the pickup and off we went.

The next morning I drove to the office in town to ask what the game branch wanted done with the lynx.

The expected instruction followed: "Tag him and turn him loose away the hell out in the bush." Then: "Where'd you park?"

"Out front."

"You should have come in the back. If he puts up a fuss when you're tagging him you'll have a crowd around in no time, and we'll have complaints about being cruel to poor wild animals."

Well, I was not about to drive all the way around into the alley to park behind the office now. Anyway, it only takes a moment to put a tag into a lynx's ear.

One of the game wardens came out to help with the task, but it soon became clear that this particular lynx was not about to let us just reach into the crate and quickly clip on the tag. In fact, he made a very noisy fuss.

I fetched some snare wire and passed a U-shaped loop of it into the crate. This I passed around the animal's head so I could draw him up firmly against the side of the crate.

As I held him securely in this way my co-worker reached in and clipped on the ear tag.

As I let the lynx loose he did some gasping for breath because I had for that short time fairly thoroughly restricted his breathing.

By now a small crowd was gathering, and we were glad to be done.

...the lynx gasped and coughed and staggered about in the cage...

Then, of all possible bad luck, the tag fell out of his ear. In the rush, the warden inadvertently had put the tag the wrong way in the pliers and the clip on the tag had not locked.

So with the crowd growing ever larger we had to repeat the process, and of course it was no easier the second time because the lynx was even less willing to be caught and held fast.

This time when I released him the tag was secure, but the lynx gasped and coughed and staggered about in the cage, making us look positively brutal. In the bargain, a reporter for the local newspaper had arrived with a camera.

So we made the front page and I had to listen to a very dry observation from the boss, "Told you you shoulda parked around the back."

The grizzly bear is the most powerful of our large animals and certainly the most dangerous in a close-quarters situation where the bear feels threatened.

Most bad encounters with grizzlies are the result of fundamental mistakes by people in the bush in bear country.

If you have reason to move quietly in bear country, be alert to the possibility of coming suddenly on a bear. If this happens, back away from the bear in the direction from which you came, and make no threatening sounds or movements. If you do not have to move quietly, make plenty of noise and stay in the open rather than in heavy brush if the choice is available.

If you see bear cubs, again back away. Do not hang around to watch the cubs.

If you smell rotting meat, avoid the source of the smell.

When you are camped out in bear country, maintain a scrupulously clean camp. Do not leave food about, and do not discard leftover food carelessly where it can rot and set up a smell.

Above all, do not pick a fight with a bear.

Although unprovoked attacks do occur, these are rare and they usually involve a spoiled bear, an animal which has grown accustomed to feeding from garbage cans or has learned to hang around campgrounds, scrounging for discarded food. In a worst case, the animal has been fed out of car windows, causing the bear to lose all fear of people.

These bears we shot, simply because the risks they presented to people were too great.

A first concern when we had report of a spoiled bear which likely must be shot was to be sure we got the right bear. By the time you reach the location, the trouble bear may have moved off and the first bear you see might be a perfectly safe one. If you shoot this bear and go away satisfied that you have solved the problem you have only made it worse. People will believe there is no reason now to be extra careful, but in fact the bear presenting the danger is still about.

When a new warden station was under construction on the Panther River, a grizzly bear moved in to terrorize the work crew. The bear stole food, broke windows and generally made a mess around the camp.

I was sent to help Ed, another warden, deal with this bear, and we agreed that shooting the bear was the only choice.

We hung a quarter of ripening elk meat from a pole, then stationed Ed's pickup truck some distance off and sideways to the bait, with the windows rolled down. From here I could take a carefully rested shot out the window and be absolutely sure of the kill.

I put my loaded rifle in the truck cab but it was too early to start my stakeout as it was still a while from evening light and early dusk.

Ed and I decided to go to the cook tent. He could bring his rifle there, so if the bear came early and we heard him we could dispatch him from the tent.

Now it happened that this was the evening of the Joe Louis versus Joe Walcott heavyweight title fight, and since I had been a boxer in the Army I was keen to hear the blow-by-blow report of the match on the radio.

We sat in the cook tent listening to the fight, not thinking much about the bear.

By the time the fight was over dusk was well upon us, and in fact I should already have been on the stand.

At any rate, as the match ended I stepped outside the tent to let my eyes grow accustomed to the poor light and there, not two feet away from me, stood a good-sized grizzly.

I thought it prudent not to make any quick movements so I said, quietly, "Ed, come out here."

Ed did just that, but he failed to bring his rifle.

Here we were in the dark close enough to this bear to rub its back and not even one firearm between us. I had that terrible feeling which you get when you find yourself in a very bad place and you know, absolutely, that you are there because you and nobody else have managed matters with disgusting incompetence.

Fortunately the bear decided there was too much company for his liking and slipped away into the night.

By the next morning I had mulled the issue over considerably and I questioned the crew.

The crew to a man swore they had been harassed by this bear to the point where they were afraid to go out of the tent.

Yet Ed and I had stood so close to the bear he could have taken both of us out with one swipe of a forepaw. Something did not add up here, but the crew insisted I track and destroy the bear. It was that or they would leave the camp.

So we set about tracking the bear up into the timber. About a quarter of a mile after we entered the timber we came on a patch of ground about twenty-five yards across which looked for all the world as though some one had dug it up in preparation for planting a garden.

Then we saw the half-buried remains of a partly eaten bear and we knew the story.

Two bears had met here and fought a terrible battle to the death. The victor had been eating for some while on his defeated foe.

We retreated quickly from that place because you do not threaten even the most benign-appearing bear by hanging around where he has cached the remains of a kill.

That discovery ended our bear hunt. We reckoned the winner had been our bear of last evening; the loser, the bear which had harassed the camp.

The camp experienced no further trouble.

Inexperienced visitors into the parks held unrealistic feelings toward bears, ranging from all-bears-are-cuddly-teddies on the one extreme to all-bears-are-dangerous-and-ought-to-be-shot on the other.

I once positioned myself on a high rock outcrop above a place we called Boulder Pass in order to search with binoculars the ground below for two grizzly bears about which I had received conflicting reports.

Into this pass a trail leads, which forks at what we called Halfway Cabin. One fork continues on through the pass, leads along Ptarmigan Lake and then comes to Baker Lake. The other fork goes off a short distance to Hidden Lake. Baker Lake offered the better fishing, and people who wanted to fish the lake would hike up the trail.

As I searched the ground below for bear I noticed three fishermen coming up the trail. At the forks, they started up the trail to Baker Lake but suddenly changed their minds and shifted over to the other fork to travel toward Hidden Lake.

I thought this strange and I searched the trail behind them. Soon I saw a small grizzly about a quarter-mile back along the trail. He was above the forks, and he too had chosen the Hidden Lake trail.

It seemed the fisherman had known the bear was on the trail behind them while they were still below the forks. They had been intending to go to the better fishing at Baker Lake but had switched to the other fork to shake the bear. By coincidence, or because he really did have some interest in the fishermen, the bear had chosen to take the same fork.

Every few feet the fishermen stopped to look back down the trail, and it was evident they were quite worried.

I was too far away to be of any immediate assistance so I continued watching the fishermen and the bear. The fishermen continued on in the direction of Hidden Lake but about half a mile before the lake, the bear left the trail to angle up the mountain to the south. I watched him until he had almost reached the summit, and he certainly posed no threat to anyone.

Later that day I was checking fishermen at Baker Lake, and here were the three men I had watched that morning. Obviously after they felt safe from the bear they had retraced their steps to reach the other fork to go to their original destination.

But what a story they had to tell of being pursued by a grizzly bear, and they told me in no uncertain terms that I had better get that bear before he killed somebody. Why, he'd stuck right on their tracks, no matter what they did to try to shake him off. They were just plain lucky they finally dodged him.

I did not let on that I had watched the entire "pursuit" and I am sure that bear story grew by leaps and bounds in the watering holes of Calgary. These men owned businesses of different sorts, one a sporting goods store. A sporting goods store is a great business in which to have a good bear story to tell.

Still, prudence is the better part of valour, and I would avoid a bear before hanging around unnecessarily to determine its intentions.

One summer Vera's mother came to visit us, and we decided to take her on a fishing trip.

At the head of the Ice River there was an old warden cabin very much in need of repair. Also, because the area was remote, the fishing was rarely tested. I thought it a good idea to do some necessary work on the cabin but also take along the fishing gear.

So we loaded our gear on a couple of packhorses and set out for the Ice River cabin. I worked on the cabin more than enough to justify the trip and in my spare time we explored the fishing.

All the pools in the river supported a good population of six- to eight-inch Rocky Mountain whitefish, but these were not exciting fish to catch.

Across the valley from the cabin we found a lake which was overflowing with good sized Dolly Varden, and they could not have been fished for years. You would soon have a fish on, and as you brought it in, a dozen others would follow it all the way to shore.

We fished for twenty or thirty minutes and each of us had landed five or so fish when I happened to turn to look behind us.

I was mildly surprised to see a very large grizzly bear standing stationary about fifty yards away.

We watched the bear for a few minutes. Grizzlies do not have good eyesight and depend heavily on their senses of smell and hearing. He was moving his nose about to catch the breeze, and I am sure he knew we were there, but apart from a grunt or two and a bit of shuffling about, he was not responding to our presence.

We returned to our fishing. After all, we had gone to some effort to get to this lake, and we were enjoying the sort of fishing you rarely come across even in our favourable circumstances.

But as I fished I found myself glancing back, and while the big bear was not moving toward us, he certainly was not moving away.

But I have come to fish, I said to myself, and fish I will.

With my mind perhaps not quite on what I was doing, I brought a fish in too fast and lost him just near shore.

Then somehow the fishing was not quite as good as it had seemed. Oh, we would still catch a fish every few casts although I was stopping to check the bear between casts. Then sometimes I would check on the bear even while I was bringing in a fish.

Then I got thinking that we had to pack these fish out of here and go a fair distance out of our way because the bear was pretty much camped on the trail.

Then I suggested perhaps we had all the fish we needed and should call it a day.

What I did not let on was that I was having a hell of a hard time thinking about fishing with the boss of the valley breathing down the back of my neck.

Grizzly bears are incredibly powerful and very swift, for all that they look like lumbering, clumsy beasts when they amble along a trail or across a hillside.

A grizzly will roll aside large boulders several feet across with casual indifference as he digs out marmots. He can overtake a running moose with ease and leap on its back in full stride to bring it down. I saw a two-year-old steer killed by a grizzly which had snapped the beast's backbone as though it were a light, dry stick.

Not only do many hunters fail to appreciate the power and speed of a grizzly bear, even some people who work as guides fail to exhibit sufficient respect.

I was working as a licensed guide on one occasion and was out in the mountains with another guide and two hunters.

We had stopped for lunch when across the valley on the lower slopes of the opposing mountain I saw colour and movement in the waist-high brush. Checking with my binoculars I identified a beautiful bear carrying an unusual off-colour coat with a bluish tinge.

The others in the party took up their binoculars but before they could locate the animal it had worked its way into heavier cover and was out of sight.

I was challenged on whether or not I had really seen a bear, and since there was only one way to prove the matter, I suggested we mount up and ride across to the opposing slope. Since I had spotted the bear, the hunter I guided was entitled to bag it. Although he had joined the others in claiming skepticism about the existence of the bear, he now grew considerably excited, and I spent some time on the trail down to the river trying to calm him down.

Not long after we splashed through the creek in the bottom of the valley and started up the other side, two cubs carrying the same off-colour as the bear I had seen popped up out of the bush ahead of us.

This ended the hunt, for you do not shoot a sow grizzly when she has cubs with her.

The cubs stayed in view and in fact were not taking alarm as well as they should have. Then, of all things, the other guide in our party took down his lariat and began to shake out a loop.

Now it is the case that a good man with a rope can drop a loop on some wild animals and get away with it. It is the sort of thing which young men full of bravado and not much common sense are known to do, and God knows how things will end up once the loop is on.

Two skilled ropers can capture a black bear by each getting a loop on him then stretching their ropes in opposite directions.

But pop a loop on a grizzly bear cub when the sow is certain to be in the vicinity?

That was bloody madness and I quickly rode over to stop it. At the very least it would force us to kill the sow when she came charging out of cover. The guide shrugged as if to say I was too cautious for his liking, but he put his rope back on his saddle where it belonged.

We rode back to the point from which we had first seen the sow and set up a powerful spotting telescope. After much searching we found her. She was lying facing downhill and flat to the ground and quite close by where we had seen the cubs. If my fellow guide had dropped a loop on a cub she would have come out at the first cry and would have been killing men and horses before anyone could have trained a rifle on her.

When we first went to the cabin at the head of the Red Deer River, I was puzzled by the door arrangement.

The cabin was equipped with the usual two-inch-thick plank door swinging in, but also with a second door swinging out. This door was made of stout peeled pine poles set in a perimeter frame with a diagonal brace. The pine poles were spaced about two inches apart. Apart from this unique spacing of the upright poles it was a very stout door. I commented to Vera that it looked as though we could expect some very large mosquitoes.

On my next trip to town I asked Jack Rae, our blacksmith, who had built the unusual pole door at our cabin.

Jack told me the story.

A man named Billy Potts was living in the cabin one summer and it was a hot summer. The only stove in the cabin was a heater and Billy had to cook on this.

In order to get the top hot enough to cook on, Billy had to build such a big fire that the heater turned the cabin into a veritable oven, so Billy would leave the door open while he was cooking. Even when it came time to go to bed the cabin was still too hot to sleep in with the door closed. So Billy would leave the door open.

One midsummer night Billy awoke in the gloom to find a big grizzly standing in the cabin.

. . . Billy awoke in the gloom to find a big grizzly standing in the cabin.

Billy sat bolt upright in bed and let out a holler. He was too scared to develop any other plan. Now sometimes such an encounter will trigger a bear to attack, but other times the bear is just as scared and anxious to get away from this unexpected confrontation as the other party.

Fortunately in this instance the latter was the case. That bear could not get out of the cabin fast enough. He headed for the open doorway but ran into the door, which slammed shut in front of him. The bear backed off to get some running room, then drove straight for the corner of the cabin which embraced the now closed door, taking out the door and the large logs which made up the stout frame around it.

That was enough for Billy. He still could not sleep in the cabin without letting in the cool night air but he aimed to have something between himself and wandering bears, so he built the ventilating pole door.

True enough, any bear who wanted to could come through it, but that was true of the solid door as well. However, given that most bears will pass by a cabin rather than break things to get into it, Billy's device made sense. It would deter the casual intruding bear, the most likely to enter the cabin if the door were open.

Black bears are not as large, powerful and fast as grizzlies, but in most respects they should be treated with similar caution.

I had been dealing with grizzlies a good deal when one day I was sent to take care of a black bear which had been raiding a work camp.

My son Hugh accompanied me, and when we arrived at the camp we set our tent and laid out our sleeping bags, then went to the cook trailer to visit the cook. I wanted to ask him about what the bear had been doing and particularly what times of the day the animal usually came around. A bear often keeps to quite a uniform daily schedule, and if he comes to your garbage can at five o'clock for a day or two, the chances are good that he will show up around the same time on the third and fourth days.

I had with me a Lee Enfield jungle carbine in .303 calibre. This was a handy rifle for the work at hand and it has a detachable magazine. I took my rifle with me to the cook trailer in order to clean it while I talked with the cook. On entering I removed the magazine, since it carried a full load of cartridges, and put it down on the table.

So far I was being sensible enough, but when I left the trailer to go back to our tent I made one of the sort of notorious oversights with which I occasionally get myself into big trouble. I brought my rifle with me but left the magazine full of cartridges sitting on the table. Perhaps I had been too much around grizzly bears lately and felt contemptuous toward black bears.

Along about five o'clock in the morning, a while after daybreak, I heard the bear in the supply tent, which was not far from our sleeping tent. I came out of the tent with my rifle in hand with the intention of dashing to the cook trailer for my magazine and cartridges.

The bear had a different plan and chased me back into the tent. Several times I tried to get to the trailer and each time the bear chased me back in the tent. Fortunately the bear did not follow me into the tent.

Finally we planned a somewhat improved strategy. On my next dash to the trailer, Hugh would set up a huge commotion of hollering and shouting as a diversion to distract the bear from such close attention to my movements.

The ploy worked, and this time I got to the trailer door. On my way I saw that the cook was looking out the window watching the events and I thought good, he'll let me in as soon as I get to the door.

But he did not let me in, for fear, I suppose that he would not get the door closed in time to stop the bear coming in as well.

There was just enough space under the trailer for me to crawl into as the bear came charging again in my direction, and fortunately the bear did not crawl after me. He just stood guard, ready to deal with me whenever I might have the audacity to come out.

Then I began a discussion with the cook through the floor of the trailer.

"Why the hell didn't you let me in?"

"The bear was right behind you."

"Of course the bear was right behind me! That's why I had to get in. My damned cartridges are in there on the table."

"Yeah. I see 'em."

"Well, put them out the door so I can get hold of them!"

"No way. That bear's out there. I ain't openin' that door."

"Open the damned door just a crack and drop the cartridges out!"

"Wait a while. Maybe the bear will go away."

"Maybe the bear will come under this trailer after me! You drop those shells out the door or I will beat the hell out of you and feed you to the bears after I get out of this mess!"

Finally I got the cook as afraid of what I would do to him later as he was of opening the door just wide enough to drop the magazine load of cartridges through. When it dropped on the ground my hand was ready and waiting to shoot out and snatch it into cover.

Never have I been so glad to hear the satisfying click of a magazine full of cartridges go home beneath the chamber of the rifle.

I went to the bolt and chambered a round. Then I sneaked out to the edge of cover again, steadied the sights just behind the bear's ears and squeezed off the round.

Then came the welcome blast and the nice recoil of the rifle into my shoulder and I could breathe again. I called Hugh out of the tent and told the cook he ought to get one behind the ear as well.

We struck our tent and left. The cook could get someone else to haul the bear away.

Destroying spoiled bears in the parks was a messy and unpleasant business.

It was a job you wanted to do without anyone watching. A bear dying or dead is a messy sight and not one about which people unaccustomed to it have any understanding.

I seldom wore a uniform at work in the park because I preferred the outdoor work at which you could not keep your clothing clean and neat — cutting trail, repairing telephone line and packing into remote locations to maintain cabins.

But on occasion I had to represent the parks service at a meeting in town and this of course called for a clean uniform, neatly pressed.

After one such meeting I returned to the Leanchoil to find a message waiting for me that the two summer students at the park gate were having bear trouble. Vera said that they had sounded very excited on the telephone.

I fetched a rifle and headed in my vehicle for the park gate. Normally the students took alternate shifts in the gate office meeting visitors. While one was on duty the other would be in the nearby residence getting some sleep. When I arrived at the gate on this occasion I found both students in the gate office.

When I enquired as to the problem they told me a bear had taken over the house and chased them out.

I walked in the front door of the house and it was a dreadful mess. The cupboards were upturned and food supplies lay strewn about. A fresh sack of flour had been torn open and bear tracks in white were everywhere about the floor.

The bear heard me come in and decided to leave by the back door. I followed him and he climbed the first tree he came to, a medium-sized lodgepole pine. He was about a two-year-old bear, still more agile and better able to climb than he would be when he was fully grown, and he made it all the way to the top of the tree.

Fortunately I was not in obvious view of the highway because I did the thing which had to be done. I shot the bear, and because he was directly above me and looking down, I shot him in the throat, immediately back of the underside of his chin.

He died instantly and began to fall, but in a piece of miserably bad luck he lodged in the branches about halfway down.

There was nothing for it but to cut down the tree. There were lots of trees in the park just like this one and we could spare it. What we could not have was a dead bear in a tree putting up a stink near the park gate for the next several weeks of hot weather.

I fetched my axe. Now when I had shot the bear I had cut his jugular vein, and his entire blood supply had drained into the space created by the wound. On the first whack with the axe to start cutting down the tree I dislodged the stored blood and it all landed on me in one dreadful splash.

The brand new uniform was ruined, the stench was terrible and as I worked it got worse. But I had no choice. I must get the tree down, load the bear into my vehicle and haul it away to some remote place to throw it out where the scavengers could clean it up.

(At the time, in fact, some dimwit in Ottawa had decreed that if we had to kill a bear we must skin it out and salt the hide, flesh and salt the head too, then ship both to Ottawa. We had no time for that, so we quietly gave the bears to the foxes and coyotes and eagles and ravens and other scavengers, then simply did not report the incident.)

The smell of that bear stayed in my nostrils for days, long after I had thrown out the uniform and scrubbed in a hot bath. Ever since, the prospect of shooting a black bear has been particularly unappealing.

If you work and travel outdoors in moose country you may, over time, see a good many moose.

In most circumstances moose are elusive animals. In country where they are hunted in the season they grow very alert. You may travel with great caution through good habitat, see much fresh sign and even hear moose moving out ahead of you yet rarely glimpse an animal.

In the parks where they are not hunted you will see them more frequently, as they have no reason to associate human activity and presence with immediate danger.

Moose are attractive animals to watch.

If you slip out on a pond in your canoe of an evening you may be rewarded with the sight of the cows emerging from the forest at the water's edge to wade in for lily roots and other aquatic food.

In late summer in a mountain basin you might watch a huge bull, grown fat from the abundant feed, beginning to condition his great neck muscles as he strips his velvet by thrashing his huge antlers against the available brush, a sure sign that the season for breeding the cows and fighting with other bulls is not far off.

In the depths of winter you might see many moose scattered

across the snow-covered sidehills where the upland willow grows, feeding on the tender shoots from last season's growth.

These sights of moose in their usually quiet attitude toward people are enjoyable, but they do not make memorable stories.

However moose are not always docile. In the time and place for it a moose can be most belligerent and aggressive and for the makings of a good moose story, here is where to look.

One friend of mine who worked in the park was walking down a road in early winter when he came upon a bull moose standing in the trail, inspecting him with apparent indifference.

My friend continued walking toward the moose. As he expected, the moose turned and trotted down the trail away from him. All well and good, he thought. Nice normal moose, just gets out of the way.

Just as my friend crossed a timbered bridge which carried the road across a small gorge, the moose reappeared. This time he was coming toward my friend with a determined pace and his head half lowered.

There was just time to get back on the bridge, then slip between the outrigger timbers to hang beneath them for what seemed an eternity while the bull stomped and snorted about on the bridge deck before finally losing interest and walking off up the trail.

On another occasion related to me reliably, a railway worker met a bull in bad humour one day along the right-of-way and spent three hours sitting on a signal arm waiting for the beast to leave.

The country around the head of the Red Deer River where we had our warden cabin was prime breeding ground for moose. Cows were there in large numbers through the summer with some resident bulls in the area as well. As the rut approached more bulls would move in, and soon you could hear moose grunting everywhere throughout the woods. It was a veritable lovers' lane.

I stepped out of the cabin one morning in early September to see a bull feeding near the lake. Soon the bulls would not be feeding at all in their intense pursuit of the cows in oestrus, and then they are reliably aggressive. But these were early days with the rut only barely begun, and I gave the bull little thought as I walked to the spring near the lake to fetch a pail of water.

I got my water, but as I turned back toward the cabin the bull came toward me. I had a good lead on him and walked briskly, but by the time I got to the cabin he had trotted up to close the distance, and even after I went into the cabin he hung around just outside.

I decided to chase him off, so I went out of the cabin to shout at him and wave an arm, but I took a rifle just the same.

My choices soon became clear: I could stay outside the cabin, although to do so safely I would have to kill the bull, or I could go back in the cabin and wait for him to lose interest. Of course I did the latter.

The next day I took a little time to go trout fishing at the outlet of the lake. I had been fishing for a while when I saw a cow moose coming down the shoreline in my direction.

I folded my rod and went into a thicket of small spruce trees where I could stay hidden but watch the cow, and predictably it was not long before the bull that had confronted me the day before came along to join her.

The air current was light and seemed to be drifting by me toward the outlet of the lake. From there the air must have been moving in a large eddy which brought my scent around to the moose. The bull grew very agitated and would move from one side of the cow to the other, constantly testing the wind and tossing his head aggressively.

Several times he charged into the brush in the direction from which he was getting the scent. I dared not move, for once I did, he would disregard the direction of the scent and charge toward the sound. On top of that, there was not enough cover nearby to stay out of sight while making a hasty retreat.

I stayed where I was while the bull continued to test the wind and make occasional rushes into the brush, fortunately not in my direction. After about twenty minutes of this the cow ambled off and the bull went with her.

The cows as well can be aggressive. A cow will defend her calf, even charging attacking wolves, futile though this may be. With her great weight, large head capable of delivering battering blows and her sharp hooves which can flail out in rapid strikes, she is not to be taken lightly.

One day I was patrolling the boundary of Kootenay Park and stopped to eat my lunch. It was early in the season with the sun gaining welcome strength after a long winter which had hung on unduly into spring. I sat with my back against a tree, facing south, and after I had eaten I dozed in the new warmth of the sun.

On feeling something touch my face I woke up but had the wit not to make a sudden movement. I opened my eyes to see a very new calf moose busily smelling my face. His mother, unaware of my presence, stood not ten feet away.

I dared not move for she would likely have been on me in the instant. I felt for the wind on my face and indeed the drift was coming from the cow to me, which would carry my scent away from her, although at that distance she should have picked it up in any case.

In a very low voice I said, "Beat it, you little bastard," but the calf only flopped his big ears about and looked more quizzical, wondering, no doubt, why this different-looking stump should also make noise.

Finally the cow moved off, the calf followed her and I got to my feet to carry on with my travels.

Close encounters of this kind are rare but they do occur. I once sat still by a trail leading around a rock outcrop in Rocky Mountain sheep country. To my surprise, and his, a young ram came around the corner to find himself immediately in front of me. He froze and so did I. He was so close that after he overcame his initial surprise he was able to lower his head and sniff at my boots. He only left some ten minutes later when I made a deliberate quick movement to frighten him off. I had agreed to meet a hunting companion at this spot and did not wish to take the chance that my companion would, as he approached, shoot the ram with which I had enjoyed this singular communion.

Back to moose, the most unusual and damaging attack known within my circle of acquaintances took place on the road between the Otter Tail district cabin and Field, BC in the Yoho Park.

Mae Tocker, the warden's wife, drove her children to school in Field and returned at the end of the day to bring them home. She travelled in a Willys car of 1940s vintage, and because she travelled early and late in the day, she was on the road at the two times when game is most often on the move. Over her years there she saw more wild animals than most people would in a lifetime.

One morning in winter Mae saw a bull moose approaching on the road ahead of her. The snowbanks on both sides of the road were very deep with the accumulated winter's ploughing and Mae knew the bull would likely be reluctant to leave the road. Since he was travelling somewhat to one side of the ploughed right-of-way, she eased her car to a stop on the other side and waited for him to go by.

But not this morning, thank you. The bull attacked the car, principally by striking down on the hood and windshield with his front hooves. He smashed the windshield and badly dented the hood, and all Mae could do was stay inside and hope he would satisfy his belligerent mood and move off.

There is no knowing how much more damage he would have

done, for luckily at that moment a large truck with a snow blade on the front came on the scene and was able to push the bull away from the front of the car and chase him back up the road.

Several times the bull turned to attack the truck, and each time the driver stopped to let the bull bash away as much as he wanted at the snow blade. Eventually the bull gave up.

Moose were an annual problem in the spring in Banff. The animals were still on winter feed and waiting, as we were, for the snow to melt. It was a time when moose which had been wintering in the vicinity of the town and grown more used to human activity than usual began drifting in around the buildings.

It was also an in-between time for the wardens. The winter patrols on skis or snowshoes were behind us, but as yet there was too much snow in the back country to begin the work for which we used the horses. So, like the moose, we were in Banff in more than usual numbers.

Banff was a small community in those years, in which everybody knew everybody else and most of their business besides. Any time a moose caused anyone a problem, people would send for a warden to deal with it. After all, if a moose was a problem it had to be some warden's fault. The moose and the wardens certainly helped each other to pass the time while waiting for the snow to melt.

One spring when I was on the moose-versus-people patrol I had several interesting adventures. Of course the object was not to have to do anything drastic to the moose but to mollify the people at the same time.

One day some school children decided to throw snowballs at a cow moose. She ran off but not very far, and when the children caught up and again threw snowballs at her, she chased them off. They ran through a yard into the next street and out of sight.

At this point the cow found herself standing in the yard with her dander thoroughly up. Now the yard belonged to an elderly lady who owned an old and overweight dog. The dog lay at this moment on the back porch. As the moose looked about for anything living to attack, she saw the dog.

The cow promptly charged the dog on the porch. The dog rolled off the porch to hide underneath it. Then the cow, with her powerful front legs and feet, tried to demolish the porch. The porch was stoutly built and held up, but the storm door took a terrible beating before the moose, her mood reduced to a less violent but still disgruntled state, stalked away.

I spent some time in diplomacy with the lady whose dog, porch and storm door had been attacked and also passed the word around that children would be well advised not to throw snowballs at moose.

Not long after that I received a message which said simply, "Jimmy's Cafe."

So I went around to Jimmy's Cafe, selected a stool at the lunch counter and ordered a cup of coffee.

When Jimmy brought the coffee, I asked, "Moose trouble?"

"Yeah," he replied, "but I'm not making an official complaint, you realize. You see, it was sort of my fault."

That I could believe. Often it was someone's fault other than the moose's. But it was good to hear this acknowledged.

So Jimmy told me the story. Because the season in Banff is so short and it is difficult to grow a good garden display, Jimmy had decided the previous spring to plant some flowering shrubs. The shrubs would green up with the spring sunshine and would brighten up his front yard with blooms long before bedding plants would be showing colour.

Jimmy spent a considerable sum of money on a selection of shrubs and spent many hours planting them in front of his house in a carefully planned arrangement.

Now moose will feed successfully on a great variety of deciduous growth, which Jimmy discovered to his horror one morning as he looked out his window to find a young bull calmly cleaning up his shrubs.

In a fury Jimmy, in his pyjamas, grabbed a broom and dashed out of the house to whack the bull on the rump with the handle. The bull headed around the house and Jimmy pursued, shouting epithets all the while.

Now the bull was faster than Jimmy and soon was out of sight, but flushed with victory in having put him to flight, Jimmy spun back to run the other way, hoping to meet the bull and have another go at him.

Well, he did meet the bull all right as he ran back around the house, but this time the bull was not about to give ground, so the next stage in this episode had Jimmy running away as fast as he could with the bull now in hot pursuit.

Jimmy reached safety through his front door just in the nick of time.

My last event before the moose, and the wardens, left Banff for the back country called for considerable discretion on my part.

Late one evening, approaching midnight, I received an anxious

...Jimmy running away as fast as he could with the bull now in hot pursuit.

call from an occupant of a motel unit.

A woman who did not identify herself but whose voice was vaguely familiar, and who must have known me because she knew exactly who to call in this predicament, said, "Please come over here. There's a moose outside the door and I can't get out."

I looked at my watch and did some thinking and then asked, "Is that a problem? The moose will likely be gone by morning."

There was a pause and then she said, "It's a little difficult to explain, but I can't wait until morning. We...I have to be out of here. I have to be somewhere else pretty soon."

Well, I did not need a whole lot more explanation than that. I made my way over to the motel and persuaded the moose to go elsewhere.

As I explained earlier, Banff was a small place in those years. By the time I'd recognized one of the cars parked a little way down the street from the motel and tied that familiar voice to a person I met occasionally in the course of business about town, I had it figured out.

There was a husband and wife in that motel all right, but the husband in question was not the husband of the wife.

From there, you can imagine the predicament.

It is a small town to start with, but you want this tryst badly enough that you are prepared to take the chance, and the only place you can go is the local motel. You cut the timing pretty fine, but you are too occupied with more intense matters to notice, until five minutes from when you have to be out of there to get back to where you are supposed to be at that time of night, that your departure is blocked by a moose.

Hence Wilf Taylor to the rescue, and of course my only business was to deal with this moose. The private activities of the people in question were outside my field of interest, as it were.

Just for added security, I did not file a report on this particular moose incident.

_____

Over the years in which I worked in the parks and for Alberta's game and forestry services, I was called many times to locate and shoot an injured animal.

Deer or elk struck on the highway or on the railway line were often reported at night.

Many of these animals were killed outright at the time of the accident; others hobbled away and only by hunting for these animals could one determine their fate and shoot them if they were still alive but with no chance of recovery.

I called this activity cleanup hunting. It was not pleasant, but it had to be done and I would go out before daybreak in the morning after the report had been received in order to be at the site of the accident in the faint light of earliest dawn.

With luck I could track the animal and shoot it while it lay up weak from its wounds and with the least chance of it being aware of me and struggling to take flight.

Over time I found on many occasions that another hunter had got there before me. Just as I would try to do, this hunter would pick up the trail, follow silently, take the injured animal by surprise and kill it swiftly. The evidence of this lay in the absence of any sign of flight or struggle where the kill took place. Often the kill occurred in the bed the injured animal had made after the initial flight from the location of the accident.

It did not take me long to conclude that this fellow cleanup hunter was the silent, elusive and rarely seen cougar.

While the cougar is a successful hunter of healthy game, he is quick to sense the presence of injured game, which he will then kill with almost certain ease and success.

Once when I was trying to get a trouble bear I used a fresh deer carcass from a highway kill as bait. I staked the carcass out in a good location and left it for long enough that the bear should be coming to it to feed. When I moved in on my bait, there was a cougar. I backed away and left him to the meat.

In a very rare event, my children watched a cougar attack a deer. They were waiting near the house for the school bus to arrive. Now the house was located in an extensive belt of excellent deer and cougar habitat and suddenly a deer broke cover, bolting by in front of them. Just at that moment a pursuing cougar leapt forward to bring the deer down.

The children of course understood the life relationship of prey and predator and that in killing prey the predator is simply making his legitimate living.

But in the heat of the moment they shouted and waved their arms at the cougar, which let go of the deer to bolt off in one direction while the deer scrambled up and sped off in another.

I was sorry to miss that event.

While the mammals around us provided most of the entertainment, fish activity in the aquatic environment was not without interest.

Largely, of course, I was concerned with enforcement of the fishing regulations. Our intervention in what went on naturally was almost totally restricted to occasional stocking of ponds and lakes with fingerling to make more fish available to the visiting anglers.

This too was limited, since the fingerlings had to be brought in on pack-horses in tanks, one tank to each side-pack and preferably on a gentle, reliable horse. Fingerling were an expensive commodity which gave little return if bucked off into the moss beside a mountain trail.

Of course we had a personal interest in the quality of fishing close to wherever we might be stationed, since the sport offered us a pleasant recreation after the day's work was done and put fresh protein on the table besides.

I did once, with Vera's help, intervene in the community of fish in a local pond near the Leanchoil cabin.

This pond lay in the middle of a swamp. The saturated peat-like soil which surrounded it supported a sedge-bound sod in which clumps of willow also grew in abundance.

The wet sod simply floated on the saturated muck below, and if you stood on one side of the pond and jumped up and down you could see the willows on the other side of the pond shaking in response.

You had to be cautious as you approached the pond, for the sedge became less dense, and between the clumps of sedge lay the exposed muck. If you got a foot into this you could be down over your boot top in no time.

But for all this, it was a pleasant pond in which to fish. The water was shallow but clear and cold because a good supply of fresh water constantly filtered into the pond to be drained away by a quick small stream at the outlet.

The pond provided good habitat for eastern brook trout, which do not need especially deep water, and of course the abundance of organic material in the muck supported plenty of the small life forms which the trout used for food. Somewhat deeper water on the near side of the pond provided a good fishing hole.

One day we discovered the quality of the fishing had dropped dramatically, and because the pond was small and the water clear it took only a short investigation to establish the reason for this.

A huge Dolly Varden—a species of char, in fact, but when grown to ten or twelve pounds often called a bull trout—had moved in.

Now a bull trout is a voracious predator with a huge mouth capable of swallowing a brook trout with ease. Not only was this predator eating the brook trout, but also he was scaring away the ones he had not yet eaten. Complaints from visiting fishermen about the quality of the fishing became numerous, although none had identified the problem.

Something, I decided, had to be done. I had tried catching this bull trout with my own fishing gear but without success. As soon as he felt the vibration in the water generated by my approach to the water's edge he would move off to the other side of the pond. I could see him lying cautiously about a hundred feet away in a couple of feet of water.

The next time we were without visiting fishermen or tourists around to watch proceedings, I rigged a snare on the end of a long, dry pole.

Then I enlisted Vera. The plan was simple. Vera would put on waders, then go around to the far side of the pond with the snare pole. She would wade out a short distance but not too far and then keep very still. The bull trout would be on the deep side of the pond, and although he would feel her movements through the water he would not be alarmed because she was on the far side of the pond.

After letting everything settle from this first part of the action, I would then approach the near side of the pond where the bull trout would be lying in the deeper water. I would tromp along with abandon, the big fish would detect that I was coming and would execute his usual evasive action: he would cross the pond to lie still in the shallow water on the far side.

Now part of this strategy took into account the fact that Vera would not be able to see the fish nor the fish see her. This had to do with the angle of the sun at the chosen time of day and the fact that Vera, having waded out into the water, would be looking into the water from too close to the surface.

However from my side of the pond I would be able to see our quarry and I would issue instructions to effect the successful placing of the snare.

Vera expressed some reservations about wading into the muck in the shallow water on the other side of the pond, but I soon reassured her that this was a safe procedure and away she went.

I waited until she was standing in the water about up to her knees and then for a while after that to ensure the pond had returned to its usual serene state. Then I stomped through the swamp to the edge of the pond on my side.

Precisely as expected, the big bull trout moved across the pond to settle in the shallow water close to where Vera stood and nicely within reach of the long, dry pole with the snare on the end.

Now began the delicate part.

"Put the snare in the water in front of you. Good. Now push it a little further out. Not quite so far. Now that's about right. Okay, but move slowly now and move the snare to your left. A little deeper. Just a little more to your left."

Gradually, by this process, I had Vera place the snare around the belly of the big fish.

Now you have to appreciate that Vera had been skeptical about this whole matter from the start. First off, she found it hard to believe that one big predator could account for such a dramatic decline in the quality of the fishing, and further, she had never seen the bull trout.

She could not see him now, yet here she was shifting this snare about in water into which she could not see, after a fish she could not see nor had ever seen.

Then I said, "Yank it up!"

And yank she did. All of a sudden Vera, who did not weigh much more than a strong wind could blow away if she got caught outdoors without her boots on, had twelve pounds of Dolly Varden thrashing away out on the end of a long pole to which she was now clinging for all she was worth.

She had not the strength to lift him from the water, given the leverage he had on her through the long pole, but I had stressed that whatever else happened, she had to keep that pole up and the snare tight or we would lose him.

And keep the snare end of the pole up she did. However, the mechanics of this resulted in Vera sinking into the soft muck in the bottom of the pond. The harder the fish thrashed, the harder Vera worked to keep the snare end of the pole up, and the further Vera settled into the muck.

. . . the harder Vera worked. . . the further Vera settled into the muck.

Of course she was hollering for help at the same time, and I was trying to make my way around the pond, but it is hard to travel through the swamp quickly when you are laughing so hard you can barely see.

By the time I got there Vera was taking water in over the tops of her waders, but she still had the fish. First I took the snare pole and got the fish safely ashore. Then I rescued Vera.

She made a hell of a fuss, of course, but after a while she forgave me, mainly, I think, because she was tremendously proud of having caught such a big fish.

Even the lowly wood tick entered our lives, mainly mine because I spent so much time out in the bush.

All species of wildlife carry a variety of parasites. Most of these you never see unless you look for them on and in the body of a dead animal.

An exception is the tick, commonly called the wood tick, which infests the larger ungulates such as moose, deer and elk and which also will attach itself to cattle and horses and to a lesser extent other domestic animals.

It will also attach itself to people, given the opportunity.

At a particular stage in its life cycle, in the warm days of late spring, the tick, no larger than the head of a match, waits on the branches of shrubs and trees for a passing animal on which to land.

Once on the host animal, the tick gravitates to certain locations where penetration of the skin is easier and blood is abundant. The top of the shoulders and the top of the neck immediately back of the skull are common locations where a heavily infested host animal may carry scores of this parasite.

The tick buries its minute head through the skin, then fills its body with blood. This complete, the tick will eventually drop away to move onto the next stage in its life cycle. A fully engorged tick will reach the size of half a measuring teaspoon.

In hotter climates, such as the Okanagan Valley in British Columbia, some ticks carry a poison which will cause paralysis in the host and, if undetected, may lead to death. In cooler climates, such as those prevailing in the regions of Banff, Yoho and Kootenay Parks, this paralysis has not been reported.

Nonetheless, the wood tick is treated with considerable respect and not a little revulsion. During the season for picking up these parasites, you check your body closely at the end of each day, particularly the hairy places, to which they tend to gravitate.

If you find one with its head buried in your skin you do not simply pull it off. If you simply pull it off, its head will break away and remain in your skin. Legend has it that if your tick does carry the paralysis poison, this will still affect you if the head is left behind, and in any case you may develop a serious infection.

How much hazard there is to simply pulling off the tick I am not certain, but I can tell you that a host of theories abound as to how you should proceed in order to safely be rid of the tick.

One of these involves putting the burning end of a cigarette on the back end of the tick's body. This will cause the tick to withdraw its head of its own accord.

One May when Vera and I were occupying our trailer in the yard behind the warden bunkhouse in Banff, I came in from a sweaty day out on the trails very keen to have a shower and put on clean clothes.

I fetched clean clothes from our trailer, then went to the bunkhouse to shower.

A couple of old hands in the parks service, Olie and Marty, were in the sitting quarters in the bunkhouse drinking overproof rum and of course they offered me a share of this strong drink.

I thanked them and said, "Not just now. I want to shower first. But I'll sure enjoy one after."

So then I showered and checked myself for ticks. Sure enough, in my armpit where I could feel but not see the offensive creature, a tick was securely attached with its head buried through my skin.

When I came out of the shower, the rum again was offered. "Not just now. I got a tick but I can't get at it. I have to get Vera to help me. But I'll sure enjoy one after."

"You got a tick?" exclaimed Olie. "Hell, I can fix your tick. All I gotta do is put the end of my cigarette on his butt and he'll back right out."

I was about to go along with this when I realized that Olie was about three sheets into the wind and not as steady as I would like for an operation requiring the end of his burning cigarette that close to my skin. I begged off, carefully, without offending him.

Olie's enthusiasm for getting rid of the tick was undiminished. "Tell you what," he said, "we'll drown him out in rum."

I could see no harm in that, although I was not certain it would work. It was certainly new. I'd heard a lot of theories but I think this one had just been invented.

So Olie poured rum into a big white enamelled cup and we went through a complicated manoeuvre in which the rim of the cup, which was held upright enough not to spill the rum, was placed securely against my skin, surrounding the tick. Then, with the cup still held firmly in place, I contrived to tilt myself over sideways until the cup was upside down on my skin. This resulted in the tick being fully submerged in the rum.

I held this position for some while, although that was not easy. Then we reversed the procedure, without spilling a drop of the rum.

Then I went to our trailer where Vera removed the tick with tweezers. The head came out readily in one piece with the body.

I then returned to the bunkhouse to accept the offered drink of rum, but I did check just to be sure that the rum used to drown the tick was still sitting on the table in the while enamelled cup and that the rum poured for me came directly from the bottle.

I do not know if anyone ever did drink the rum from the white enamelled cup.

V

THE FAR NORTH

Following two years of forestry school, Wilf applied for work as a forestry officer in the Northwest Territories.

In 1967 he moved north. The four younger children, now ranging in age from ten to seventeen, moved north with their parents; the older two, nineteen and twenty, were now out on their own.

Wilf's employer now was the Northern Affairs Program, a division of the federal Department of Indian Affairs and Northern Development. He continued in this employment until 1982. During this time he was stationed first at Inuvik in the Northwest Territories and later at Whitehorse in the Yukon Territory. The stories from this interval are, however, all drawn from events in the Northwest Territories.

Going North

By 1965 fifteen years had passed since I had joined the parks service in Banff. I had moved between three principle employers in that time: the National Parks Service, the Alberta Forest Service and the Alberta Game Branch.

These employments had offered a range of experiences in dealing with a forest and mountain environment, with wildlife and with people. During these years we lived in the spectacular mountain and foothill country of eastern British Columbia and western Alberta and never more than a day's drive from the foothills area in which I had grown up and first made my living as a market hunter.

By 1965 I felt the need for a change, although I hardly foresaw where this would lead. I decided to improve my basic qualifications and took leave of absence to attend forestry school for two years.

Successful completion of this course of studies opened new doors. Suddenly I had more choices than seemed possible. I could go back into the parks service in a well-paid specialty. In Alberta the game branch and the forestry service both offered jobs, and two offers came in from the Northwest Territories.

These latter were a choice between working as a development officer with the game branch in Fort Smith or as the forest management officer in the Mackenzie district with headquarters at Inuvik.

And so it happened that in the last week of May of 1967 I flew north to Inuvik to plunge immediately into fire suppression duties, since, as I soon discovered, the northern fire season comes on almost the instant the long winter gives way to the twenty-four-hour-a-day presence of the summer sun.

We had only twenty-five fires that season, but it was hectic just the same. There had been little training in the small native settlements thinly scattered throughout the district, mainly along the Mackenzie River, and no contingent organization of crews among the trappers and hunters most likely to wish to take advantage of summer employment as firefighters.

196

I had no administrative quarters in Inuvik and no warehouse. I found most of the equipment piled up on the river bank. Fire pumps had not been drained, hoses had not been properly dried after last being used and small tools lay scattered about.

I found a willing ally in Ron Williams, the game management officer in Inuvik. I shared office space with him for the two years it took to get capital funds into my own budget to build an office and warehouse complex for forest service use.

Ron had been in the north for some time and helped me find my way around and understand the people. In that first fire season his district wardens in the settlements were invaluable in helping to organize local fire crews.

Of course I had much to learn.

I had been somewhat surprised when I was offered a forest service job on the Arctic coast. I was astounded to see how much forest cover prevails in the western Arctic, where the tree line reaches the northern ocean.

Permafrost was a new experience, and it did not take long to see that it imposes serious constraints on such everyday matters as disposing of waste, securing a safe water supply, constructing foundations under buildings and building roads.

The means of supply had much impact on the tempo of life.

Light supplies could come in regularly by air although at considerable expense.

The great bulk of supplies, including all heavy material and equipment, came in by barge. These were piloted down river with their heavy loads by well-powered tugboats which could push them back up river after they were empty.

Often when you needed some item in the north, particularly one which you did not foresee needing well ahead of time, the dealer from whom you sought the item would not have it but would assure you that he would have it on the next barge. The phrase had become a stock northern joke. If anything needed could not be found to hand, some wag would suggest it must be on the next barge.

Of course through the winter increasing numbers of essential daily items were going to be on the first barge, that is to say the first barge down the river after the ice goes out. By the end of winter just about anything you could think of that was too heavy or bulky to bring in by air was going to be on the first barge.

If everything that was going to be on the first barge actually was on the it, that first barge would have stretched from Tuktoyaktuk to Point Separation.

The barges left Hay River as soon as Great Slave Lake was free of ice, then navigated down the river from Fort Providence to Tuktoyaktuk, calling at Fort Simpson, Wrigley, Fort Norman, Norman Wells, Fort Good Hope, Arctic Red River, Inuvik, Aklavik and Fort McPherson. From there they would head south again.

One spring Ron and I had occasion to fly out to Arctic Red River. On our way back to our surprise we saw the first barge making its way down the east channel, well ahead of schedule.

"This will take everybody by surprise," Ron observed. "She shouldn't be in town for another four days."

Then we flew over the town, in which there was not a soul to be seen. Whether word had preceded the barge or whether the town was simply growing anxious enough that four days was an intolerable wait I was not sure, but the entire population was out on the riverbank straining for a first glimpse of the first barge, the barge which had on it everything promised for delivery since last October.

And Yes, It Does Get Cold

Anyone raised in outdoor work in the foothills and prairies of Alberta knows about cold weather, particularly how wind will suck away body heat.

You do not have to be caught in many prairie blizzards to know that thirty below with a high wind is a lot worse than fifty below with no air moving.

So the extremes of cold in the Arctic were no shock to me and I was glad of my previous experience in cold weather.

People in the north have many stories and jokes about cold weather.

"How do you stand the long, cold winters?" asks the southern visitor.

"Well, I just let my functions freeze, then thaw 'em out again in the spring," replies the old northern hand.

Of necessity, much work continued in the north which in the south would be put on hold until the weather warmed up. The reason is obvious enough: if you stop an activity in the north until the weather warms up you simply will not get your work done. The exception to the rule is that you stop working when it is no longer safe to continue.

Cold weather is harder on equipment than on people. Provided people are well dressed and know how to behave in cold weather, it will not hasten their aging or damage their health. On the other hand, equipment operated in cold weather wears out, goes wrong and breaks down at a far greater rate than in normal operating temperatures.

One morning when it was seventy-four below I went out to see if my truck would start. It was fitted with the usual electrical devices to assist winter starting, and I had plugged the lead from these into an electrical outlet.

When I opened the door the steering wheel split. The rush of cold air into the cab was more than the material in the wheel could take. The truck was down until a new wheel could come in on the next supply flight from Edmonton.

Work did continue, much of it calling for travel.

One January, with temperatures around the delta running from sixty to seventy below, I had a final inspection on a seismic camp to complete near the Horton River, some two hundred air miles out of Inuvik. Delaying a final inspection is not good since the more time that passes the more trouble you will have getting the company back in to deal with deficiencies in the cleanup.

The only plane I could charter fit for the trip was a single-engine Otter, so the pilot and I loaded on extra fuel and survival gear and got ready for a long, cold flight.

The Canadian Wildlife Service biologist in Inuvik asked me if I would stop by the camp of a trapper, Billie, to pick up some car-casses which he had arranged to have saved for him. I agreed readily as it was essential in the north for the various government services to cooperate in this way to cut down on aircraft charter costs.

Now often when it is extremely cold at ground level, it is much warmer at some altitude above. In consequence we did considerable searching up and down for warmer air but without much luck. It was cold outside, and it was far from warm in the plane.

We landed at the inspection site and while I did my work the pilot refueled. He left the spare fuel containers in the plane and extended a fueling hose from the containers out through the door and into the

I stood in the prop blast holding the door open. . . . At the same time, I entered a stroke on a tally sheet . . .

fuel port. All the while he left the engine running for fear that it would not start again if he shut it down for even a short while. I thought the procedure somewhat dangerous, but I have to confess it worked without mishap.

On our way back we stopped to pick up the carcasses of marten, fox and lynx at Billie the trapper's camp. The air temperature at this point was sixty below. I stood in the prop blast holding the door open while Billie loaded the cargo, a process which took all of twenty minutes. At the same time, I entered a stroke on a tally sheet for each carcass as it went on board.

After twenty minutes standing still in the prop blast I was glad to be back in the aircraft for the flight home. It was a very cold place, but everything is relative; it had been a good deal colder in the prop blast.

We arrived home safely at Inuvik, another uneventful flight in an Arctic winter successfully completed.

Sometimes, of course, you are forced by circumstance to camp out somewhere on the tundra. In that case, all your survival gear serves its purpose: it enables you to survive.

In the winter of 1967–68 the Canadian Wildlife Service took over responsibility for one of the major reindeer herds which ranged not far from Inuvik.

Officials with the service wanted to make a count of the herd and asked Ron Williams if he could help them, but when they told him they expected the work to take six weeks he had to refuse. He simply could not take that much time away from his regular duties.

When Ron told me about this I suggested we could get a count on the herd in less than a day's flying by using a camera. I had a good camera, easily capable of high-resolution photographs from the air. We could haze the reindeer out onto Sitidgi Lake, a large lake in the area where the herd was wintering, and start them milling, a herd behaviour in which reindeer agitated by aircraft or herders on the ground circle in a compact mass.

To better ensure the success of the operation we would have another aircraft help us so that the herd could be kept milling while we made our photographing run at the right altitude.

The pictures we would take could be enlarged to a suitable size and used to develop the count in the comfort of a laboratory.

The powers that be agreed to this, so we blow-potted Ron's plane.

A blow-pot is an oil-fired heater used in cold weather to warm an aircraft engine to the point at which it will start. A canopy is used to convey the flow of hot air to the engine. Sometimes the engine oil is drained when the aircraft is shut down, then heated on a heater in the radio shack. This heated oil is put back in the oil sump after the engine has been warmed up with the blow-pot, just before attempting to start.

We left our blow-pot and canopy on the river bank in front of the office of Reindeer Air Services where the owner and chief pilot, Freddie Carmichael, could keep an eye on our equipment, then flew out to the lake. We had taken off at an air temperature of forty-five below, but we suspected the temperature might be dropping and were hoping to get the job done promptly.

Unfortunately our helper plane did not rendezvous with us. It was a privately owned craft volunteered for the work, but the owner-pilot and friend on board had spotted some wolves and decided to go wolf hunting instead, offering to help us another day.

To conserve fuel we landed, and by the time we became aware that the other airplane would not be joining us we found we could not restart the engine. The temperature had dropped and the engine had cooled more quickly than expected.

We got on the radio to ask Freddie to start his aircraft and bring us out our blow-pot and canopy.

He replied, "Sure. But let's let it warm up a bit first if you guys are safe. It's sixty-seven below here in town, and I'd rather wait until it warms up to maybe forty below."

So we set up our camp, scrounged up some firewood and settled in to wait for the weather to moderate.

We were there for ten days before we saw forty below again, but as soon as the weather was suitably warm our help arrived. We thawed out our plane and cameras, milled the reindeer, shot our photographs and returned to Inuvik.

It had been a pleasant ten days, in fact, with no telephone ringing and no people coming into the office with problems. All we had to do was cut firewood and eat meat.

Still, it was just as well we got out after ten days, because we had cut all the firewood within easy reach of the camp.

––––––––––––––––––   ––––––––––––––––––

My closest brush with disaster in cold weather came about through an unexpected combination of rather ordinary factors.

On a winter inspection tour for which I had chartered a Beaver aircraft, the pilot and I had to land for the night at Fort Good Hope.

The next morning the temperature had dropped from forty below to somewhere on the cold side of sixty below. We were two hours with two blow-pots starting the aircraft.

I had only one inspection to do on the trip home to Inuvik, a routine ground inspection of a seismic road.

To achieve this I had the pilot land on a small lake near one end of the road. Our plan was simple: I would hike the road on snow-shoes while the pilot would keep the engine running. At the time I estimated I would finish the inspection the pilot would fly the Beaver to another lake where I would come out on the ice to be picked up. The route of the road was such that the distance between the two lakes was only a mile and a half as the crow flies, although the road itself was much longer.

Numerous small lakes of the sort we were on and the one from which I would be picked up dotted the landscape around us, so we spent some time trying to ensure that we had a common understanding about which of the many lakes was my destination.

I found the travelling easier than I had expected and arrived at the lake where I was to be picked up about an hour ahead of time.

I also discovered overflow on the lake, water which has come over the ice to soak into the lower layers of the snow. As is most often the case, the water was not visible at the surface of the snow.

Landing an aircraft on overflow causes dreadful problems. The skis settle into the saturated snow and ice quickly forms over and around the skis. Hours of work can be required to get the craft off again and at sixty below it is crucial to avoid this.

Now a pilot can test the surface by bringing the aircraft down until the skis are on the surface but under sufficient power to pre-vent the skis settling into the snow. After testing a long strip, the pilot then lifts the plane off again. The test strip can then be inspect-ed from the air, and if no water is visible in the ski tracks landing will likely be safe.

We had no reason to anticipate overflow on the lakes in this area at this time of winter, and I was immediately worried that the pilot would not test the snow before landing. I decided at once to try to get back to the other lake before he would take off.

I set off on my snowshoes to run the mile and a half. Since I was well dressed for cold weather and carried a pack besides, it was not long before I broke into a sweat.

Now getting up a sweat in extremely cold weather is dangerous, which I well knew, but I had to weigh the risk of that against the chance of getting the aircraft stuck in overflow.

I kept on running and kept on sweating, and as luck would have it, just as I broke out of timber on one side of the lake, the pilot had the aircraft into the take-off run on the other.

I could only hope now that he would not land on any lake unless he saw me waiting. With luck he would conclude that he had misunderstood what lake I would wait on and would progressively search each lake in the area until he saw me. This procedure should in time bring him back to this lake which he had just left.

Now I had two options: stay out on the ice where the pilot could see me or go into the timber to light a fire and dry out my clothing. I decided if I could get a fire going as close to the lake as possible I might stay by the fire but dash out on the lake on hearing the aircraft.

Unfortunately this was not workable. Because there were so many lakes in the vicinity I was constantly hearing the sound of the aircraft approaching then receding then approaching again. I had no way to know when on one of his passes over the area, the pilot would again fly over this lake. If I missed him on the first pass, how long might it be before he would come by again?

Every time I headed for the timber to light a fire I would hear the aircraft again, the sound growing stronger each time that I would head back out on the ice. Correctly as it turned out, I judged from the sound of the engine that he was inspecting the lakes in a progression which was bringing him closer by stages.

At an alarming rate, I was becoming more and more chilled as my sweat-soaked clothing could no longer conserve my body heat. I knew I was losing body heat faster than I could replace it, the classic process of hypothermia, which can kill a healthy person within hours.

Finally the pilot flew over, saw me and landed. Now would have been the time to have the pilot wait, again with the engine running, while I could build a big fire to dry out my clothing and warm myself, but now we had barely enough time left to return to Inuvik before dark.

So I boarded at once. Through chattering teeth I explained about the overflow, then settled down for the 180-mile ride home in the Beaver.

The interior of the aircraft cabin was only barely warmer than the outside air temperature and I continued losing body heat. By the time we landed in Inuvik I could not have been many minutes away from the critical point in hypothermia where rewarming the body core becomes virtually impossible.

I was too numb in mind as well as body to fully appreciate the risk at the time but it was abundantly clear when I thought it over the next day.

Bureaucratic Stuff & Nonsense

Anyone who has worked for government has witnessed outrageous instances of costly nonsense.

Sometimes the issue is trivial. Once in the parks service I had been sent with another employee to reduce an elk herd. We were to shoot a specified number of animals, maintaining a ratio of bulls to cows. We were to field dress each animal as we killed it and a truck would pick up the meat for immediate transfer to the processing plant in Banff. We had been provided an entire case of ammunition, an abundance neither of us had experienced before.

We also knew the government purchased the ammunition in large quantities at a low cost, so we set up some targets at our campsite, not only to ensure the accuracy of the sight settings on our rifles, but also to improve our shooting skills.

We had a good practice session before we went out shooting elk, and each day on our return we would expend on our targets whatever ammunition we had left in the magazines in our rifles. We had an abundance of ammunition for the required days of elk shooting as well as our target practice and when we were done we turned a large remainder back to stores.

Now we were obliged to keep a diary which we turned in each month as a record of our activities. I do not know what my partner wrote in his diary, but each day I wrote simply, "Elk hunting."

We kept a running tally of the elk we shot, and when we reached our assigned total the job was over.

A few days after I had turned in my diary my supervisor called me in to discuss its contents.

"Wilf, your diary is not adequate."

"That right?" I was not at all interested, but I did my best to appear concerned.

"That's right. You didn't mark down the number of elk you shot each day and also you didn't show how much ammunition you used."

"Oh."

"Well, you'd better take it back and do it over and turn it in properly."

"You serious?"

"I certainly am."

I debated about explaining that I no longer had the least idea how many elk I had shot on each particular day, although I knew the total from our tally, and that I had not the least idea how much ammunition I had used, either each day or in total. Then I decided against this because obviously my supervisor already knew these facts, yet he still wanted me to rebuild my diary.

So I took back the diary and started over.

First I went to the tally sheet, divided it in half to establish my share of the elk killed, and then distributed the result evenly over the days we had hunted.

Then I asked the person in charge of stores how much ammunition was still in the carton. From this I calculated how much we had used, and again assuming I had used half of that, I distributed the number of cartridges evenly over the days of hunting.

It was obvious at once that either I was the world's worst rifle shot or I had done something else with a fair amount of ammunition but I refrained from doing the remaining calculation which would tell me how many rounds I had used per elk I had shot.

I left that to my supervisor. He made the calculation, and the answer was nineteen rounds.

"Thought you were a good shot," he observed.

"Thought so myself," I replied.

Some days later he enquired, "Did you guys dismantle your target setup yet? It won't look very good for the tourists next summer."

I said, "Oh, we never leave anything like that lying around."

Now I had to agree, quietly to myself, that we need not have used all that ammunition, although anyone whose work depends on accurate shooting must do a certain amount of practising on a regular basis to remain a good shot. Any good hunter will put many rounds on a target for every round on game, but my ratio of nineteen to one in the span of one elk hunt sounded a little high.

Still, it hardly made sense to require me to fabricate a diary when my supervisor and I both knew exactly what had happened.

Less trivial was the matter of purchasing a boat for forest service work in Inuvik in 1967.

The service had not previously owned a boat, but so much use had to be made of rented riverboats or canoes of whatever sort could be had that finally the watchdogs of the public purse in Ottawa authorized forty-five hundred dollars in my capital budget to purchase a boat.

Pleased about how useful a good riverboat would be in my work, I set about collecting the advice of knowledgeable local river travellers. My sources of advice settled me on a thirty-six foot riverboat of a design widely used in the lower reaches of the Mackenzie River and the channels of the Delta. I then settled on an experienced local builder whose boats best stood up in hard use.

But my plans soon went awry. That year of 1967 was, you may remember, Centennial Year, the year in which we all celebrated the hundredth birthday of Confederation.

The Northern Affairs Administrator in Inuvik saw that I had funds in my budget for a boat and he asked me to come around to his office.

Now although I had charge of forest service functions, the administrator had a good deal to say on general administrative and financial matters.

As it turned out, the administrator also had much to do with the Centennial celebrations, and when he saw that I had money in my budget for a boat he wanted to discuss the sort of boat I would buy.

I explained this to him, but he then explained to me that the department had no suitable boat in Inuvik to meet the Centennial Barge when it came down the river, calling at all the settlements as it proceeded. In the south, dignitaries crossed the country in the Centennial Train. Here, we would have the Centennial Barge. We needed a suitable boat with which to meet the barge and give the visiting dignitaries a comfortable small tour around the area.

I explained that my thirty-six-foot open riverboat might not be the most comfortable for the purpose, and the administrator certainly agreed with that, which is why it would be necessary for me to buy a sleek cabin boat with a planing hull and a high-speed motor.

When I explained that a sleek cabin boat with a planing hull and a high-speed motor would be inefficient for my work even in the local area and useless on longer river trips, the administrator only smiled in the way that such administrators do smile when they know they will have their way in the end and do not really want to listen your tedious arguments.

Of course he did have his way in the end because, finally, the powerful people in the department, to whom he had access and I did not, were far more concerned about a suitable performance for visiting dignitaries on one special day than they would ever be about efficiency in carrying on our work during the whole of the season for the next many years.

I bought the prescribed boat and the great day came. Along with thirty privately owned boats of every description we went out to meet the barge, horns tooting and flags waving, a very patriotic lot.

After the great day was over and forgotten I had a splendid boat which I could use only for short trips in the local area. The bulk of my work was done as it had been before, by renting whatever suitable riverboat or canoe I could find when I needed one.

Among the more blatant cases of bureaucratic stuff and nonsense ever to come to my attention had to do with a house fire at Reindeer Station in 1968. This case illustrates the well known bureaucratic game, often played at considerable cost to the taxpayer, known as Cover Your Ass. Note how the game situation develops, requiring in its closing stages the appropriate protective manoeuvres.

Every Monday morning in Inuvik we had a staff meeting. The officer in charge of each section of the Northern Affairs Program — game, forestry, education, engineering and so on — would attend. The administrator would chair the meeting.

One Monday morning the administrator read out a letter dated the previous Friday from the schoolteacher at Reindeer Station.

In the letter the teacher complained of a strong smell of fuel oil throughout the house and of finding, on investigation, that the ground in the crawlspace area under the house was soaked in oil. He said further that he had advised the engineer of the situation, but no action had been taken, and he now felt the condition was unsafe for his family.

As stated by the teacher the facts suggested to me a serious leak in the oil line between the storage tank and the heating unit in the house, but since the engineer was sitting across the table in our meeting I decided to keep my conclusions to myself. I was, after all, only the forestry officer.

The engineer tendered the opinion that the teacher was just playing amateur engineer but that he would be looking into the matter in due course.

All of this except the reference to the teacher playing amateur engineer was entered in the minutes and the meeting turned to other matters.

The essential first phase of Cover Your Ass was now complete. A potentially dangerous or costly situation had been brought to the attention of the responsible bureaucrat only to be discounted, with disparaging remarks made as well about the source of the information.

On Wednesday morning the house burned to the ground. The teacher and his family got out safely but lost all their personal possessions. The bulk of the loss fell to the taxpayer since not only the house but the furnishings as well, right down to the knives and forks, were government property.

Now the panic was on. The prompt action which might have prevented the fire would have been trifling compared to the flurry of activity which occurred after it. With the facts recorded in the teacher's letter as well as in the minutes of the meeting it was imperative that the teacher be assured of new quarters at once. Otherwise he might complain to higher levels in the department, with the negligence of the engineer shining out like a grand display of northern lights.

As luck would have it there was already a house on a barge coming down the Mackenzie River. It was destined for Fort Good Hope, to be placed on a concrete basement to replace a very old department building judged to be well beyond its usable life.

It took some juggling of funds between budgets and some pacification of an employee in Fort Good Hope who had to endure another winter in an old house, but of course that barge kept on coming down the Mackenzie. The house that was designed to sit on a concrete basement in Fort Good Hope ended up three hundred miles farther north on a gravel pad in windswept country, having to

. . . but of course that barge kept on coming down the Mackenzie

be re-insulated at a steep additional cost to make it tolerably live-able.

But everybody was happy except the disgruntled employee in Fort Good Hope, who did not know enough of the facts to make waves in any case. The game of Cover Your Ass was complete and by the time Reindeer Station was closed for good the following year, with all the buildings abandoned, everyone's attention was taken up with more immediate matters.

Firefighters

While the north is locked up in ice and snow and darkness for the long winter months, it enjoys summers of seemingly endless sunshine and extended dry spells.

This leads to frequent periods of high fire hazard both in the forests and in the open tundra.

Also, the spring transition is very abrupt. The last of the snow will melt beneath the twenty-four-hour sun, and virtually at once the bush can be tinder dry. A fire can take you by surprise while you are still stowing away your winter gear.

Throughout most of the Mackenzie district for which I had responsibility hundreds of lakes dotted the landscape. This helped us in two major ways: first, we could get a crew with equipment into a fire using float-equipped aircraft very soon after it had been spotted and second, we often had water so close to hand that we could lay it on the fire with pumps and hoses.

We had another advantage. In the inland communities within my district—Fort Norman, Norman Wells, Fort Good Hope, Arctic Red River, Fort McPherson, Aklavik, and Inuvik—lived many people whose lives were anchored in the northern bush and the tundra and the waterways.

These people hunted and trapped for much of their living, and most hunting and trapping takes place in the fall, winter and spring. Consequently these people had time to spare in the season when I frequently needed fire crews. It was also a season in which they most needed the chance to earn some cash income.

I was surprised that no organized firefighting training had been done in these communities, and I started training programs at once. By the onset of my second fire season in the district I had well-trained people in every community, over 130 in all, and knew those with the leadership qualities necessary to take charge of a crew on the fire line.

These people were very committed to the work. Wherever a fire might start, it was in someone's trapping or hunting ground, and although fire is a natural event which is followed by a new succession of plant communities, the immediate effect is a loss of habitat for important fur and food species.

The most important single factor in low-cost fire suppression is early arrival with adequate crew and equipment before the fire gets out of control.

For this reason I stressed that whenever I called a crew boss on the radio to advise him of the crew needed and of the time I expected to have equipment, supplies and an aircraft at the dock ready for departure to the fire, the crew must also be at the dock without fail.

One season I had many fires in the Fort Good Hope area and frequently I would arrive in a plane to dispatch crews.

On one occasion I called ahead on the radio to advise of the crew I would like and the time of departure.

On arrival I saw some crew members already on hand and expected the rest would be there by the time I had made a quick trip to the Hudson's Bay store for grub supplies. On my return, however, I saw we were missing one man.

"Where is Dolphus?" I asked my crew boss, John. "If you couldn't get Dolphus you should have got a replacement."

John said, "I got Dolphus."

"Where is he?"

"He just went to say goodbye to Dorie." Dolphus was very attached to Dorie.

I said, "You'd better go tell him to cut short the goodbye. We have to get on that fire right away."

John dashed off to Dorie's house and soon came back with Dolphus who had a sheepish and apologetic look on his face and off we went.

It was later I learned through the crew what had happened. Dolphus had thought he had time to get in a little more than just a quick goodbye, and when John had rapped on the door and got no answer, he had simply walked in to find Dolphus and Dorie most occupied on the couch.

John knew Dolphus and Dorie well enough to get away with it and promptly gave Dolphus a resounding whack on his exposed backside with the admonition, "No time for this. Wilf is ready to go."

Dolphus leapt up, did up his trousers and hurried down to the dock with John.

Now you have to agree, that is a well-trained firefighter.

The native men on my fire crews and my native crew bosses often impressed me with their resourcefulness. In their bush life they constantly had to make do and improvise with whatever lay at hand, and they would tackle a problem on the fire line with a similar ingenuity. It was not in their nature to conclude that something could not be done even if it looked that way. Instead they would set about figuring out how it could be done.

It was not uncommon to have twenty-five or thirty fires burning at one time out of Fort Good Hope, and I would require at least one crew on each fire.

Although I spent as much time as I could close to the action on the fire lines, I could not always be out because of the time needed in the settlement to organize crews and expedite supplies and equipment.

On one such occasion I was in Fort Good Hope with a number of crews out in the surrounding bush. Leon, our pilot at the time, was due in to the dock from a flight with supplies to one of the crews, and on hearing the airplane I walked down to the dock to help him tie up.

It was then that I saw, lying on the dock, the intake hose for a fire pump.

This was bad news. Every crew had a gasoline-powered pump with a sufficient length of delivery hose but required also a short length of intake hose. One crew had to be out there without an intake hose because the damned thing was lying there on the dock in front of me.

Now you cannot substitute delivery hose for intake hose. When you set the pump at the water's edge you need a short hose to go from the intake port into the water, and unless of a properly reinforced type it will collapse when the pump develops suction on the intake side. It also requires a foot valve so it won't drain the water from the pump back into the lake during intervals when the pump is not in use.

I tied the aircraft float to the dock as it nudged in, and when Leon stepped out I said, "Look what we've here. Any idea which crew left it behind?"

Leon inspected the hose. "No," he said, thoughtfully. Then, "Maybe you should get on the radio and ask who's missing their suction hose."

That was a good suggestion, but these crews were very competitive, and I did not wish to broadcast to everyone that one particular crew had left behind such a vital piece of gear. It would be deeply

embarrassing and difficult for that crew to take the inevitable ribbing.

When I went on the radio I asked each crew boss in turn how he
was making out with the fire. As each replied I then enquired if the
pump was operating properly.

Without exception every fire boss reported his fire under control
and his pump running just fine. That did not make sense. A Gor-
man Rupp pump does not run "just fine" without a suction hose.

I went back to the dock where Leon was standing by. "Let's go," I
said. "I'm doing fire inspections until I find out who's missing a
hose." I picked up the crucial piece of equipment as I boarded.

As we started our round of inspections I was greeted at each landing by the familiar sound of a pump running. Any problems? No
problems. Missing anything? Nothing anyone could think of. I kept
secret the well-hidden intake hose on the floor of the aircraft, but I
stole increasingly puzzled glances at it as this tour progressed.

We came to John's fire. John was by any reckoning a thorough
fire boss. His pump could be heard a short way off from where we
had drawn in to the water's edge.

"Any problems, John?"

"No." A short pause, then, "Not now, anyway."

Not now. Not *now*. That was different. It implied he had had
some problem earlier.

I put the next question, "Missing anything?"

John did not answer. Something was wrong. I enquired, gently,
"Suction hose?"

"Yeh," he said, a note of chagrin in his voice. "Must have left 'er
on the dock."

"This," I said, "I have to see."

I climbed out of the aircraft, jumped ashore and struck off in the
direction of the obviously running pump. It was set up no more
than a few minutes' walk away along the beach.

Indeed there it was, pushing water as efficiently as it ever had.

John and his crew had cut two long poles, then forced them, side
by side, into the mud of the lake bottom at about a forty-five degree
angle to the surface with a few feet of the poles extending above the
surface.

Then they had lashed the pump to the poles so that the intake
port was actually in the water but with the rest of the pump, including the vital motor, safely out of it. Then above the pump they had
stationed the fuel tank, lashing it to the poles as well.

This was a fine piece of improvisation all around. It was so good,

. . . a fine piece of improvisation all around.

in fact, that I wanted the other crews to know about it in case they should ever be without an intake hose for whatever reason. But I could not tell them without also disclosing that John had left his intake hose behind on the dock in the first place.

"John," I said, "I'd like you to do me a favour."

"What's that?"

"Tell the other crews about this setup. How you put it together. Just in case someone else ever gets caught without a hose, he'll know what to do."

John did not reply immediately and I knew he was weighing the implications of what I had asked him to do and thinking about the ribbing he would get. Undoubtedly, for years to come, every time a few men would be together and get to reminiscing about firefighting, someone would be bound to say, "Remember the time old John left his suction hose on the dock?"

But maybe it occurred to John as well that someone else would perhaps then say, "Yeh. Remember that all right. But pretty smart, though, how he rigged his pump on those poles."

In any case John said to me then, "Sure. I'll tell the boys. Be just as well if they know how to do 'er, too."

I felt I was in good hands with people like that.

The fact that native people were accustomed to the hardships of the bush gave them an added advantage on the fire line. They could concentrate on fighting fire because they were not distracted by being in the bush to begin with.

The point was well illustrated on one occasion when I had a non-native man with me to help gain quick control of a small fire.

Our maintenance people were located in Fort Smith. Tommy, a very skilled mechanic, repaired our pumps and outboard motors while Art, an expert on radios, kept our large number of portable two-way radios, vital on the fire lines, in good working order.

One day these two helpful people came to Inuvik to look over my pumps and radios and then we chartered an aircraft to take us on tour to check the equipment which we had stored in the settlements for quick access by the fire crews.

On the way to Arctic Red River (there was no road in those days) we spotted a fire near Campbell Lake. I asked the pilot to put us on the ground at once as I had enough equipment with me to take early action on the blaze and perhaps get it under control before it grew.

My plan was that one man should go with me to tackle the fire while the other should go with the pilot to Arctic Red River to gather a crew and equipment and return as soon as possible. Three men with a pump would be sufficient.

Now Tommy knew a fair bit about fighting fire, but Art had never been on a fire line. Perhaps for these reasons it was Tommy who quickly volunteered to go with the aircraft to fetch a crew while Art agreed that he would stay to give me a hand.

Together Art and I slashed our way through thick alders and willows to reach the fire, which was underway in a stand of spruce. We worked quickly and soon had the blaze in check, and I knew we could easily put it out once our small crew and pump arrived.

When we heard the aircraft returning to come down on the lake we stopped working for the first time and I took a look at my companion.

He was a sad sight. The mosquitoes and the black flies were in his ears and his nose and his eyebrows and even getting into his mouth as he gasped for air. A cloud of the insects which could not find room to settle on him yet were hovering about his head waiting their turn to feed on him. He slapped at them in a futile attempt to drive them off. Green caterpillars hung from his hat and clung to his shirt. I could see that fighting fire had not been a good experience.

Then he said, emphatically, "Wilf, this is three fires for me: my first, my last, and my only one."

. . . green caterpillars hung from his hat.

He was true to his word. Nobody ever got him out on a fire again.

We had our mishaps but these were rarely serious.

We had a big fire burning one time near a large lake with many bays. I organized a crew to fight the blaze, but it was moving fairly quickly and I decided we would only get it under control with a back fire. In any case I wanted to demonstrate to this crew the effectiveness of back firing in controlling a large, moving fire.

We moved away along the lake and into one of the bays, then followed up a stream which flowed into the bay. I strung the crew members out along the stream, instructing them to set fires on the side of the stream facing the fire we wanted to control.

By lighting a series of small fires beside the stream which we could prevent from crossing the stream we gradually burned the fuel from a belt of ground across the front of the main fire and around its flank. When the main fire, swiftly moving, reached this belt of burned out ground it had nothing left to feed on. Having robbed the fire of fuel we had brought it under control.

Now as it happened, a local trapper had some time earlier left his canoe ashore not far from where we started our back fire. As we often did with canoes, he had pulled it half out of the water into the bush and tied it to a tree.

Our back fire went through, badly damaging the half of his canoe which lay out of the water while the other half simply sank in the shallow water to rest on the bottom.

It was not long before this man came to me asking compensation so he could buy another canoe. Of course the main fire might have burned his canoe if our back fire had not, but I thought this a niggardly point and agreed that I should do something to help him secure another canoe.

However, the prospect of explaining this situation to the administrators who would have to approve compensation did not appeal to me, and if I did finally get compensation paid to the trapper, the season in which he needed the canoe would be over.

Fortunately, I had a solution. There was in stores a canoe belonging to the department which had seen better days and was in for write-off, a laborious procedure we had to go through to have a piece of equipment declared no longer serviceable and taken off inventory.

So I asked the trapper to bring in the burned half of his canoe, which I then persuaded the man in stores to exchange for the old department canoe with the argument that since it was to be written off, all he needed was a canoe or the remains of one. It did not make any difference what canoe. The process of write-off only required the presence of a canoe which could be sworn to be of no further use.

I helped the trapper rebuild the old department canoe and he ended up with a rather better craft than the one which had been burned. The government came out ahead because we did not have to pay compensation in cash, and I came out ahead because I did not have to go through a tangle of red tape to obtain the compensation.

Only the stores man was a little disgruntled, because I did not explain to him exactly how it happened that only half a canoe got burned.

A fire which threatens a settlement is a serious fire by any definition.

For ten days in August of 1968 such a fire threatened the village of Inuvik and the military, transport and communications facilities located nearby. By the time the fire came under control 450 people had worked on the fire lines or in communications and support activities. In addition, six Caterpillar tractors and a water bomber had been in use.

Inuvik lies on the northeast bank of the East Branch of the Mackenzie River. A road leads southeast to the Inuvik airport, which is eight miles from the village. The Department of Transport transmitter site lies by this road a little better than halfway to the airport. The Canadian Forces Service base, the administrative centre for NORAD operations in the Western Arctic, lay to the northeast on Navy Road, about eight miles from the outskirts of the village.

The early summer had been dry. Only one-third of an inch of rain had fallen in the area between May 12th and August 18th.

On August 8th at 2 p.m. a brush fire was reported burning on the northeast side of the airport road about two miles southeast of the village.

I joined the village fire brigade in responding. We had with us both a pumper truck belonging to the village and pumps belonging to the forest service.

The fire was only fifty feet in diameter on our arrival and located near two adjoining lakes, but it moved away from us faster than we could lay hose. The area was tinder dry.

It was now my fire, with the village fire brigade providing all the help it could. In my next attempt to confine the fire I dispatched a D7 Caterpillar tractor to travel up the south flank of the fire and then to cut a fire-break along a ridge at the top of the high ground. This would hold the moving front of the fire at the ridge and give us time to enclose it on the north. When in a short while I followed the cat trail on foot to assess our progress, I met the operator, who gave me the bad news that the fire was out of reach, to hell and gone as he put it.

I then mobilized crews to work on cut lines and to man pumps where water was available. I brought further bulldozers into service to push in fire-breaks. Since I no longer had any chance to surround the fire I had to build defensive lines to protect every installation from the Forces Station on the northwest to the airport on the southeast.

By 6:30 p.m. the fire had travelled a mile to the northwest and much closer to the village. By 9 p.m. the fire was threatening the water facilities above the village. The fire-breaks and pump crews kept the fire at bay at this location, however the head of the fire continued moving north-westward above the village.

I also dispatched aircraft to Aklavik, Fort McPherson and Reindeer Station to bring in more equipment, which arrived around midnight.

At about 9 p.m. I had a first meeting with key managers of the village and various government services. These included, among others, the mayor, the RCMP Superintendent, the Forces Station Commander and the Department of Transport Superintendent.

I briefed everyone on the present state of the fire and the defensive works now in place or being extended.

We reached agreement that I would be solely responsible for firefighting operations while the village, the government departments and other agencies would provide me all the resources at their disposal.

The fire was relatively quiet in the cool and calm conditions overnight.

On the morning of the 9th I had additional firefighters brought in from Aklavik, and by noon I had a primary system of fire-breaks around the village.

I now had to strengthen our ability to fight the fire since it would almost certainly continue to grow and begin jumping the fire-breaks. Virtually all government and village resources came into the effort. I asked for and soon was provided a twenty-four-hour communications centre which could maintain radio contact with crew bosses on fire lines and receive and transmit all vital information. Maps were posted and kept current showing the progress of the fire and the location and adequacy of fire-breaks. Crew strength and crew locations were tracked so that resources could be moved quickly to respond to shifts in the activity of the fire.

Round-the-clock shifts were working and expanding in strength. A kitchen went into operation to ensure full meals for each shift, and accommodation was found for the firefighters who had come in from Aklavik.

Through the communications centre and by occasional air reconnaissance when smoke conditions allowed it I was informed at all times of the progress of the fire. This allowed me to deploy men and equipment to the more threatening points on the fire front. Also I could anticipate developing danger points where my own presence on the fire line would be imperative.

One unusual problem developed. Firefighters are desperately thirsty by the end of a shift, but back in the bush this is no problem. Here in Inuvik the crews, exhausted and tired, could go into the bars at the end of the shift to slake their thirst with cold beer, and it was hard to suggest they should not. These men were working desperately hard and giving me their best, but unfortunately too many lacked the judgement to have only a couple of cold beers and a good meal before resting up for the next shift. Too many were staying for far more beer than was healthy.

I discussed the problem with the RCMP but they could only close the bars on receipt of direct orders from Divisional Headquarters in Yellowknife, a process which could take days to effect.

So I approached the operators of the bars, who understandably were reluctant to close down. They were doing a booming business with the huge influx of thirsty firefighters. But I had the final ace up my sleeve. I offered that if they stayed open I would come around and conscript to the fire line all bar employees and all customers who were not already on my fire crews.

This brought the necessary cooperation, and as it turned out I only required the town to go dry for the most critical forty-eight hours of the fire.

Our moment of greatest danger came on the 10th. We had extended the fire-break above the village considerably to the northeast to protect the Forces Station. However, aided by desperately hot weather and a capricious wind, the fire moved along the fire-break to eventually come around it and back toward the station. By 4 p.m. the fire was on the hills only a mile east of the facility.

When the station had been set up ten years earlier some ten acres around the site had been cleared and the slash had not been removed but only scattered on the ground. Each year saplings and other plant growth came up through the scattered slash, and each year the station personnel sprayed this growth with a chemical brush killer to keep it down.

By the time of the Inuvik fire this collection of old slash and chemically controlled annual growth was a pile of tinder, not a fire-break at all.

I organized a fresh crew with two bulldozers and proceeded to the site. The fire came down on us swiftly and when it hit the clearing it came through, sending up a thick, yellow, acrid smoke. We hosed the building down thoroughly and pushed as much debris back toward the advancing fire as we could.

Meanwhile the fire reached the road between the station and the village and jumped it, bringing several power poles down across it. The power had been shut off earlier and the NORAD control centre at the station converted to emergency power generated on the site.

For several perilous hours we stood our ground, and indeed there was little else we could do since the fire had cut off any retreat toward the village. I doubt if I have ever owed so much to the hard work and determination of a sweating, dirty, exhausted and anxious crew.

On arriving, while the fire was still advancing toward us, I had suggested to the very worried commander that I would hold the fire and in return he would owe me a case of beer. He accepted this proposition on the basis that if I did not stop the fire I would owe him ten million dollars.

These were staggering odds but I accepted and happily, by the time the smoke cleared and the fire around the site had burned down, he owed me that case of beer. Needless to say, I had no intention of collecting on this wager until the Inuvik fire was snuffed out to the last ember.

We were soon able to clear the road back to the village and I organized a mop-up operation of the remaining fire inside our defended perimeter.

At 11 that evening, further to the southeast, the fire was reported within two miles of the Department of Transport transmitter site. I had an additional fire-break put in by the night shift to secure this front against further advance.

We could not be certain of it then, but the worst moments of the fire were behind us at the point that we had saved the Canadian Forces Station. From the morning of the 11th onward I extended and improved fire-breaks along what was now a main front nine miles long.

The weather remained dreadfully hot and dry with unpredictable winds. Spot fires inside the defended perimeter continued to break out from embers blown across the fire-breaks. Three shifts of firefighters remained in key locations along the lines with personnel shifting from time to time as needed to mop up the spot fires. We had obtained a water bomber, but smoke for the most part was so dense we could neither use the bomber nor make aerial surveys of the fire.

By the 17th the fire was dormant along the major fire-breaks, but at 11:50 that morning a spot fire was reported on the south side of the airport road between the airport and the transmitter site. This was so distant from the main fire that we could only conclude it had been caused by a cigarette butt thrown from a car window.

On the 18th, rain began to fall and the Inuvik fire soon was history.

I was pleasantly surprised later to receive a letter from the deputy minister of our department in Ottawa commending me for organizing and directing the efforts of several hundred people in saving the town of Inuvik from fire. I was even more surprised when later yet I was commanded to put on my uniform to be paraded before the minister himself, the Honourable Judd Buchanan, to receive a Merit Award.

I wished there had been a way to share these acknowledgements with hundreds of hard-working crews and volunteers, most of them soaked in sweat, smothered in smoke and soot, desperately thirsty, and all the while working their backsides off for a guy who, in their most desperate hours, cut off their cold beer.

Big Oil Comes North

The major oil companies operating in the north today have learned, sometimes very much the hard way, that they need a good relationship with the Indian and Inuit people.

In the earlier days of oil exploration most oil company employees not only felt they did not need good relationships with natives, they disdained for the most part to suppose they needed a relationship at all.

In this respect they were not much different from many non-natives who had preceded them.

A major impediment to good relationships stemmed from the fact that whites talked mainly to whites, Indians mainly to Indians, and Inuit mainly to Inuit.

Public servants from the larger centres such as Yellowknife, Inuvik, Fort Smith and Cambridge Bay would, on arrival in a small, isolated settlement, be taken over by the one or two or three non-natives living there. Unless the public servant made a particular effort to talk with native people, they could come and go from the settlement with virtually no contact.

Colville Lake was an extreme example. Two non-natives lived there and each had a dock. When an aircraft would land, each would go out to discover to which dock the pilot would direct the aircraft to tie up. Once this was clear, the person whose dock was not chosen would retire to his quarters while the other would engage the visitors. It would occur to neither of them that the people on the aircraft might have any need or desire to see anyone else in the settlement.

Sadly, all too many visiting officials were happier with this arrangement than with the effort required to establish effective communication with native people in remote settlements.

Unfortunately, the early representatives and on-site managers for the oil exploration companies were too often satisfied to go the same, seemingly easier, route. When native people felt grieved by the actions of an oil company, they were left to seethe while the oil people went blithely on their way.

Also, few native people could raise an issue of potential conflict with a non-native unless the non-native first demonstrated that he or she would listen and could be trusted.

I soon found myself in a triangle: the oil people ignored the natives but frequently offended them through some action, the native people would tell me of their grievance or it would come to my attention indirectly, I would go to the oil people to try to sort the matter out and, in the step which completed the round, the oil people would insist there could be nothing wrong because the natives had not said anything to them.

Although I had come north to be a forestry officer I soon was responsible for monitoring major exploration activity for its impact on both the environment and the native communities. In the early stages, few enforceable obligations were placed on the industry.

In 1970 one of the companies began a new exploration program in the Delta region, and before long I began to hear of incidents implying a disregard of native interests.

I talked to the most senior company executive available, who agreed to meet with the people. There were, he said, no problems to discuss but he would be glad to explain the program.

We had our meeting in the hall in Aklavik and I was pleased to see a good turnout. I introduced the company executive, who explained in good detail why his company was exploring in the delta. Everyone was quiet and attentive, and when he was done and asked if there were questions, nobody had anything to say.

This, of course, confirmed for the company man that he had been right — there were no problems. If there were problems, the people would tell him.

I realized this process had to be helped along if it was going to work, so I spoke to the meeting briefly and then I asked if anyone had any problems. In response the meeting went on for several stormy hours while the people addressed directly to me their complaints and concerns while the company man listened.

One trapper had taken a load of supplies many miles in on a dead-end channel to his trapping cabin in his thirty-six-foot river boat. On returning the next day he found the channel blocked by a huge fill made with bulldozers. One man cannot drag a thirty-six-foot riverboat over such an obstruction and so he was stranded forty miles from home.

Another trapper was away from home freighting supplies on a

river barge. His home was on the delta, his modest house set back fifty feet or so from the bank of the river channel. His young wife and four small children were at home and his team of valuable Mackenzie River huskies were tethered in front of the house where his wife could watch them and provide them feed and water.

Now dog teams of the very large Mackenzie River husky type must be tethered out with sufficient spacing that they cannot reach each other. Each dog must be securely tethered to a heavy stake well driven into the ground with a light but strong chain leading from the stake to the dog's collar. The collar also must be strong.

If anything goes wrong with this arrangement and one or more dogs get loose, you are in trouble. One hell of a fight breaks out, dogs become seriously injured very quickly and you are at risk yourself while you separate the combatants.

One morning in this trapper's absence a large bulldozer came along the river bank, about thirty feet in from the channel, with the blade down making a rudimentary road. The machine travelled quickly in the light cover. The dogs grew alarmed and all moved toward the house as far as their tethering chains would let them.

The machine marched onward, passing close to the dogs, with the blade tearing out all the tethering stakes.

The consequent dogfight got underway at once.

The consequent dog fight got under way at once.

The trapper's wife and small children dashed from the house to try to separate the dogs and drag them off to any object heavy enough to tie them to until the stakes could be re-set.

The operator on the bulldozer merely watched this scene for a while, then put his machine back in gear and carried on his way.

As these and other stories came out, the meeting grew more intense as people shared indignation at how they had been treated. By the end of the day, through telling me their grievances, they had given a strong message to an oil company.

Many years went by before the oil companies achieved a workable relationship with the native people, but on looking back I believe that stormy meeting made a good beginning.

Two oil companies set up on Banks Island that winter, one at Johnson's Point on the northeast coast about two hundred miles from Sachs Harbour and the other in the vicinity of Sachs Harbour.

The Inuit were not happy about the distant camp but were willing to tolerate it. But the operation near Sachs Harbour soon became intolerable.

To begin with the party chief wanted to hire local labour at a dollar and sixty cents an hour. The Inuit had enjoyed an excellent white fox season and were not interested. Who wants a tedious job at a dollar and sixty cents an hour when he has twenty-five thousand dollars sitting on the kitchen shelf?

In response to this the oil company people began talking about how the Sachs Harbour people were a lazy lot, an accusation which was grossly unfair. To live successfully by the land in the Arctic, which the Banks Island people were doing, takes plenty of determination and resourcefulness. The oil people refused to accept this and, like many non-natives, they interpreted the native reluctance to endure the boredom of industrial employment as laziness.

Then to make matters worse, the oil company moved farther out of Sachs Harbour to set up a main camp between two lakes known locally as Fish Lakes, so called because they are a primary source of the arctic char which are a large part of the diet of the Sachs Harbour people. In doing this, the company took over the whole of the available camping ground, the same ground the people used each season for their fish camps

Now that put the dirt in the fan. Word reached Ottawa by some means other than department channels. I suspect that feeling in the community had erupted so quickly that one of the few non-natives, in a legitimate state of alarm, had alerted the bureaucracy at a senior level.

The first word I received came from my superintendent in Fort Smith telling me to expect instructions directly from Ottawa. How quickly the red tape can be cut when real trouble starts!

The instructions arrived. Go to Sachs Harbour, find out what is wrong, do something about it.

I chartered a light aircraft for the flight to Banks Island and when I got there I gathered the people together for a meeting. My message was simple: tell me what the problems are and I'll do what I can to set things right.

The problems were plenty.

Whoever in Ottawa had issued the seismic permits obviously viewed Banks Island as a wasteland and the settlement of Sachs Harbour of no importance. Perhaps, the people suggested, officials in Ottawa thought that since they were not mailing welfare cheques there by the planeload nobody much occupied the place.

Further, the party chief had not asked anybody about anything, just planted his unwanted seismic camp right on the ground where the Inuit had their vitally important fishing site.

On top of all that, it had not escaped the notice of the Inuit that the party chief thought of them as lazy and good for nothing.

Now Banks Island was no wasteland. It abounded in game such as caribou, muskox, white fox and arctic hare with good char fishing in the bargain. To feel their land and themselves belittled had stirred these ordinarily easy-going people to visible anger.

It became clear that nothing short of relocation of the seismic camp would be sufficient to restore a measure of co-existence with the oil company's operations.

I left to do what I could, proceeding to the camp to talk with the party chief.

He said he could not see what the fuss was about.

I asked him who he had consulted before he chose the site for the camp.

Well, he had consulted one of the local RCMP officers and he thought that was all he was obliged to do, thank you very much.

The police officer in question I knew to be unsympathetic toward the Inuit and ignorant of their needs and their use of the land.

So that he might understand the problem as the Inuit perceived it, I tried to explain the critical importance of the site to the Inuit in their annual food gathering.

Unfortunately, this party chief had a "so what" attitude and Inuit perceptions did not matter a damn to him.

Finally I made the direct suggestion that he move the camp.

He scoffed at this.

I countered that I would make his field conditions so tough that he would be unable to operate. I reminded him that although Ottawa issued the permits, I would be doing the inspections.

He protested that I was not giving him much choice.

I agreed and added that I did not intend him to have any choice.

Reluctantly he moved the camp, but too much damage had been done to restore anything like good will. The oil company did its work, and the Inuit community smoldered.

Part of our difficulty with the exploration people on the ground grew out of their assumption that the conditions of their permits and other regulations were only a formality on paper and were, in any case, unenforceable by lesser officials thinly spread about the north.

Often the most difficult step in enforcement was to convince an offending party that we could make anything stick, to use the common phrase.

Sometimes, indeed, one had to innovate.

I was returning to Inuvik from Fort Good Hope one fine summer day in a chartered Beachcraft when Air Radio called to ask the pilot if he had Wilf Taylor on board.

"Positive on that," the pilot replied.

"Tell him we've got a fire report. About forty miles north of here. Small fire."

Since we were already in the air it made sense to inspect the fire before landing in Inuvik, so we altered course.

In time we spotted the column of smoke. The location coincided with an exploration well site at which drilling had been completed and cleaning up was in progress. As we overflew the fire we saw three men on the ground attempting to control it. To burn debris was a common practice during these cleaning up operations, but of course extreme care had to be taken to prevent the fire getting out of control. This one had got away.

We returned to Inuvik where I had a summer student working in the office who had been anxious to try his hand at running a fire crew. I had taken him out earlier for basic fire training and this small fire seemed ideal for his first experience in charge, so I delighted him by telling him to charter a Jet Ranger, take a couple of men with equipment and go put out the blaze. With three men already on the site he would have five men and himself, quite sufficient for a fire of that size. There was no serious wind in the offing.

I was surprised when after the crew had been out for only an hour to get a call on the radio from the student, advising that the fire was now half a mile in length and that he could not control it. The crux of the problem was that the three men previously on the site had left as soon as the student and his two men had arrived, leaving insufficient manpower to do the job.

I quickly gathered more crew and flew to the site. Soon we had the fire out.

Now leaving a fire before it is under control without a very compelling reason is poor behaviour.

It borders on despicable when the people whose carelessness started the fire in the first place do not have the common decency to stay on hand until the fire is secure.

But here again we were faced with the indifference of an oil company or its contractors.

I knew the company expediter who had charge of local operations so I called him on the telephone. He knew already of the fire so I explained that our legislation did provide for reimbursement to the Crown for firefighting costs where responsibility for starting the fire can be established.

I had calculated our costs at $2,760 and said I would be pleased to receive a cheque to the Receiver General of Canada in this amount. I added that had the cleanup crew stayed on the fire to help control it, the costs would have been much less and reimbursement would not have come up.

It clearly amused the expediter that a Northern Affairs forestry officer would have the temerity to expect such things of the major oil company which he represented.

"Wilf," he said, in a good natured voice, "I have to tell you to go to hell."

I replied, in my best good natured voice, "That's fine. In that case I have only one further question."

"What's that?"

"In which newspaper would you like to read all about it first? Choose one that your head office in Calgary reads on a regular basis." Senior management people in the oil companies may not have been enforcing good practice everywhere in the field, but they were becoming highly sensitive to public perception of their environmental performance.

"Wilf! You wouldn't do that!"

"You're damned right I would."

There followed a silence on the other end of the telephone and then in a significantly different tone of voice the expediter said, "Wilf, give me a little time on this, will you? I've got to do some phoning."

I agreed to that, and exactly sixteen minutes later he called back to ask me to please not take further action until his company's resource man could get to Inuvik at eleven o'clock that evening.

I had had a very long day and I was tired, but I said that would be fine with me.

Indeed, the company executive arrived as promised, and he had with him the necessary cheque.

I believe he also discussed operating attitudes and practices with his local personnel, because we enjoyed a much improved working relationship after that.

The oil companies were not alone in creating problems for northerners in those early days of exploration. The Government of Canada contributed substantially to the confusion.

In fairness, global market conditions and Canadian anxiety to find more oil combined to create an exploration rush in the north which neither the companies nor the government were adequately organized to manage.

Early exploration permits were issued without consultation with local communities or government employees familiar with the ground. Provisions in the permits were insufficient for protection of the environment or the interests of native people.

An exploration permit issued in 1969 for exploration in the Old Crow flats was among the first to include sufficient and enforceable safeguards yet the story there is fraught with communications breakdowns in which, particularly in industry, the left hand did not know what the right hand was up to.

I returned to Inuvik from a four-day field trip one day in early winter with the temperature running to fifty below to find a telephone message had been left at my home. A department official from Ottawa we shall call Dave was lodged at the Eskimo Inn and wanted me to call him.

I called him and he wanted to know did I have the aircraft chartered for the trip to Old Crow and did I have the meeting arranged.

To which I had to reply that I did not and in fact had no idea
what he was talking about.

"But didn't you get my telex?"

"I've been in the field for the last four days. I've just landed. I
won't be in the office until morning. The telex will still be in the
radio office, which is now closed."

Dave informed me that the department in Ottawa had issued an
oil exploration permit for a program in the Old Crow flats and that
he and a representative from the company were here to meet with
the people in Old Crow tomorrow to explain matters.

Obviously I had work to do in what was left of the day if we were
to go to Old Crow the next day. I went to the curling rink to get the
radio operator out of a game long enough to open the radio office
and get me the telex.

I made a telephone call to arrange the aircraft charter and then,
through the RCMP in Inuvik by radio to the detachment in Old
Crow, I asked for a meeting with the Old Crow people.

Then I read the telex, which was about three feet long. Much of it
was devoted to the conditions of the permit, and it provided specific
controls which were better than any I had seen before.

Considering the nature of the Old Crow flats, that was important.

The native community of Old Crow is located where the Old
Crow River flows into the Porcupine River from the north. The
village lies seventy miles inside the Arctic Circle.

Some twenty miles up the Old Crow River from the village the
flats begin. Five tributaries, meandering through a flat basin with
barely perceptible relief, drain hundreds of square miles of some of
the most sensitive terrain in North America. The main flats contain
thousands of ponds and small lakes.

The area is rich in wildlife. The ponds provide nesting grounds
for huge numbers of waterfowl and as well support a major population of muskrat. Muskrat trapping has provided the people of Old
Crow with their principal cash income for generations.

Caribou frequent the area and salmon migrate up the Yukon River, through the Porcupine River and thence to spawn in the tributa-
ry streams of the Old Crow River.

Motorized vehicles can only travel in this terrain when the ground
is solidly frozen during the winter months. Equipment and supplies
for exploration must come in on winter roads from where the
Dempster Highway crosses the Eagle Plains 150 miles to the south-

east. However, the winter is long, winter roads can be quickly constructed and equipment can be in place for several months of exploration.

Four key conditions in the permit provided environmental protection: no wheeled vehicles were to be used, no earth fills would be used in stream crossings, shoes must be installed on all cat blades (to ensure the cat could only move snow, not dig into the frozen tundra) and no refuse would be dumped on ice (to protect lakes and streams).

To ensure enforcement, no work was start without Wilf Taylor in Inuvik being notified.

The meeting in Old Crow achieved about what it could in the circumstances. The oil company representative explained what work was planned. The department official from Ottawa explained the permit and that I would be responsible for inspections. I emphasized the conditions which I believed were crucial to protection of the land.

The glaring deficiency in the process became abundantly clear when the people of Old Crow, polite and considerate in the greatest degree, said they would like some time to think about the proposal.

It then had to be explained that they had no decision to make, the government had issued the permit, the work would go ahead and this meeting was only to inform them of what was going on.

We returned to Inuvik, the department official returned to Ottawa, the oil company executive went south and I attended to other pressing matters.

Some weeks went by, and I began to think it was time I heard from the oil company if indeed they were going to do the work on the Old Crow Flats.

Then one day I met a trapper from Old Crow who was visiting in Inuvik. After the usual social chat I asked if he had heard or seen anything of people from the company.

Indeed he had. He could report that the company had been at work for some time on the flats.

I chartered an aircraft immediately, and when we flew over the flats I could see substantial progress on several seismic lines. Before even landing I could identify breaches of the permit.

No wheeled vehicles were to be used, but Kenworth trucks were on site.

No earth fills were to be used in creek crossings, but an earth fill on a salmon spawning stream could be seen.

The earth fill on the stream and exposed earth along the cut lines indicated there were no shoes on the cat blades.

Refuse was scattered indiscriminately.

I had the pilot land near the leading bulldozer on a new line and approached the operator. I identified myself and asked where I could find the party chief.

The operator explained that everyone but the bulldozer operators had gone out to Whitehorse for a break.

So I asked the next question, "Who is in charge in the absence of the party chief?"

"I am."

"Good. I have to instruct you to shut down as this operation is in violation of several conditions of the permit."

"Suppose I don't?"

"I will arrange that very shortly after that you meet a magistrate." I hoped that my confidence in the stop work provision in the permit was as enforceable as the permit made it sound but in any case this was enough for the operator in charge.

Now we were making history. This was the first time an oil company had been shut down during a program and of course, given the time limits imposed by the approaching end of winter, it was serious for the company.

Communications began to fly between Old Crow Flats, White-horse, the company's main headquarters in the United States, its subsidiary offices in Canada and our department offices in Ottawa, Yellowknife, Fort Smith and of course Inuvik.

The company's first move was to protest the shutdown and lobby at senior levels for immediate permission to return to work due to the short time frame.

When clarification was sought through the department chain of command, that is to say from Ottawa to Yellowknife to Fort Smith to Inuvik, both the Yellowknife and Fort Smith offices wanted no part of the problem. If they supported me and the oil company won the lobbying effort, they would find themselves on the wrong side of the fence. On the other hand I would not back down, and neither office wanted to overrule me in case I won in the end.

This left me dealing with the Ottawa office, and when I reiterated how clearly the company had violated the permit, the Ottawa office stood fast.

The company spent two weeks of their precious time trying to have the stop work order overruled, and then the party chief arrived in my office.

If I can believe what he said, and I do, he was not even aware of the conditions of the permit.

When I showed him these he said he could comply and I promised him an inspection followed by permission to return to work as soon as he had shoes on the dozer blades and had moved the wheeled vehicles out. This was achieved almost immediately, and the program was completed with no further violations.

After the thaw I took vertical photographs of the site from two thousand feet, which showed vividly the difference in environmental disturbance before and after the operation complied with the permit.

Later in the summer the president of the company visited Inuvik and asked me why I had shut down his seismic operation. I showed him the permit and drew his attention to the important conditions which had not been met.

That was the first he had ever seen of the permit. He shook my hand and offered apologies for the behaviour of his people.

The Old Crow Flats experience was a forerunner to more comprehensive land use regulations to which all companies subsequently had to adhere.

This ensured more uniform environmental protection, a clear set of rules for the industry to work by and a more manageable enforcement task for the people in the field.

An interesting postscript to this story: I later received a letter of commendation from the department in Ottawa for the success of the inspection and enforcement aspect of the operation, including advice that "the Old Crow Flats operation has become well known in the petroleum industry."

Adventures in the Air

I first flew in an aircraft in 1944. Carried on a stretcher, I was loaded into an ancient Lockheed for an evacuation flight from Brussels to a military hospital in England.

I did not fly again until I boarded a Pacific Western Airlines flight to Inuvik to take up duty there.

In matters of transport, my life changed profoundly. From almost never having flown, I now spent what seemed like the greater part of my time in small airplanes chartered to take me from one part of my sprawling district to another in pursuit of my various tasks. This was certainly a change from horse transport in the national parks.

Ron, the game officer, had two planes: first an Aeronca Sedan and later a Stinson 108. I travelled with him on many flights in these. More regularly, of course, I flew in chartered aircraft with professional charter pilots.

Within my first few flights as a passenger in the seat beside the pilot I began to understand how these machines were driven and believe me, I wanted to understand.

In large aircraft, upward from a DC-3, you perhaps can separate yourself mentally from the technology which suspends you thousands of feet up in the air; but if you have any imagination at all you have to be concerned when you are suspended a long way above jumping distance without a parachute in a craft which can be perceived as little more than a specially designed tin can with an engine attached to its front end.

Ron gave me some informal introductory lessons and on longer flights my charter pilots often gave me the controls during the tedious hours at cruising altitude.

But I felt compelled to understand more than could be achieved by these limited instructions.

On a couple of occasions I believed I had come close to disaster due to pilot error and I wanted to develop an independent understanding of what was happening in flight. This seemed the only way that I could judge the competence of the pilots in whose hands I so frequently placed my life.

A mobile aircraft training school came to Inuvik in March of the year following my move to the north, and busy though I was I signed up. "Teach me to fly," was my imperative message.

I was flying in charters most of the days, then taking ground school and flying instruction in the evenings and on weekends.

After fifty hours of ground school and fifty hours of flight instruction I realized I did not know much, partly because I am a slow learner and partly because such a short period of instruction could only provide the minimum necessary training to get anyone airborne at the controls.

But like the horses I grew up with, I may be slow to learn but I am long on memory, and I set about to learn everything I could about aircraft maintenance, aerodynamics, instrument specialties, safety and small aircraft construction.

I attended a number of short courses, including two three-week aircraft management seminars with the US Forest Service in Portland, Oregon and in Arizona and a three-week course at the University of Southern California on aircraft safety.

From these and the constant hours in the air in small airplanes over the tundra and the Beaufort Sea, I could make better judgements about the airworthiness of the machines and the competence of the pilots.

Sorting out pilots was most important.

Some were just drivers, pushing their metal chariots around the sky. They read their instruments and seldom looked out the window. If a wheel fell off they would have had to be told it was missing.

Then there were the pilots who buckled up their seat belts and become part of their aircraft. They always knew where they were, where the wind was coming from, what the wind was doing to their plane, the problems glassy water presented in a landing, the significance of rim ice and many other factors which bore on the safe operation of an aircraft in the north.

They also had an ear tuned to the performance of the machine, they could report an odd sound or an unusual control response to a mechanic and they could tell if the mechanic understood and could deal with what they had reported.

One day I was in the right front passenger seat next to the pilot in a chartered airplane as he put on sufficient power for a takeoff from moderately choppy water. He was a good pilot in whom I had plenty of confidence, and still do.

We were on the step, the point at which the aircraft can be lifted out of contact with the water by easing back on the yolk, then placed securely in flight by gently easing forward. It is a delicate moment in takeoff in a float-equipped plane.

At the point of easing back on the yolk my pilot's seat fastenings broke and he fell backward, pulling the yolk all the way with him.

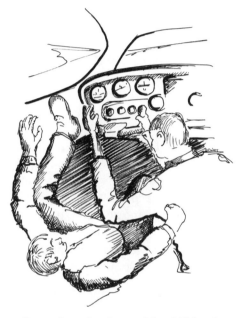

. . . my pilot's seat fastenings broke and he fell backwards . . .

This was a recipe for disaster. With the yolk all the way back, the aircraft would stand on its tail and in the impossible attempt to take off straight up, would drop back into the water on its tail and sink. No one inside would have a chance to get out.

I lunged across from my seat beside the pilot, grabbed the yolk and pushed it forward. I set the craft in a low angle of climb until the pilot was able to recover his seating arrangements and once more take control.

I recovered the cost of my flying licence in that one brief event.

The pilots with whom I flew appreciated that I had taken the trouble to learn to fly. They also possessed the usual northern sense of humour and were not beyond putting my knowledge to the test.

One season I had several fires burning in the northern part of my district, one near a place we called Little Chicago.

I put a crew on this fire, then went on to place crews and expedite supplies to other fires.

When I flew back to the fire at Little Chicago I found it had moved on considerably. The crew had no way to get to the fire front and were simply protecting the camp.

I asked Leon, the pilot who was providing transport on this particular round of fires, to fly the crew to the fire front and put them down on the nearest lake large enough to fly out of safely. In the meantime I would help the cook pack up the camp.

Leon made four trips to relocate the crew and all the equipment and then came to fetch me last. I wanted to spend some time on the ground at the new location ensuring an effective attack on the fire.

As we approached the new site and were flying through the smoke we came to a small slough. Leon circled the slough, put on ten degrees of flap and began to position for a landing. He notched on a little more flap, circled the slough again and put on full flaps.

Now Leon was a good pilot and he had already made four trips, but I could not for the life of me see how he could ever fly out of this dribble of a slough.

Finally I could not stand any longer what he appeared to be about to do. Of course I had been keeping track of where we were on a map on my knees.

"Leon!" I shouted above the roar of the engine. "There's a lake just over the hill!"

He gave me a blandly innocent look and said, "Is there now?" and at the same time lifted the aircraft easily over the rise to begin a landing on the lake where at once I could see my crew waiting for us.

A disadvantage of working too many years in back country is that one may grow too independent; more independent, sometimes, than regulations allow.

There was the time we crashed a Beaver aircraft, then did our own repairs.

I needed to move some fire equipment and supplies from Inuvik out to a forest fire crew on the Arctic Red River near Marten House. I chartered a Beaver with a pilot from Great Northern Airways, and while the pilot did some last-minute errands of his own I started loading gear from a pickup truck onto the wharf and then into the aircraft.

As I finished loading, Don, the game officer from Fort McPherson, came trudging out on the wharf.

"Wilf," he asked, "which way are you travelling?"

"Arctic Red," I replied. "I've got a fire crew near Marten House. They need this pile of outfit."

"Can I get a ride as far as Fort McPherson?"

"Fine with me but you'll have to sit on this load of gear. You won't have a seat belt." Now it is against regulations to ride in a small aircraft without a seat belt fastened, but out of practical necessity it sometimes is done. The chance to catch a flight going your way outweighs the discomfort and the risk of being loose in the cabin with a heap of freight if something goes wrong.

"Fine with me," came Don's reply. "I just want to get back to McPherson. I'd ride a loon if there was one flying."

We finished loading, the pilot came down and we got on board, then made a routine takeoff. We enjoyed an uneventful flight on a perfectly calm and beautiful day all the way to Fort McPherson.

It was that perfectly calm quality which started our problems at Fort McPherson. The pilot came down over the water, then made a low-level turn to take the craft back over the ground in order to make his landing run out from the shore into the width of the stream.

But absolutely still water, glassy water as we call it, is deceptive. You cannot get a sense of depth, of how far below you the surface lies. On this occasion we were much too close. The pilot almost dipped a wing tip in the water on the turn, shattering his own composure with the realization of how close he had brought us to a disastrous accident.

Before he could recover his wits he had put himself into the landing run with very poor position, had missed the approach and struck the ground a glancing blow with the float on my side of the plane at about twenty feet before the water's edge and perhaps fifteen feet above it.

He quickly increased power to lift the craft and regain control then proceeded to make a successful landing a short distance down river.

Now as we had struck the bank that glancing blow, everything loose inside, including Don and the pile of freight and the dust and grit of many cargoes which had collected about the floor and the corners of the compartment, came adrift at once. You could hardly see. The confusion was terrible. Don had come to rest with half the cargo on top of him.

The pilot shouted to no one in particular, "How is that float?"

I reckoned the float was all right as nearly as I could see it out my window, but before I could say anything Don, from under the cargo where he could not possibly see anything, cried out, "We're sinking!"

That was too much for the pilot to sort out, so he gunned the motor and rammed the airplane up onto a sandbar, as far as the thrust would push it.

At least now we could get out and assess the damage. The float which had made ground contact had been driven back about six inches, with a seven-eighths inch front strut bolt having been sheared off in the process.

Well, here we were downstream of Fort McPherson, well up on a dry sandbar and with a damaged aircraft. As you can imagine, we soon also had the RCMP from the settlement on hand as they had heard the plane land downstream and, sensing something was wrong, had come down in their outboard-powered river skiff.

We did not find any damage other than the dislocation of the float so I rigged a Spanish windlass, a crude but effective drawing device contrived with ropes and a twisting stick, to pull the float back into

. . . I rigged a Spanish windlass. . .

place, then tied it there with wire. After that we rigged a fire pump and some hose in order to wash sand out from behind the floats to create twin channels back into the stream. The channels thus made, we floated our aircraft backwards and soon were ready for takeoff.

Don, the game officer, wanted no part of flying any farther in that airplane so he caught a ride to Fort McPherson with the police.

Now that was where our luck ran out. The police called Inuvik to advise that we were flying back there in a crippled aircraft. I am sure they only meant us well, and in any case it was their duty.

But as it happened there was a Department of Transport inspection team in Inuvik on a routine trip, and we were certainly well met on our arrival: the DOT inspectors, the chief engineer for Great Northern Airways and the RCMP were all on the wharf looking exceedingly stern.

Once more the dirt was in the fan. A board of inquiry was held at once. The pilot suffered a six-week suspension for taking off with a damaged aircraft, and I got one of the more severe lectures of my life for repairing the plane and influencing the pilot.

The sobering fact is that these stern-faced inspectors were absolutely right to dress us down and deliver punishment. The chief engineer called me to his shop the next day to show me the damage we had not detected back on the sandbar. Among other lesser items were two breaks in the motor mounts.

Had the motor fallen off this story would have to be told by some one else, if at all.

It is a failing of old packhorse men that they think they can fix anything.

———————————————   ———————————————

With the increase in oil company activity on Banks Island together with the unrest among the Inuit over these intrusions into their country I was having to fly there as often as four times a month, rarely less than twice.

Now this was a year-round requirement and anything you do off the Arctic coast year round you are doing more in winter weather than any other.

We had a major problem getting aircraft. The increase in exploration activity used up most of the air time available from local charter operators and I had to fly in whatever I could find, anything from a Cessna 180 to a Twin Otter. Often I flew in bad weather because I could find nothing to charter in good weather.

I was building a collection of yarns to tell later, such as blow-potting an Aztec all morning to get it started, then scrambling to eleven thousand feet to clear the fog bank, or having a battery, overdue for replacement, explode in mid-flight.

These sort of experiences make better telling later than they are worth at the time and, given the temperature of the water in that part of the world and the hours of my life spent flying over it, I wanted assured regular access to a twin-engine aircraft. This way I would be flying in a safe machine, and could go in the better weather rather than the worst.

The solution was to enter into a standby contract with a local charter company. We would pay a flat rate in exchange for assurance that the craft would always be available to us on a few hours' notice, plus the usual charter rate for flight time.

I tried explaining this through department channels but I found in my time in the north that many people in the distant east were hard of hearing and that most of them worked for the government in Ottawa. You could repeat the facts to them over and over again, but they could not hear what you were saying.

Mind you, these same people certainly did like the north. They could impress their friends by telling how they worked for Northern Affairs and boast about their trips, all in good weather in large aircraft, of course. These people liked the north for its showplace qualities but did not want it to cost more to look after than absolutely necessary.

So I continued asking for a twin-engine aircraft on a standby contract for use out of Inuvik, but with little hope of anyone paying serious attention.

One winter day a well-dressed bureaucrat came in on the flight from the south. I had no idea of his purposes. I had been told only that he was coming and that I was to meet him and place myself at his service.

And my goodness, he certainly was a refreshing sight, all dressed up in his business suit with a tie on and a southern-style topcoat and flimsy overshoes over his oxfords. It was running sixty below with a light breeze and that is cold, even when you are dressed for it. Clearly this man knew as much about the weather in the north and how to dress for it as I knew about why he was here in the first place.

Then he said, with no enlightening preliminaries, that he wanted me to charter an airplane and that we were to fly at once to Tuktoyaktuk.

I said right back that this was not a safe proposition, that his clothing was totally inadequate and that we could not possibly, on such short notice, locate a suitable aircraft.

He insisted. We must fly to Tuktoyaktuk.

So I thought to myself, all right, if you want to fly to Tuk we'll see what we can do, and off we went to the office of the local charter service.

My friend Freddie, in charge there, was no more impressed with this venture than I was, but he offered little comment other than to state the facts about his aircraft that particular day, "The only machine available is a 180 we've been working on in the shop. It still wants more work, but it's safe to fly."

I mulled that over briefly, then said to my visitor, "Look, I have to say again, you are not dressed for the trip, but if you insist on going we can take this 180 to Aklavik which is only thirty-five miles out of here. If you still want to go to Tuk after you try it that far, then we'll go to Tuk."

He agreed and we all boarded. Since I had decided that if we must make this trip I might as well bring my assistant along for some work he could do in Tuktoyaktuk, there were four of us on the flight, counting Mac the pilot.

All you could say for the flight was that we got what we asked for. She was an old 180, she was dirty, half her floorboards were out and you had to take care to keep your feet out of the cables, the tachometer was not working (the pilot hushed me in a hurry when he saw my eyes widen on noticing that!), the pitot tube was frozen up so we had no idea of air speed and there was not enough heat in the cabin to decently defrost the windshield, much less keep the occupants comfortable. I was well dressed and I felt cold; there was no doubt about how thoroughly we were chilling our bureaucrat.

We landed at Aklavik and went directly to the nursing station to have some hot coffee. Mac warned us that we must be quick about it. If the aircraft sat too long we would not get it started up again.

We enjoyed our coffee and our visit with the resident nurse, but even in the short time we stopped there Mac's boots, which he had left in the hallway on entering, had frozen to the floor. As he pried them loose I stole a glance at our Ottawa chap. The look on his face suggested that life in the north at sixty below was getting to him.

"Still want to go to Tuk?" I enquired.

"No. Back to Inuvik. This is madness."

I did not mind at all hearing that. The return flight was every bit as cold as the hop over had been and we were glad to gather around the stove in the charter office in Inuvik. We had to stop by so that I

. . .Mac's boots. . .had frozen to the floor.

could sign the charter ticket.

As he completed the ticket for my signature Mac said, "I need another three hours flying time. Have you got anything at all to make a trip for?"

"Not now," I replied.

"Not even three hours?"

"Sorry. But why three hours, Mac?"

"It'll put me over the thousand mark. I think it might help if I can tell the judge I'm a thousand-hour pilot."

I knew of the matter to which he referred, so no more explanation was necessary. I said again I was sorry not to be able to charter another three hours, and with my Ottawa visitor and my assistant returned to my office.

Once there, of course, the inevitable question was asked. "What was that all about, that reference to being able to tell the judge he's a thousand-hour pilot?"

It was a long story but I made it short. "He had some trouble back east before he came up here. Some outfit underbid him on a job and he was a little upset so he buzzed one of their aircraft while it was on a take-off run. He miscalculated and caught the tail structure. He's a good pilot but a little hot-headed I guess. I don't think that thousand-hour mark would help him much. It's a serious charge."

For the first time our man from Ottawa showed some intensity of emotion and now he all but shouted at me, "Do you mean to tell me that without so much as batting an eye you are prepared to fly with pilots like that, in ramshackle aircraft like that, in weather like this? You have to be out of your mind!"

I pointed out quietly, "You did insist."

"You should have refused."

"My friend," I replied, "in this part of the country these days we fly with whoever we can, in whatever we can, whenever we can. We don't like it, but it's the only way we have of getting our work done."

It now came out that the purpose of this visit was to assess whether in fact we needed a twin-engine craft on a standby contract or whether Wilf Taylor was just selling headquarters a bill of goods so he might travel around in extra style.

My visitor returned to the comfort of Ottawa, I am sure with a wild story of how I had put his life at risk in a rickety aircraft with a mad pilot in weather so cold that a man's boots froze to the floor.

But all turned out well in the end. I received authority to enter into the necessary standby contract for a twin-engine aircraft and visitors out of Ottawa began showing up with issued winter kit including down-filled coveralls and five-star sleeping bags.

AFTERWARDS

In 1971 Wilf transferred to Whitehorse in the Yukon Territory and rather abruptly the nature of his work changed. Although he still directed fire control activity and later worked as a safety officer, for the first time in his life he became significantly desk-bound. Although his work retained a bush connection, he no longer enjoyed the daily experience of bush life.

Consequently Wilf no longer collected the memories which provided the sort of anecdotes he has given us here. Perhaps we sensed the approach of this in his days working out of Inuvik where, for the first time, a significant administrative role crept in to compete with life in the bush.

Wilf was fortunate to have fended this off for as long as he did. Many rural boys of his generation got little formal schooling before the war, then returned to find themselves in some indoor job where "pushing paper" made up some or all of their tasks. I was too young for the war but I met many of these men after the war, wrestling with paper competently enough but seldom happily.

We are fortunate that Wilf fended off the paper for so long, for in doing so he had the chance to gather, in his memories, splendid snapshots of a way of life now either gone for good or fast disappearing.

When he should have been in school, he lived in the hills. When later he might have been making money in some indoor job, he was moving his young family into a remote cabin in the park with saddle and packhorses. When it would have paid him more to upgrade his formal schooling with night courses and shift into park administration, he chose to stay out in the bush in daily interaction with wildlife.

But finally the paper caught him, in Whitehorse behind an eight-drawer desk, and so his lively anecdotes of outdoor life, unknown and out of reach to most people today, come to an end.

In 1982 Wilf left government service.

He and Vera stayed in the north for a while, living in the historic village of Carcross and later at Marsh Lake, a few miles south of Whitehorse. Wilf went prospecting and mined a little placer gold and occasionally went out hunting. With Vera he puzzled over the question of what to do next.

Finally they bought three hundred acres of land in the Peace River country of British Columbia, twenty miles outside of Dawson Creek, where Wilf grows hay, does some modest horse-trading and keeps a few horses for family use.

The family now includes grandchildren who visit from time to time. There are sixteen, ranging in age from one to twenty-two years. When the occasion calls for it, Wilf saddles the required number of horses and puts packs with camp gear and grub on a few others, then makes a short journey into the hills with one or more grandchildren.

While he's at it, I don't doubt he tells them stories of years gone by when he packed into remote cabins in the park with their grandmother—along with their mother, father, uncle or aunt as the case might be—for the season's work as a warden.

Or even of the time, fifty-six years ago now, when with his brother and a friend, he went camping with a pony and cart and "borrowed" a little cream to go with the Saskatoon berries they had picked.

Or perhaps the time, having run out of the grub they had brought with them, he and his brother resorted to snaring fish for camp food and got a little friendly advice from the game warden about how they should catch fish in future.

I also don't doubt Wilf is having a pretty good time as a grandfather. After all, there are not many grandfathers these days who have the chance to build memories of pack horse trips with their grandchildren.